SHAKESPEARE'S
WORKMANSHIP

Shakespeare's Workmanship

by

Sir Arthur Quiller-Couch

THIS IS A LIMITED EDITION OF 150 COPIES

ARDEN LIBRARY

1980

Shakespeare's Workmanship

by

Sir Arthur Quiller-Couch

CAMBRIDGE

AT THE UNIVERSITY PRESS

1931

First published
 (T. Fisher Unwin, Ltd) *October* 1918
   Reprinted (six times)   1918–1930
Pocket Edition
 (Cambridge University Press)   1931

To

PROFESSOR BARRETT WENDELL

AND NOW TO HIS MEMORY

In gratitude for many pleasures of insight
directed by
his illuminating common sense

PREFACE

THE following papers were first written as Lectures and so spoken before an audience in the University of Cambridge. Being shy of repeating myself too often in print in the guise of a lecturer, I have turned my second persons plural into third persons singular. But I am sensible that the change will only commend itself by help of the reader's good-will in his remembering all the while that these are familiar discourses rather than learned inquiries.

They seek to discover, in some of his plays, just what Shakespeare was trying to do as a playwright. This has always seemed to me a sensible way of approaching him, and one worth reverting to from time to time. For it is no disparagement to the erudition and scholarship that have so piously been heaped about Shakespeare to say that we shall sometimes find it salutary to disengage our minds from it all, and recollect that the poet was a playwright.

I must thank my brother-in-law, Mr John Hay Lobban, for reading these pages in proof and making an index for me.

ARTHUR QUILLER-COUCH

1918

PREFACE

TO THIS EDITION

I HOPE that since this book first appeared (in 1918) I have learnt, in the process of helping to edit *The New Shakespeare*, some few things to correct previous confidence. But the main argument stands as defined above. Nor am I daunted at all by the frowns of those scholars— all their learning admitted—who claim an ability to pick out any passage from the Shakespearean canon and announce 'This is Kyd, that Marlowe, this other Chapman.' To be frank, I must, after examination, deny that they can do it, save on a claim to have access to sources of inspiration denied to ordinary men who (even as they) have never achieved superlative Drama.

My conviction at any rate persists that we may all approach Shakespeare in our several ways; and in each of them may usefully remind ourselves that the man we consent to admire was, by consent, a man of gentle manners.

Q.

1931

CONTENTS

CONTENTS

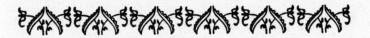

SHAKESPEARE'S WORKMANSHIP

CHAPTER I

MACBETH

I

Ways of studying Shakespeare—Method proposed for these notes—*Macbeth* to be considered as a piece of workmanship—The Elizabethan theatre, its audience and its stage—Shakespeare's 'conditions'—His 'material'—The 'material' of *Macbeth*—The capital difficulty of *Macbeth* as a tragedy—How Shakespeare might have extenuated it—How, rather, before setting to work, he made his problem as hard as possible.

(1)

I PROPOSE to take a single work of art, of admitted excellence, and consider its workmanship. I choose Shakespeare's tragedy of *Macbeth* as being eminently such a work: single or complete in itself, strongly imagined, simply constructed, and in its way excellent beyond any challenging.

There are, of course, many other aspects from which so unchallengeable a masterpiece deserves to be studied. We may seek, for example, and seek usefully, to fix its date and define its place in order of time among Shakespeare's writings; but this has been done for us, nearly enough. Or we may search it for light on Shakespeare, the man himself, and on his history, so obscure in the main, though here and there lit up by flashes of evidence, contemporary and convincing so far as they go. For my part, while admitting such curiosity to be human, and suffering myself now and again to be intrigued by it, I could never believe in it as a pursuit that really mattered. All literature must be personal: yet the artist—the great artist—dies into his work, and in that survives. What dread hand designed the Sphinx? What dread brain conceived its site, there, overlooking the desert? What sort of man was he who contrived Memnon, with a voice to answer the sunrise? What were the domestic or extra-domestic habits of Pheidias? Whom did Villon rob or Cellini cheat or Molière mock? Why did Shakespeare bequeath to his wife his second-best bed? These are questions which, as Sir Thomas Browne would say, admit a wide solution, and I allow some of them to be fascinating. 'Men are we,' and must needs wonder, a little wistfully, concerning the forerunners, our kinsmen who, having achieved certain things we despair to improve or even to rival, have gone their way, leaving so much to be guessed. 'How splendid,' we say, 'to have known them! Let us delve back and discover all we can about them!'

> Brave lads in olden musical centuries
> Sang, night by night, adorable choruses,
> 　Sat late by alehouse doors in April,
> Chaunting in joy as the moon was rising.
>
> Moon-seen and merry, under the trellises,
> Flush-faced they played with old polysyllables;
> 　Spring scents inspired, old wine diluted,
> Love and Apollo were there to chorus.
>
> Now these, the songs, remain to eternity,
> Those, only those, the bountiful choristers
> 　Gone—those are gone, those unremembered
> Sleep and are silent in earth for ever.

No: it is no ignoble quarrel we hold with Time over these men. But, after all, the moral of it is but summed up in a set of verses ascribed to Homer, in which he addresses the Delian Women. 'Farewell to you all,' he says, 'and remember me in time to come: and when any one of men on earth, a stranger from afar, shall inquire of you, "O maidens, who is the sweetest of minstrels here about? and in whom do you most delight?" then make answer modestly, "Sir, it is a blind man, and he lives in steep Chios."'

But the shutters are up at *The Mermaid*: and, after all, it is the masterpiece that matters—the Sphinx herself, the *Iliad*, the Parthenon, the Perseus, the song of the Old Héaulmières, *Tartufe*, *Macbeth*.

Lastly, I shall not attempt a *general* criticism of *Macbeth*, because that work has been done, exquisitely and (I think) perdurably, by Dr Bradley, in his published *Lectures on Shakespearean Tragedy*, a book which I can hardly start to praise without using the language of extravagance: a book which I hold to belong to the first order of criticism, to be a true ornament of our times. Here and there, to be sure, I cannot accept Dr Bradley's judgment: but it would profit my readers little to be taken point by point through these smaller questions at issue, and (what is more) I have not the necessary self-confidence.

If, however, we spend a little while in considering *Macbeth* as a *piece of workmanship* (or artistry, if you prefer it), we shall be following a new road which seems worth a trial —perhaps better worth a trial just because it lies off the trodden way; and whether it happen or not to lead us out upon some fresh and lively view of this particular drama, it will at least help us by the way to clear our thoughts upon dramatic writing and its method: while I shall not be false to my belief in the virtue of starting upon any chosen work of literature *absolutely*, with minds intent on discovering just that upon which the author's mind was intent.

I shall assume that *Macbeth* is an eminently effective play; that, by consent, it produces a great, and intended, impression on the mind. It is the shortest of Shakespeare's plays, save only *The Comedy of Errors*. It is told in just under 2000 lines—scarcely more than half the length of Hamlet. We may attribute this brevity in part—and we shall attribute it rightly—to its simplicity of plot, but that does not matter; or, rather, it goes all to *Macbeth's* credit. The half of artistry consists in learning to make one stroke better than two. The more simply, economically, you produce the impression aimed at, the better workman you may call yourself.

Now what had Shakespeare to *do*? He—a tried and competent dramatist—had to write a play: and if it be answered that everybody knew this without my telling it, I reply that it is the first thing some commentators forget. This play had to be an 'acting play': by which of course I mean a play to succeed on the boards and entertain, for three hours or so,[1] an audience which had paid to be entertained. This differentiates it at once from a literary composition meant to be read by the fireside, where the kettle does all the hissing. Therefore, to understand what Shakespeare as a workman was driving at, we must in imagination seat ourselves amid the audience he had in mind as he worked.

Moreover we must imagine ourselves in the Globe Theatre, Southwark, different in so many respects from the playhouses we know: because at every point of difference we meet with some condition of which Shakespeare had to

[1] In the Prologue to *Romeo and Juliet* Shakespeare talks of 'the two hours' traffic of our stage.' But the actual performance must have taken longer than two hours.

take account. The stage, raised pretty much as it is nowadays, was bare and ran out for some way into the auditorium, the central area of which was unroofed. Thus—the fashionable time for the theatre being the afternoon—the action, or a part of it, took place in daylight. When daylight waned, lanterns were called in, and some may agree with me, after studying Shakespeare's sense of darkness and its artistic value, that it were worth while, with this in mind, to tabulate the times of year, so far as we can ascertain them, at which his several plays were first performed. For my part, I am pretty sure that, among other conditions, he worked with an eye on the almanac.

To return to the stage of the Globe Theatre.—Not only did it run out into the auditorium: the audience returned the compliment by overflowing *it*. Stools, ranged along either side of it, were much in demand by young gentlemen who wished to show off their fine clothes. These young gentlemen smoked—or, as they put it, 'drank'—tobacco in clay pipes. So the atmosphere was free and easy; in its way (I suspect) not much unlike that of the old music-halls I frequented in graceless days, where a corpulent chairman called for drinks for which, if privileged to know him and sit beside him, you subsequently paid; where all joined companionably in a chorus; where a wink from the singer would travel—I know not how—around four-fifths of a complete circle.

The Elizabethan theatre had no painted scenery;[1] or

---

[1] 'The Elizabethan Stage,' 'the Elizabethan Drama,' are terms which actually cover a considerable period of time. It is certain that—say between 1550 and 1620—the theatre enormously improved its apparatus: upon the masques, as we know, very large sums of money were spent; and I make no doubt that before the close of Shakespeare's theatrical career, painted scenes and tapestries were the fashion.

little, and that of the rudest. At the back of the stage, at
some little height above the heads of the players, projected a
narrow gallery, or platform, with (as I suppose) a small
doorway behind it, and a 'practicable' ladder to give access
to it or be removed, as occasion demanded. Fix the ladder,
and it became the stairway leading to Duncan's sleeping-
chamber: take it away, and the gallery became the battlements of Dunsinane, or Juliet's balcony, or Brabantio's
window, or Shylock's from which Jessica drops the coffer,
or Cleopatra's up to which she hales dying Antony. From
the floor of this gallery to the floor of the stage depended
draperies which, as they were drawn close or opened, gave
you the arras behind which Falstaff was discovered in
slumber, or Polonius stabbed, the tomb of Juliet, Desdemona's bed, the stage for the play-scenes in *Hamlet* and the
Midsummer-Night's Dream, the cave of Prospero or of
Hecate.

To right and left of this draped alcove, beyond the pillars
supporting the gallery, were two doors giving on the back
and the green-room—*mimorum aedes*—for the entrances
and exits of the players.

Such was the Elizabethan theatre, with an audience so
disposed that, as Sir Walter Raleigh puts it, 'the groups of
players were seen from many points of view, and had to
aim at statuesque rather than pictorial effect.' When we take
the arrangements into account with the daylight and the lack
of scenic back-ground, we at once realise that it *must* have
been so, and that these were the conditions under which
Shakespeare wrought for success.

I must add another, though without asking it to be
taken into account just here. I must add it because, the
more we consider it, the more we are likely to count
it the heaviest handicap of all. All female parts were

taken by boys. Reflect upon this, and listen to Lady
Macbeth:

I have given suck, and know
How tender 'tis to love the babe that milks me:
I would, while it was smiling in my face,
Have pluck'd my nipple from his boneless gums
And dash'd the brains out, had I so sworn as you
Have done to this.

That in the mouth of a boy! Shakespeare's triumph over
this condition will remain a wonder, however closely it be
studied. Nevertheless, there it was: a condition which,
having to lay account with it, he magnificently overrode.

It were pedantic, of course, to lay upon a modern man
the strain of constantly visualising that old theatre on the
Bankside when reading Shakespeare, or, when seeing him
acted, of perpetually reminding himself, 'He did not write
it for *this*.' He did not, to be sure. But so potent was his
genius that it has carried his work past the conditions of his
own age to reincarnate, to revive, it in unabated vigour in
later ages and under new conditions, even as the *Iliad* has
survived the harp and the warriors' feast. This adaptable
vitality is the test of first-rate genius; and, save Shakespeare's,
few dramas even of the great Elizabethan age have passed
it. But, as for Shakespeare, I verily believe that, could his
large masculine spirit revisit London, it would—whatever
the *dilettante* and the superior person may say—rejoice in
what has been done to amplify that cage against which we
have his own word that he fretted, and would be proud of
the care his countrymen, after three centuries, take to interpret him worthily: and this although I seem to catch,
together with a faint smell of brimstone, his comments on
the 'star' performer of these days, with the limelight following him about the stage and analysing the rainbow upon his

glittering eye. These things, however, Shakespeare could not foresee: and we must seek back to the limitations of *his* theatre for our present purpose, to understand what a workman he was.

(2)

We pass, then, from the *conditions* under which he built his plays to the *material* out of which he had to build this particular one. The material of *Macbeth*, as we know, he found in Raphael Holinshed's *Chronicles of Scotland*, first published in 1578 (but he appears to have read the second edition, of 1587). It lies scattered about in various passages in the separate chronicles of King Duncan, King Duff, King Kenneth, King Macbeth; but we get the gist of it in two passages from the *Chronicle of King Duncan*. There is no need to quote them in full: but the purport of the first may be gathered from its opening:

Shortly after happened a strange and uncouth wonder....It fortuned as Macbeth and Banquho journeyed towards Fores, where the king as then lay, they went sporting by the way together without other companie save only themselves, passing through the woodes and fieldes, when sodenly, in the middes of a launde, there met them 3 women in strange and ferly apparell, resembling creatures of an elder worlde; whom they attentively behelde, wondering much at the sight.

Then follow the prophecies: 'All hayle, Makbeth, Thane of Glamis,' etc., with the promise to Banquho that 'contrarily thou in deede shalt not reigne at all, but of thee shall be borne which shall governe the Scottish Kingdome by long order of continuall descent.' I pause on that for a moment, merely because it gives a reason, if a secondary one, why the story should attract Shakespeare: for James I, a descendant of Banquho, had come to be King of England:

actors and playwrights have ever an eye for 'topical' opportunity, and value that opportunity none the less if it be one to flatter a reigning house.

I take up the quotation at a later point:

The same night at supper Banquho jested with him and sayde, Nowe Makbeth thou hast obtayned those things which the two former sisters prophesied, there remayneth onely for thee to purchase that which the thyrd sayd should come to passe. Whereupon Makbeth, revolving the thing in his mind even then, began to devise how he mighte attayne to the kingdome.

Next we read that Duncan, by appointing his young son, Malcolm, Prince of Cumberland, 'as it were thereby to appoint him his successor in the Kingdome,' sorely troubled Macbeth's ambition, insomuch that he now began to think of usurping the kingdom by force. The *Chronicle* goes on:

The wordes of the three weird sisters also (of whome before ye have heard) greatly encouraged him hereunto, but specially his wife lay sore upon him to attempt the thing, as she that was very ambitious burning in unquenchable desire to beare the name of a Queene. At length, therefore, communicating his proposed intent with his trustie friendes, amongst whom Banquho was the chiefest, upon confidence of their promised ayde, he slewe the king at Envernes (or as some say at Botgosuane) in the VI year of his reygne.

The *Chronicle* proceeds to tell how Macbeth had himself crowned at Scone; how he reigned (actually for a considerable time); how he got rid of Banquho; how Banquho's son escaped; how Birnam Wood came to Dunsinane, with much more that is handled in the tragedy; and ends (so far as we are concerned) as the play ends:

But Makduffe...answered (with his naked sworde in his hande) saying: it is true, Makbeth, and now shall thine insatiable crueltie have an ende, for I am even he that thy wysards have tolde thee of, who was never borne of my mother, but ripped out of her wombe: therewithall he stept unto him, and slue him in the place. Then cutting his heade from the shoulders, he set it upon a poll, and brought it unto Malcolme. This was the end of Makbeth, after he had reigned XVII years over the Scottish-men. In the beginning of his raigne he accomplished many worthie actes, right profitable to the common wealth (as ye have heard), but afterwards, by illusion of the Divell, he defamed the same with most horrible crueltie.

There, in brief, we have Shakespeare's material: and patently it holds one element on which an artist's mind (if I understand the artistic mind) would by attraction at once inevitably seize. I mean the element of the supernatural. It is the element which almost every commentator, almost every critic, has done his best to belittle. I shall recur to it, and recur with stress upon it; because, writing as diffidently as a man may who has spent thirty years of his life in learning to understand how stories are begotten, and being old enough to desire to communicate what of knowledge, though too late for me, may yet profit others, I can make affidavit that what first arrested Shakespeare's mind as he read the *Chronicle* was that passage concerning the 'three weird sisters'—'All hayle, Makbeth, Thane of Glamis!' and the rest.

Let us consider the *Chronicle* with this supernatural element left out, and what have we? An ordinary sordid story of a disloyal general murdering his king, usurping the throne, reigning with cruelty for seventeen years, and being overcome at length amid everyone's approval. There is no material for tragedy in that. 'Had Zimri peace, who slew his master?' Well (if we exclude the supernatural in the *Chronicle*), yes, he had; and for seventeen years: which, for a bloody tyrant, is no short run.

Still, let us exclude the supernatural for a moment. Having excluded it, we shall straightway perceive that the story of the *Chronicle* has one fatal defect as a theme of tragedy. For tragedy demands some sympathy with the fortunes of its hero: but where is there room for sympathy in the fortunes of a disloyal, self-seeking murderer?

Just there lay Shakespeare's capital difficulty.

(3)

Before we follow his genius in coming to grips with it, let us realise the importance as well as the magnitude of that difficulty. 'Tragedy (says Aristotle) is the imitation of an action: and an action implies personal agents, who necessarily possess certain qualities both of character and thought. It is these that determine the qualities of actions themselves: these—thought and character—are the two natural causes from which actions spring: on these causes, again, all success or failure depends.'[1]

But it comes to this—the success or failure of a tragedy depends on what sort of person we represent; and principally, of course, on what sort of person we make our chief tragic figure, our protagonist. Everything depends really on our protagonist: and it was his true critical insight that directed Dr Bradley, examining the substance of Shakespearean tragedy, to lead off with these words:

Such a tragedy brings before us a considerable number of persons (many more than the persons in a Greek play, unless the members of the Chorus are reckoned among them); but it is pre-eminently the story of one person, the 'hero,' or at most of two,

[1] I quote from Butcher's rendering, which gives the sense clearly enough; though, actually, Aristotle's language is simpler, and for 'thought' I should substitute 'understanding' as a translation of διάνοια.

the 'hero' and 'heroine.' Moreover, it is only in the love-tragedies, *Romeo and Juliet, Antony and Cleopatra*, that the heroine is as much the centre of the action as the hero. The rest, including *Macbeth*, are single stars. So that, having noticed the peculiarity of these two dramas, we may henceforth, for the sake of brevity, ignore it, and may speak of the tragic story as being concerned primarily with one person.

So, it makes no difference to this essential of tragedy whether we write our play for an audience of Athenians or of Londoners gathered in the Globe Theatre, Southwark: whether we crowd our *dramatis personæ* or are content with a cast of three or four. There must be one central figure (or at most two), and on this figure, as the story unfolds itself, we must concentrate the spectators' emotions of pity or terror, or both.

Now, I am going, for handiness, to quote Aristotle again, because he lays down very succinctly some rules concerning this 'hero' or protagonist, or central figure (call him what we will—I shall use the word 'hero' merely because it is the shortest). But let us understand that though these so-called 'rules' of Aristotle are marvellously enforced—though their wisdom is marvellously confirmed—by Dr Bradley's examination of the 'rules' which Shakespeare, consciously or unconsciously, obeyed, they do no more than turn into precept, with reasons given, certain inductions drawn by Aristotle from the approved masterpieces of his time. There is no reason to suppose that Shakespeare had ever heard of them; rather, there is good reason to suppose that he had not.

But Aristotle says this concerning the hero, or protagonist, of tragic drama, and Shakespeare's practice at every point supports him:

(1) A Tragedy must not be the spectacle of a perfectly good

man brought from prosperity to adversity. For this merely shocks us.

(2) Nor, of course, must it be that of a bad man passing from adversity to prosperity: for that is not tragedy at all, but the perversion of tragedy, and revolts the moral sense.

(3) Nor, again, should it exhibit the downfall of an utter villain: since pity is aroused by undeserved misfortunes, terror by misfortunes befalling a man like ourselves.

(4) There remains, then, as the only proper subject for Tragedy, the spectacle of a man not absolutely or eminently good or wise, who is brought to disaster not by sheer depravity but by some error or frailty.

(5) Lastly, this man must be highly renowned and prosperous —an Œdipus, a Thyestes, or some other illustrious person.

Before dealing with the others, let us get this last rule out of the way; for, to begin with, it presents no difficulty in *Macbeth*, since in the original—in Holinshed's *Chronicles*— Macbeth is an illustrious warrior who makes himself a king; and moreover the rule is patently a secondary one, of artistic expediency rather than of artistic right or wrong. It amounts but to this, that the more eminent we make our persons in Tragedy, the more evident we make the disaster —the dizzier the height, the longer way to fall, and the greater shock on our audience's mind. Dr Bradley goes further, and remarks, 'The pangs of despised love and the anguish of remorse, we say, are the same in a peasant and a prince: but (not to insist that they cannot be so when the prince is really a prince) the story of the prince, the triumvir, or the general, has a greatness and dignity of its own. His fate affects the welfare of a whole; and when he falls suddenly from the height of earthly greatness to the dust, his fall produces a sense of contrast, of the powerlessness of man, and of the omnipotence—perhaps the caprice—of

Fortune or Fate, which no tale of private life can possibly rival.' In this wider view Dr Bradley may be right, though some modern dramatists would disagree with him. But we are dealing more humbly with Shakespeare as a *workman*; and for our purpose it is more economical, as well as sufficient, to say that downfall from a high eminence is more spectacular than downfall from a low one; that Shakespeare, who knew most of the tricks of his art, knew this as well as ever did Aristotle, and those who adduce to us Shakespeare's constant selection of kings and princes for his *dramatis personæ*, as evidence of his having been a 'snob,' might as triumphantly prove it snobbish in a Greek tragedian to write of Agamemnon and Clytemnestra, or of Cadmus and Harmonia, because

> The gods had to their marriage come,
> And at the banquet all the Muses sang.

But, touching the other and more essential rules laid down by Aristotle, let me—very fearfully, knowing how temerarious it is, how imprudent to offer to condense so great and close a thinker—suggest that, after all, they work down into one:—that a hero of Tragic Drama must, whatever else he miss, engage our sympathy; that, however gross his error or grievous his frailty, it must not exclude our feeling that he is a man like ourselves; that, sitting in the audience, we must know in our hearts that what is befalling him might conceivably in the circumstances have befallen us, and say in our hearts, 'There, but for the grace of God, go I.'

I think, anticipating a little, I can drive this point home by a single illustration. When the ghost of Banquo seats itself at that dreadful supper, who sees it? Not the company. Not even Lady Macbeth. Whom does it accuse? Not the company, and, again, not even Lady Macbeth. Those who

see it are Macbeth and you and I. Those into whom it
strikes terror are Macbeth and you and I. Those whom it
accuses are Macbeth and you and I. And what it accuses is
what, of Macbeth, you and I are hiding in our own breasts.

So, if this be granted, I come back upon the capital
difficulty that faced Shakespeare as an artist.

(1) It was not to make Macbeth a grandiose or a
conspicuous figure. He was already that in the *Chronicle*.

(2) It was not to clothe him in something to illude us
with the appearance of real greatness. Shakespeare, with
his command of majestic poetical speech, had that in his
work-bag surely enough, and knew it. When a writer can
make an imaginary person talk like this:

> She should have died hereafter;
> There would have been a time for such a word.
> To-morrow, and to-morrow, and to-morrow
> Creeps in this petty pace from day to day
> To the last syllable of recorded time;
> And all our yesterdays have lighted fools
> The way to dusty death—

I say, when a man knows he can make his Macbeth talk like
that, he needs not distrust his power to drape his Macbeth
in an illusion of greatness. Moreover, Shakespeare—artist
that he was—had other tricks up his sleeve to convince us of
Macbeth's greatness. One of these I hope to discuss in a
subsequent chapter.

But (here lies the crux) how could he make us sympathise
with him—make us, sitting or standing in the Globe
Theatre some time (say) in the year 1610, feel that Macbeth
was even such a man as you or I? He was a murderer, and
a murderer for his private profit—a combination which
does not appeal to most of us, to unlock the flood-gates of
sympathy or (I hope) as striking home upon any private

and pardonable frailty. The *Chronicle* does, indeed, allow just one loop-hole for pardon. It hints that Duncan, nominating his boy to succeed him, thereby cut off Macbeth from a reasonable hope of the crown, which he thereupon (and not until then) by process of murder usurped, 'having,' says Holinshed, 'a juste quarrell so to do (as he took the mater).'

Did Shakespeare use that one hint, enlarge that loop-hole? He did not.

The more we study Shakespeare as an artist, the more we must worship the splendid audacity of what he did, just here, in this play of *Macbeth*.

Instead of using a paltry chance to condone Macbeth's guilt, he seized on it and plunged it threefold deeper, so that it might verily

> the multitudinous seas incarnadine.

Think of it:

He made this man, a sworn soldier, murder Duncan, his liege-lord.

He made this man, a host, murder Duncan, a guest within his gates.

He made this man, strong and hale, murder Duncan, old, weak, asleep and defenceless.

He made this man commit murder for nothing but his own advancement.

He made this man murder Duncan, who had steadily advanced him hitherto, who had never been aught but trustful, and who (that no detail of reproach might be wanting) had that very night, as he retired, sent, in most kindly thought, the gift of a diamond to his hostess.

To sum up: instead of extenuating Macbeth's criminality, Shakespeare doubles and redoubles it. Deliberately this

magnificent artist locks every door on condonation, plunges
the guilt deep as hell, and then—tucks up his sleeves.

There was once another man, called John Milton, a
Cambridge man of Christ's College; and, as most of us
know, he once thought of rewriting this very story of
Macbeth. The evidence that he thought of it—the entry in
Milton's handwriting—may be examined in the library of
Trinity College, Cambridge.

Milton did not eventually write a play on the story of
Macbeth. Eventually he preferred to write an epic upon
the Fall of Man, and of that poem critics have been found
to say that Satan, 'enemy of mankind,' is in fact the hero and
the personage that most claims our sympathy.

Now (still bearing in mind how the subject of Macbeth
attracted Milton) let us open *Paradise Lost* at Book IV
upon the soliloquy of Satan, which between lines 32–113
admittedly holds the *clou* of the poem:

O! thou that, with surpassing glory crown'd—

Still thinking of Shakespeare and of Milton—of Satan and
of Macbeth—let us ponder every line: but especially these:

Lifted up so high,
I 'sdain'd subjection, and thought one step higher
Would set me highest, and in a moment quit
The debt immense of endless gratitude,
So burdensome, still paying, still to owe:
Forgetful what from him I still receiv'd;
And understood not that a grateful mind
By owing owes not, but still pays at once
Indebted and discharg'd....

And yet more especially this:

Farewell, remorse! All good to me is lost:
Evil, be thou my good.

CHAPTER II

MACBETH

II

The criminal hero—Hallucination—What is witchcraft?—Dr Johnson on the witches in *Macbeth*—'Evil, be thou my good' —The use of darkness and its suggestions in Shakespeare's tragedies—Schiller and Schlegel—Vagueness of the witches— 'A deed without a name'—Deliberate enfeebling of all characters, save in the two protagonists—The critical word in this drama—The knocking at the gate.

(1)

WE left off upon the question, How could it lie within the compass even of Shakespeare, master-workman though he was and lord of all noble persuasive language, to make a tragic hero of this Macbeth—traitor to his king, murderer of his sleeping guest, breaker of most sacred trust, ingrate, self-seeker, false kinsman, perjured soldier? Why, it is sin of this quality that in *Hamlet*, for example, outlaws the guilty wretch beyond range of pardon—our pardon, if not God's.

> Upon my secure hour thy uncle stole....

Why, so did Macbeth upon Duncan's. Hear the wretch himself on his knees:

> Forgive me my foul murder?
> That cannot be; since I am still possess'd
> Of those effects for which I did the murder....

Why, so was Macbeth again.

> O bosom black as death!
> O limèd soul, that, struggling to be free,
> Art more engag'd!

How could Shakespeare make his audience feel pity or terror for such a man? Not for the deed, not for Duncan; but for Macbeth, doer of the deed; how make them sympathise, saying inwardly, 'There, but for the grace of God, might you go, or I'?

He could, by majesty of diction, make them feel that Macbeth was somehow a great man: and this he did. He could conciliate their sympathy at the start by presenting Macbeth as a brave and victorious soldier: and this he did. He could show him drawn to the deed, against will and conscience, by persuasion of another, a woman: and this—though it is extremely dangerous, since all submission of will forfeits something of manliness, lying apparently on the side of cowardice, and ever so little of cowardice forfeits sympathy—this, too, Shakespeare did. He could trace the desperate act to ambition, 'last infirmity of noble minds': and this again he did. All these artifices, and more, Shakespeare used. But yet are they artifices and little more. They do not begin—they do not pretend—to surmount the main difficulty which I have indicated, How of such a criminal to make a hero?

Shakespeare did it: *solutum est agendo*. How?

There is (I suppose) only one possible way. It is to make our hero—supposed great, supposed brave, supposed of certain winning natural gifts—proceed to his crime *under some fatal hallucination*. It must not be an hallucination of mere madness: for that merely revolts. In our treatment of lunatics we have come to be far tenderer than the Eliza-

2-2

bethans. (We recall Malvolio in the dark cellar.) Still, to us madness remains unaccountable; a human breakdown, out of which anything may happen. No: the hallucination, the dreadful mistake, must be one that can seize on a mind yet powerful and lead it logically to a doom that we, seated in the audience, understand, awfully forebode, yet cannot arrest—unless by breaking through the whole illusion heroically, as did a young woman of my acquaintance who, on her second or third visit to the theatre, arose from her seat in the gallery and shouted to Othello, 'Oh, you great black fool! Can't you *see*?'

Further, such an hallucination once established upon a strong mind, the more forcibly that mind reasons the more desperate will be the conclusion of its error; the more powerful is the will, or combination of wills, the more irreparable will be the deed to which it drives, as with the more anguish we shall follow the once-noble soul step by step to its ruin.

Now, of all forms of human error, which is the most fatal? Surely that of exchanging Moral Order, Righteousness, the Will of God (call it what we will) for something directly opposed to it: in other words, of assigning the soul to Satan's terrible resolve, 'Evil, be thou my good.'

By a great soul such a resolve cannot be taken save under hallucination. But if Shakespeare could fix that hallucination upon Macbeth and plausibly establish him in it, he held the key to unlock his difficulty. I have no doubt at all where he found it, or how he grasped it.

(2)

What is Witchcraft? Or first let us ask, What *was* Witchcraft?

Well, to begin with, it was something in which the mass

of any given audience in the Globe Theatre devoutly believed; and of the educated few less than one in ten, perhaps, utterly disbelieved. I shall not here inquire if Shakespeare believed in it; or, if at all, how far: but if Shakespeare did utterly disbelieve when he wrote (if he wrote) the First Part of *King Henry VI*, then it adds—what we could thankfully spare—one more feature of disgrace to his treatment of Joan of Arc.

Women were burnt for witches in Shakespeare's time, and throughout the seventeenth century and some way on into the eighteenth. We may read (and soon have our fill) in the pious abominable works of Cotton and Increase Mather of what these poor women suffered publicly, in New England and Massachusetts, at the hands of Puritan Fathers. We may find in Sinclair's *Satan's Invisible World Discovered* more than any Christian should bargain for concerning our home-grown beldames, and specially those of Scotland. To go right back to Shakespeare's time, we may study the prevalent, almost general, belief in Reginald Scot's *Discovery of Witchcraft* (1584). To the Elizabethans witchcraft was an accepted thing: their drama reeks of it. We need only call to mind Marlowe's *Faustus*, Greene's *Friar Bacon*, Middleton's *Witch*, Dekker's *Witch of Edmonton*.

I shall not labour this, because it has been seized on by Dr Johnson with his usual straight insight and expounded with his usual common sense. This play of *Macbeth* peculiarly attracted him. In 1745, long before he annotated the complete Shakespeare, he put forth a pamphlet entitled *Miscellaneous Observations on the Tragedy of Macbeth, with Remarks on Sir T. H.'s* (Sir Thomas Hanmer's) *Edition of Shakespeare*. To that pamphlet (says Boswell) he affixed proposals for a new edition of his own: and though no copy survives which contains them, he had certainly advertised his intention somehow and somewhere. As all the world knows, twenty years elapsed before, in October 1765, his constitutional lethargy at length overcome, there appeared his edition of Shakespeare in eight volumes.

Now what has Johnson to tell us of this his favourite play?

He begins on Act I, Scene 1, line i—nay, before it: on the stage direction, 'Enter Three Witches.' Says he:

In order to make a true estimate of the abilities and merits of a writer, it is always necessary to examine the spirit of his age and the opinions of his contemporaries. A poet who should now make the whole action of his tragedy depend upon enchantment, and produce the chief events by the assistance of supernatural agents, would be censored as transgressing the bounds of probability, be banished from the Theatre to the nursery, and condemned to write fairy-tales instead of tragedies.

Here I submit that Johnson talks too loudly. I may not actually believe in Jove or Apollo or Venus, 'mother of the Æneid race divine,' any more than I believe in Puck or in Oberon, or in ghosts as vulgarly conceived. Yet Jove, Apollo and Venus remain for me symbols of things in which I do firmly and even passionately believe: of things for which neither Christian doctrine nor modern Natural Science provides me with symbols that are equivalent or even begin to be comparable. Tradition has consecrated them: and an author to-day may invoke these names of gods once authentic; as an author to-day may employ ghosts, fairies, even witches, to convey a spiritual truth, without being suspected by anyone, not a fool, of literal belief in his machinery, of practising Walpurgis or Corybantic dances in his closet or drenching his garden at night with the blood of black goats.

But a survey [proceeds Johnson] of the notions that prevailed at the time when this play was written, will prove that *Shakespeare* was in no danger of such censures, since he only turned the system that was then universally admitted to his advantage, and was far from overburthening the credulity of his audience.

Some learned observations follow, on the Dark Ages and their credence in witchcraft; among which is introduced a story from Olympiodorus, of a wizard, one Libanius, who promised the Empress Placidia to defeat her enemies without aid of soldiery, and was promptly on his promise put to death by that strong-minded lady: 'who,' adds Johnson, 'shewed some kindness in her anger, by cutting him off at a time so convenient for his reputation.'

He continues:

The Reformation did not immediately arrive at its meridian, and tho' day was gradually increasing upon us, the goblins of witchcraft still continued to hover in the twilight. In the time of Queen *Elizabeth* was the remarkable trial of the witches of *Warbois*, whose conviction is still commemorated in an annual sermon at *Huntingdon*. But in the reign of King *James*, in which this tragedy was written, many circumstances concurred to propagate and confirm this opinion. The King, who was much celebrated for his knowledge, had, before his arrival in *England*, not only examined in person a woman accused of witchcraft, but had given a very formal account of the practices and illusions of evil spirits, the compacts of witches, the ceremonies used by them, the manner of detecting them, and the justice of punishing them, in his Dialogues of *Dæmonologie*, written in the *Scottish* dialect, and published at *Edinburgh*. This book was, soon after his accession, reprinted in London, and as the ready way to gain King *James's* favour was to flatter his speculations, the system of *Dæmonologie* was immediately adopted by all who desired either to gain preferment or not to lose it. Thus the doctrine of witchcraft was very powerfully inculcated; and as the greatest part of mankind have no other reason for their opinions than that they are in fashion, it cannot be doubted but this persuasion made a rapid progress, since vanity and credulity co-operated in its favour. The infection soon reached the parliament, who in the first year of King *James*, made a law by which it was enacted, chap. xii, that 'if any person shall use any invocation or conjuration of any evil or wicked spirit; 2, or shall consult, covenant with, entertain, employ, feed or reward any evil or cursed spirit to or for any intent or purpose; 3, or take up any dead man, woman or child out of the grave—or the skin, bone, or any part of the dead person—to be employed or used in any manner of witchcraft, sorcery, charm, or enchantment; 4, or shall use, practise or exercise any sort of witchcraft, sorcery, charm, or enchantment; 5, whereby any person shall be destroyed, killed, wasted, consumed, pined, or lamed in any part of the body; 6, that every such person being convicted shall suffer death.' This law was repealed in our own time.

Thus, in the time of *Shakespeare*, was the doctrine of witchcraft at once established by law and by the fashion, and it became not only unpolite, but criminal, to doubt it.

Upon this general infatuation *Shakespeare* might be easily allowed to found a play, especially since he has followed with great exactness such histories as were then thought true; nor can it be doubted that the scenes of enchantment, however they may now be ridiculed, were both by himself and his audience thought awful and affecting.

Thus wrote Johnson in the middle of the eighteenth century, 'the age of reason'; and, assuming that he talks sense, I put the further, more important question: 'What is, or was, Witchcraft?' 'What did men hold it, essentially and precisely, to mean?'

It meant, essentially and precisely, that the person who embraced witchcraft sold his soul to the devil, to become his servitor; that, for a price, he committed himself to direct reversal of the moral order; that he consented to say, 'Evil, be thou my good.' 'Satan, be thou my God.' It meant this, and nothing short of this.

Now let us return to Holinshed. The *Chronicle* relates that Macbeth and Banquo 'went sporting by the way together without other companie save only themselves, passing through the woodes and fieldes, when sodenly, in the middes of a launde there met them 3 women in strange and ferly apparell, resembling creatures of an elder worlde': and it adds that by common opinion these women 'were eyther the weird sisters, that is (as ye would say) ye Goddesses of destinee, or else some Nimphes or Faieries.' I have already announced my readiness to make affidavit that Shakespeare's mind, as he read, seized on this passage at once. Following this up, I will suggest (as a diversion from my main argument) a process—rough indeed, yet practical— by which a dramatist's mind would operate.

He would say to himself, 'I have to treat of a murder; which is, of its nature, a deed of darkness. Here to my hand is a passage which, whether I can find or not in it the motive of my plot, already drapes it in the supernatural, and so in mystery, which is next door to darkness.'

Let us pause here and remind ourselves how constantly Shakespeare uses darkness to aid the effect of his tragedies upon the spectator. To omit *Romeo and Juliet*—of which the tragic action really starts under a moonlit balcony and ends in a vaulted tomb—of the four tragedies by general consent preferred as greatest, *Hamlet* opens on the dark battlements of Elsinore, with a colloquy in whispers, such as night constrains, between sentinels who report a ghost visiting their watch: *Othello* opens with the mutter of voices in a dark street, and ends by the bedside lit by one candle: the total impression of *Lear* is of a dark heath upon which three or four men wander blindly, lit only at intervals by flashes from the dark elements; and the physical blindness of Kent (the one morally sane character in the piece) enhances our sense of impotent moral groping. Of *Macbeth* I cannot do better than quote Dr Bradley:

Darkness, we may even say blackness, broods over this tragedy. It is remarkable that almost all the scenes which at once recur to the memory take place either at night or in some dark spot. The vision of the dagger, the murder of Duncan, the murder of Banquo, the sleep-walking of Lady Macbeth, all come in night-scenes. The witches dance in the thick air of a storm, or 'black and midnight hags' receive Macbeth in a cavern. The blackness of night is to the hero a thing of fear, even of horror; and that which he feels becomes the spirit of the play. The faint glimmerings of the western sky at twilight are here menacing: it is the hour when the traveller hastens to reach safety in his inn, and when Banquo rides homeward to meet his assassins: the hour when 'light thickens,' when 'night's black agents to their prey do rouse,' when the wolf begins to howl, and the owl to scream, and withered murder steals forth to his work. Macbeth bids the stars hide their fires that his 'black' desires may be concealed: Lady Macbeth calls on thick night to come, palled in the dunnest smoke of hell. The moon is down and no stars shine when Banquo, dreading the dreams of the coming night, goes unwillingly to bed, and leaves Macbeth to wait for the summons of the little bell. When the next day should dawn, its light is 'strangled' and 'darkness does the face of earth entomb.' In the whole drama the sun seems to shine only twice: first, in the beautiful but ironical passage where Duncan sees the swallows flitting round the castle of death; and afterwards, when at the close the avenging army gathers to rid the earth of its shame. Of the many slighter touches which deepen this effect I notice only one. The failure of nature in Lady Macbeth is marked by her fear of darkness; 'she has light by her continually.' And in the one phrase of fear that escapes her lips even in sleep, it is of the darkness of the place of torment that she speaks.

'Hell is murky.' Yes, and upon the crucial test of the guilty king's soul in *Hamlet*—the play-scene—what is the cry?

    King. Give me some light—away!
    All. Lights, lights, lights!

What, again, is the scene that gives quality to *Julius Cæsar* but the brooding night in Brutus' garden? What, again (to go back among the plays), retrieves *The Merchant of Venice* from tragedy—from the surcharged air of the trial scene—to comedy, but the Fifth Act, with placid night shimmering towards dawn, and the birds starting to sing in the shrubberies, as Portia, mistress of the house and the play, says in four words what concludes all?—

    It is almost morning.

It may well be that Shakespeare, as a stage-manager, had means of employing darkness at will, say by a curtain pulled overhead across the auditorium, or part of it. If he had not —and the first account of the play by a spectator is by one Dr Forman, an astrologer, who paid for his seat in the Globe on Saturday, April 20th, 1610—that is, at a time of year when the sky over the theatre would be day-lit—I frankly confess my ignorance of how it was managed. But that Shakespeare saw the play in darkness, no one who has studied it can have any doubt at all.

He saw the whole thing in darkness, or at best in the murk light of the Scottish highlands. He saw it (as the play proves) a thing of night. Now, always and everlastingly, amongst men, as day typifies sight and sanity, night typifies blindness and evil. In the night-time murder stalks, witches ride, men doubt of God in their dreams—doubt even, lying awake—and wait for dawn to bring reassurance.

In darkness—in a horror of darkness only—can one mistake and purchase evil for good.

So, as I reason, Shakespeare saw his chance. I am weary, and over-weary, of commentators who dispute whether his witches were real witches or fates or what-not. Schiller, as all know, adapted *Macbeth*; and Schiller was a poet: but Schiller was no Shakespeare, and by philosophising Shakespeare's witches, as by other means, he produced a *Macbeth* remarkably unlike Shakespeare's *Macbeth*. Why, when he came to the knocking at the gate, Schiller omitted the Porter —in deference (I believe) to the genteel taste of his age— and substituted a Watchman, with a song to the rising dawn; and a charming song, too, with the one drawback that it ruins the great dramatic moment of the play. Schlegel rates Schiller roundly for his witches; and Gervinus says that Schlegel's censure is not a half-pennyworth too harsh. But Schlegel proceeds to evolve out of his inner consciousness a new kind of witch of his own; and this too has the merit of being a witch of Schlegel's own with the defect of being as much like Shakespeare's as any other camel. Thereupon starts up Gervinus, and says that Schlegel 'gives throughout an opposite idea of Shakespeare's meaning'; and forthwith proceeds in his turn to evolve his own camel, leading off with the observation that 'the poet, in the actual text of the play, calls these beings "witches" only derogatorily: they call themselves weird sisters.' Profoundly true!—and has anyone, by the way, ever known a usurer who called himself a usurer, or a receiver of stolen goods who called himself a receiver, or a pandar who called himself a pandar, or a swindler who called himself anything but a victim of circumstances? A few days ago, some enterprising firm sent me a letter which began (as I thought with gratuitous abruptness) 'We are not money-lenders'—and went on to suggest that if, however, I should need 'temporary financial accommodation,' they were prepared to advance any sum between £5 and £50,000.

But, as everybody knows who has studied the etiquette of traffic with Satan, it is the rule never to mention names. If Professor Gervinus had never, to ponder it, studied the tale of *Rumpelstiltskin*, he might at any rate have remembered the answer given to Macbeth's salutation in Act IV, Scene 1:

> *Macbeth.* How now, you secret, black, and midnight hags!
>   What is't you do?
> *All.*   A deed without a name.

—and if the deed be nameless, why not the doer? But if the reader insist on my being definite, when a lady wears a beard on her chin, and sails to Aleppo in a sieve, and sits at midnight boiling a *ragoût* of poisoned entrails, newt's eyes, frog's toes, liver of blaspheming Jew, nose of Turk and Tartar's lips, finger of birth-strangled babe, to make a gruel thick and slab for a charm of powerful trouble—I say, if he insist on my giving that lady a name, I for one am content with that given in the stage-direction, and to call her 'witch.'

But if these philosophising critics would leave their talk about Northern Fates, Norns, Valkyries—beings of which it is even possible that, save for the hint in Holinshed, Shakespeare had never heard, and certain that not one in ten of the Globe audience had ever heard—and would turn their learned attention to what Shakespeare as a workman *had to do*, could they miss seeing that a part of his very secret of success lay in leaving these creatures vague, the full extent of their influence dreadfully indeterminate? Coleridge on this, as not seldom, has the right word:

The Weird Sisters are as true a creation of Shakespeare's as his Ariel and Caliban—fates, furies, and materialising witches being the *elements*. They are wholly different from any representation of witches in the contemporary writers, and yet presented a sufficient external resemblance to the creatures of vulgar prejudice to act immediately on the audience. Their character consists in the imaginative disconnected from the good; they are the shadowy obscure and fearfully anomalous of physical nature, the lawless of human nature—elemental avengers without sex or kin.

> 'Fair is foul, and foul is fair;
> Hover through the fog and filthy air.'

I will put it in another way. Suppose that Shakespeare as a workman had never improved on what Marlowe taught. Suppose, having to make Macbeth choose evil for good, he had introduced Satan, definite, incarnate, as Marlowe did. Suppose he had made the man assign his soul, by deed or gift, on a piece of parchment and sign it with his blood, as Marlowe made Faustus do. What sort of play would *Macbeth* be?

But we know, and Shakespeare has helped to teach us, that the very soul of horror lies in the vague, the impalpable: that nothing in the world or out of it can so daunt and cow us as the dread of *we know not what*. Of darkness, again—of such darkness as this tragedy is cast in—we know that its menace lies in *suggestion* of the hooded eye watching us, the hand feeling to clutch us by the hair. No; Shakespeare knew what he was about when he left his witches vague.

Can we not see that very vagueness operating on Macbeth's soul? For a certainty, standing near in succession to the throne, he has, before ever the action begins, let his mind run on his chances. We need not say, with Coleridge, that 'he who wishes a temporal end for itself does in truth will the means:' but at least Macbeth has let his mind toy with the means. He has been on the stage scarce two minutes when, at the Third Witch's salutation—'All hail, Macbeth, that shalt be king hereafter'—he starts,

'betrayed by what is false within.'

'Good sir,' says Banquo,

'why do you start, and seem to fear
Things that do sound so fair?'

If we read and ponder Macbeth's letter to his wife; if we read and ponder what they say—yes, and specially ponder what they *omit* to say—when she greets his return; we see beyond shadow of doubt that certain things are understood between them. They had talked of the chance, even if, until this moment, they had forborne to speak of the way to it. These are things which, until the necessary moment arrives —the moment that summons action, now or never—cannot be uttered aloud, even between husband and wife.

Let us pause here, on the brink of the deed, and summarise:

(1) Shakespeare, as artificer of this play, meant the Witches, with their suggestions, to be of capital importance.

(2) Shakespeare, as a workman, purposely left vague the extent of their influence; purposely left vague the proportions of their influence; and Macbeth's own guilty promptings, his own acceptance of the hallucination, contribute to persuade him; vague as the penumbra about him in which— for he is a man of imagination—he sees that visionary dagger. For (let us remember) it is not on Macbeth alone that this horrible dubiety has to be produced; but on us also,

seated in the audience. We see what he does not see, and yearn to warn him; but we also see what he sees—the dagger, Banquo's ghost—and understand why he doubts.

(3) As witchcraft implies a direct reversal of the moral order, so the sight and remembrance of the witches, with the strange fulfilment of the Second Witch's prophecy, constantly impose the hallucination upon him—'Fair is foul, and foul is fair.' 'Evil, be thou my good.'

(3)

And now let us mark the daring of the great workman! So far he has carefully piled up shadows, doubts, darkness, half-meanings upon the distraught mind of Macbeth. Now, of a sudden, he confronts him with a will that has no doubts at all, but is all for evil: this in his wife, his 'dearest partner of greatness.' She, poor soul, is to suffer hereafter: but for the moment she sees the way—which is the evil way—with absolute conviction. May I, without undue levity, illustrate her clearness of purpose by this comparison?—

'Dearest Emma' (wrote a young lady), 'you will congratulate me when I tell you that Papa has this morning been offered the Bishopric of ——. It was quite unexpected. He is even now in the library, asking for guidance. Dear Mamma is upstairs, packing.'

So before the First Act closes—for actually, though our reluctant horror drags upon it, the action moves with a curious (nay, for an Elizabethan drama, with a singular) rapidity—the hallucination is established, the scene is set, and we behold this man and this woman groping their road to certain doom. So cunningly has Shakespeare, to heighten our interest in these, flattened down the other figures in the drama that none of them really matters to us. Duncan's

murder matters, but not Duncan. He sleeps, and anon after
life's fitful fever he is to sleep well : but the only fever *we* feel
burns or shivers in that tremendous pair. The thick walls of
Inverness Castle fence in the stealthy, damnable work. The
gate is closed, barred. Around and outside broods darkness;
yet even this is aware of something monstrous at work within.
An owl screams: 'there's husbandry in heaven': the stars,
'as troubled by man's act,' dare but peer through it as
through slits in a covering blanket: in the stables the horses
catch a panic and gnaw each other's flesh in their madness.
For within, up the stair, past the snoring grooms, a murderer
creeps to his deed, a woman prompting. In part, no doubt
—mostly, if we will—themselves have betrayed themselves:
but the powers of evil have their way and reign in that
horrible house.

So! and so—when it is done—as Lady Macbeth takes the
dagger and Macbeth still stares at his bloody hands, the
hour strikes and the word is spoken.

What word? It is the critical word of the drama: and yet
no voice utters it. As befits the horrible, impalpable, en-
closing darkness, it is no articulate word at all. What is it?

It is this:—*Knock! knock! knock! knock!*

A knocking at the gate—but *who* knocks? Can we suppose it is Macduff or Lennox? Who cares more than a
farthing for Macduff? Who cares even less than a farthing
for Lennox?

Then *who* is it—or, shall I say, *what* is it—stands without, on the other side of the gate, in the breaking dawn,
clamouring to be admitted? What hand is on the hammer?
Whose step on the threshold?

It is, if we will, God. It is, if we will, the Moral Order.
It is, whatever be our religion, that which holds humankind
together by law of sanity and righteousness. It is all that this

man and this woman have outraged. It is daylight, revealing things as they are and evil different from good. It is the tread of vengeance, *pede claudo*, marching on the house. Macbeth is king, or is to be. But that knock insists on what his soul now begins to know, too surely. Evil is *not* good; and from this moment the moral order asserts itself to roll back the crime to its last expiation.

Knock, knock! 'Here's a knocking indeed!' growls the Porter as he tumbles out. 'If a man were porter of hell-gate, he should have old turning the key....' 'Ay, my good fellow: *and that is precisely what you are!*'

CHAPTER III

MACBETH

III

De Quincey on the knocking at the gate—Dramatic effect of the 'closed door'—Inside and outside—The Porter—'Flattening' of minor characters—Banquo's part in the drama—The point of rest in art—Macduff, Lady Macduff, and the child—Lady Macbeth and the broken spring—Tragic 'irony'—Peculiar 'irony' of *Macbeth*—Relation of this play to Greek tragedy—Its greatness.

(1)

WE have examined at some length the means by which Shakespeare overcame his main difficulty—that of reconciling Macbeth as hero or protagonist with the 'deep damnation' of Duncan's taking-off. I do not think we have extenuated that damnation, as I am sure that Shakespeare has not extenuated it. Rather—to use a favourite word of Johnson's—he has 'inspissated' it, like a strong man glorying in his strength. If now we see how, accepting the murder, and all the murder, he has forced us into terrified sympathy—into actual *fellow-feeling* with the murderer—we hold the artistic secret of the drama.

I propose in this third chapter to take some specimens of his workmanship in this play and attempt to show how excellent it is in detail; not pretending to be exhaustive choossing more or less at random from the heap of excellence, seeing that, in Dryden's phrase, 'here is God's plenty.'

Nevertheless let us preserve the semblance of good order by starting afresh just where we left off—with the knocking at the gate.

Embedded in the works of De Quincey, like a prize in a bran-pie (the late William Ernest Henley used to call him, unjustly yet with some justice, 'De Sawdust'), there is to be found a little paper six pages long, and prolix at that, which contains the last word of criticism on this knocking at the gate.

De Quincey starts by confessing that 'from his boyish days' this knocking produced an effect on his mind for which he could never account. 'The effect was, that it reflected back upon the murderer a peculiar awfulness and depth of solemnity.' He goes on to tell us (as he told us elsewhere, in his *Murder Considered as One of the Fine Arts*) how in the dreadful business of the murders in the Ratcliffe Highway—a series of crimes so fiendish that nothing like them again thrilled London until the days of Jack the Ripper —there did actually happen what the genius of Shakespeare had invented two hundred years before. The murderer, one Williams, who had entered the house of the Marrs and locked the door behind him, was startled, right on the close of his bloody work, as he had butchered the last member of the family, by the knocking of a poor little servant-girl, the Marrs' maid-of-all-work, who had been sent out on an errand. De Quincey draws a wonderful picture of these two, one on either side of that thin street door, breathing close and listening: the little maid on the pavement, the stealthy devil in the passage, with his hand on the key, which, mercifully, he did not turn.

And here let us note, in parenthesis, how fashionable this

effect of the closed door has since become with dramatists. If we study Maeterlinck, for example, we shall find it his favourite master-trick. It is the whole secret of *L'Intruse*, of *The Death of Tintagiles*—the door with something dark, uncanny, foreboding, something that threatens doom on the other side. Maeterlinck has variants, to be sure. In *Les Aveugles* he makes it the shutter of physical darkness in a company of old people, all blind. Sometimes, as in *Intérieur* and *Les Sept Princesses*, he rarefies the partition to a glass screen through which one set of characters, held powerless to interfere, watches another set unconscious of observation. But in one way or another always the dramatic effect hangs on our sense of this barrier, whether impalpable or solid, whether transparent as glass or dense as a door of oak, locked, bolted, barred.

Now let De Quincey go on. In what happened to the Marrs' murderer he says he found the solution of what had always puzzled him—the effect wrought on his feelings by the knocking in *Macbeth*. A murderer—even such a murderer as a poet will condescend to—exhibits human nature in its most abject and humiliating attitude. Yet if, as in *Macbeth*, the murderer is to be the protagonist, upon him our interest *must* be thrown. But how?

In *Macbeth*, for the sake of gratifying his own enormous and teeming faculty of creation, Shakespeare has introduced two murderers: and, as usual in his hands, they are remarkably discriminated; but, though in Macbeth the strife of mind is greater than in his wife, the tiger spirit not so awake, and his feelings caught chiefly by contagion from her—yet, as both were finally involved in the guilt of murder, the murderous mind of necessity is finally to be presumed in both. This was to be expressed.... And, as this effect is marvellously accomplished in the *dialogues* and *soliloquies* themselves, so it is finally consummated by the expedient under consideration; and it is to this that I now solicit the reader's attention. If the reader has ever witnessed a wife, daughter, or sister in a fainting-fit, he may chance to have observed that the most affecting moment in such a spectacle is that in which a sigh and a stirring announce the recommencement of suspended life. Or, if the reader has ever been present in a vast metropolis on the day when some great national idol was carried in funeral pomp to his grave, and, chancing to walk near the course through which it passed, has felt powerfully in the silence and desertion of the streets, and in the stagnation of ordinary business, the deep interest which at that moment was possessing the heart of man—if, all at once, he should hear the death-like stillness broken up by the sound of wheels rattling away from the scene, and making known that the transitory vision was dissolved, he will be aware that at no moment was his sense of the complete suspension and pause in ordinary human concerns so full and affecting as at that moment when the suspension ceases and the goings-on of human life are suddenly resumed. All action in any direction is best expounded, measured, and made apprehensible, by reaction. Now apply this to the case in *Macbeth*. Here, as I have said, the retiring of the human heart, and the entrance of the fiendish heart, were to be expressed and made sensible. Another world has stept in; and the murderers are taken out of the region of human beings, human purposes, human desires. Macbeth has forgot that he was born of woman; both are conformed to the image of devils; and the world of devils is suddenly revealed. But how shall this be conveyed and made palpable? In order that a new world may step in, this world must for a time disappear. The murderers and the murder must be insulated—cut off by an immeasurable gulf from the ordinary tide and succession of human affairs—locked up and sequestered in some deep recess; we must be made sensible that the world of ordinary life is suddenly arrested—laid aside—tranced—racked into a dread armistice. [Time must be annihilated; relation to things without abolished; and all must pass self-withdrawn into a deep syncope and suspension of earthly passion.] Hence it is that when the deed is done, when the work of darkness is perfect, then the world of darkness passes away like a pageantry in the clouds: the knocking at the gate is heard; and it makes known audibly that the reaction has commenced; the human has made its reflux upon the fiendish; the pulses of life are beginning to beat again; and the re-establishment of the goings-on of the world in which we live first makes us profoundly sensible of the awful paren-thesis that had suspended them.

We perceive, then, with how right an artistry Shake-speare throws all the effect of this knocking upon the souls *within*. Suppose an inferior artist at work writing a play on this theme. Suppose he sets the scene on the outside of the door. Suppose Macduff and Lennox to arrive in the dawn, after the night of tempest, and to stand there, Macduff with his hand on the knocker, the pair chatting lightly before they ask admission. That were a situation with no little of tragic irony in it, since we, the spectators, know upon what they are to knock. Suppose the door to open upon a sudden cry and the sight of Duncan's body borne down by his sons into the daylight of the courtyard. That were a 'situation' indeed; yet how flat in comparison with Shake-speare's!

Let me give a special reason, too, why it would have been flat: for this also illustrates workmanship. It is that, except-ing only Banquo (and I am to talk of Banquo), he has deliberately flattened down every other character to throw up Macbeth and Lady Macbeth into high relief. For why? Because he had, against odds, to interest us in them, and only in them. As I demanded before, who cares more than a farthing for Macduff or even less than a farthing for Lennox? Says Dr Bradley of the Macduffs, 'Neither they,

nor Duncan, nor Malcolm, nor even Banquo himself have
been imagined intensely, and therefore they do not produce
that sense of unique personality which Shakespeare could
convey in a much smaller number of lines than he gives to
most of them. And this is, of course, even more the case
with persons like Ross, Angus and Lennox, though each of
these has distinguishable features. I doubt if any other great
play of Shakespeare's contains so many speeches which a
student of the play, if they were quoted to him, would be
puzzled to assign to the speakers. Let the reader turn, for
instance, to the Second Scene of the Fifth Act, and ask
himself why the names of the persons should not be inter-
changed in all the ways mathematically possible.' To be
sure they could: because Shakespeare was taking good care
all the time that not one of these puppets should engage our
interest, to compete in it for one moment with the two great
figures of guilt in whom (as I have tried to show) he had so
jealously to keep us absorbed.

(2)

I wish to pursue a little further this effect of flattening (as
I call it) the subsidiary characters. But first let me deal with
the Porter, and so get this business of the knocking out of the
way.

There are critics who find the Porter's humour offensive
and irrelevant: who complain (Heaven help them!) that it
is a low humour and ordinary. As Charles Lamb said of the
Surveyor, 'O, let me feel the gentleman's bumps—I *must*
feel his bumps.' For answer to these critics (if answer be
seriously required) I would refer them to a play entitled
Hamlet, Prince of Denmark, written about the same time
as *Macbeth* and, oddly enough, by the same author, and
invite them to explain why this same Prince of Denmark,

after an agonising colloquy with his father's ghost, should break out into shouting back on it, 'Art thou there, true-penny?' 'Well said, old mole!' and swearing his comrades to secrecy upon the profound remark that

> 'There's ne'er a villain dwelling in all Denmark
> But he's an arrant knave.'

This is the laughter in which surcharged hysteria breaks and expends itself. I have scarce patience to enlarge that ex-planation. Some who read these lines are too young, per-haps, to have yet suffered a great tension such as must sooner or later befall every man, though his life be ever so happy. He who has not known that tension stretched may-be over weeks, say by the almost desperate illness of a wife or a child, cannot know upon what sheer craziness the delivered soul recoils. Yet he may *guess*, as, alas! he will assuredly *learn*, and as Shakespeare *knew*.

To be brief, the Porter's speech is just such a discharge, vicarious, of the spectator's overwrought emotion; and it is quite accurately cast into low, everyday language, because that which knocks at the gate is not any dark terrific doom—for all the darkness, all the terror, is cooped within—but the sane, clear, broad, ordinary, common workaday order of the world reasserting itself, and none the more relentingly for being workaday, and common, and ordinary, and broad, clear, sane.

(3)

Let us now return to Shakespeare's clever—as it seems to me, his immensely clever—flattening of the virtuous charac-ters in this play. I have suggested the word for them—for your Rosses and Lennoxes. They are ordinary, and of purpose ordinary.

If we consider this carefully, we shall see that one or two consequences flow from it.

To begin with a very practical piece of workmanship—the Elizabethan stage, as I have remarked, had not a straight-drawn front, with footlights, but thrust forward from its broad platform a sort of horn upon the auditorium. Along this horn, or isthmus, a player who had some specially fine passage to declaim advanced and began, laying his hand to his heart—

'All the world's a stage...'

or

'The quality of mercy is not strained...'

or (raising his hand to his brow)

'To be, or not to be: that is the question'—

and, having delivered himself, pressed his hand to his heart again, bowed to the discriminating applause, and retired into the frame of the play. An Elizabethan audience loved these bravuras of conscious rhetoric, and in most of his plays Shakespeare was careful to provide opportunities for them. But we shall hardly find any in Macbeth. Here, by flattening the virtuous characters almost to figures on tapestry, Shakespeare flattened back his whole stage. Obviously, neither Macbeth nor his lady, with their known antecedents, was the kind of person to stalk forward and spout virtue: and the virtuous receive no chance, because virtue has all the while to be kept uninteresting.

Further, this flattening of the virtuous characters gives *Macbeth* (already Greek in its simplicity of plot) a further resemblance to Greek tragedy in its sense of fatality. I reiterate that nobody can care more than a farthing for Macduff on his own account. He had, to be sure, an unusual start in the world; but he has not quite lived up to it.

His escape, which leaves his wife and children at Macbeth's merciless mercy, is (to say the least) unheroic. Here again I suggest that Shakespeare's workmanship was sure. By effecting Macbeth's discomfiture through such men of straw, he impresses on us the conviction—or, rather, he leaves us no room for anything but the conviction—that Heaven has taken charge over the work of retribution; and the process of retribution is made the more imposing as its agents are seen in themselves to be naught.

(4)

I come now to Banquo, who really *has* individual character: and the more we study Banquo (limned for us in a very few strokes, by the way), the more, I think, we find cause to wonder at Shakespeare as a workman. The *Chronicle* makes Banquo guilty as an accomplice before the fact. Here are Holinshed's words:

At length therefore communicating his purposed intent with his trustie friendes, amongst whom Banquho was the chiefest, upon confidence of theyr promised ayde, he (Macbeth) slewe the King at Envernes, etc.

Now, in the play, on the eve of the murder, Macbeth does seem to hang for a moment on the edge of imparting his purpose to Banquo, who has just brought him the King's diamond. 'I dreamt,' says Banquo,

'I dreamt last night of the three weird sisters—
To you they have showed much truth.'

Macbeth returns:

'I think not of them:
Yet, when we can extract an hour to serve,
We would spend it in some words upon this business,
If you would grant the time.'

And Banquo replies:

> 'At your kindest leisure.'

His leisure! Macbeth's 'kindest leisure' at that moment! Let the reader remember it when I come to say a word on the all-pervading irony of this play. The dialogue goes on:

Macbeth. If you should cleave to my consent, when 'tis,
It shall make honour for you.

Banquo.   So I lose none
In seeking to augment it, but still keep
My bosom franchis'd and allegiance clear,
I shall be counsell'd.

Macbeth.   Good repose the while!
Banquo.   Thanks, sir: the like to you!

Now, why did Shakespeare avoid the *Chronicle* at this point and send Banquo to bed with a clear conscience? The commentators are ready, as usual. 'Why, don't you see? Banquo was to be father to a line of kings, the last of whom, in 1603, had inherited the throne of England also, "and two-fold balls and treble sceptres swayed." It would never do, in a play written some time before 1610 for performance by His Majesty's Servants, to depict His Majesty's Scottish forbear as an accomplice in treason.'

O Tweedledum! O Tweedledee! how near we came to forget something so profoundly true! Yet, though profoundly true, and even illuminating in its way, it scarcely illustrates the way in which dramatic masterpieces are constructed. At least, I think not.

Let us try again, and we shall find two most potent artistic reasons—one simple, the other subtler, but both (as I say) potent—why Shakespeare did not involve Banquo in Macbeth's guilt.

In the first place, it is surely obvious that by sharing the

plot up with Banquo and other 'trustie friendes' (in Holinshed's phrase) Shakespeare would have destroyed the im-
pressiveness of Macbeth and his wife. In proportion as he
dragged in that crowd, and just so far, would he have
shortened the stature, blurred the outlines, marred the effect
of that tremendous pair, who, as it is, command us by the
very isolation of their grandeur in guilt.

The second reason is subtler, though scarcely less strong.
In all great literature there is always a sense of the norm.
Even in Shakespeare's most terrific and seismic inventions—
when, as in *Hamlet* or in *Lear*, he seems to be breaking up
the solid earth under our feet—there is always some point
and standard of sanity to which all enormities and passionate
errors are referred by us, albeit unconsciously, for correc-
tion; on which the agitated mind of the spectator settles back
as upon its centre of gravity.

It was Coventry Patmore who first taught me to see this
clearly, in his little book *Principle in Art*. He calls it the
punctum indifferens, or Point of Rest. In a painting (he
shows) it may be—often is—something apparently insigni-
ficant: a sawn-off stump in a landscape of Constable's; in
the Dresden Madonna of Raphael, the heel of the Infant—
which yet, as we know, was to bruise, yea, to crush, the
Serpent's head. 'Cover these from sight,' says he, 'and, to
the moderately sensitive and cultivated eye, the whole life
of the picture will be found to have been lowered.' But, he
continues, it is

in the most elaborate plays of Shakespeare that we find this
device in its fullest value; and it is from two or three of these
that I shall draw my main illustration of a little noticed but
very important principle of art. In *King Lear* it is by the
character of Kent; in *Romeo and Juliet* by Friar Laurence; in
Hamlet by Horatio; in *Othello* by Cassio, and in *The Merchant*

of Venice by Bassanio,[1] that the point of rest is supplied....Thus Horatio is the exact *punctum indifferens* between the opposite excesses of the characters of Hamlet and Laertes—over-reasoning inaction and unreasoning action—between which extremes the whole interest of the play vibrates. The unobtrusive character of Kent is, as it were, the eye of the tragic storm which rages round it; and the departure, in various directions, of every character more or less from moderation, rectitude or sanity, is the more clearly understood or felt from our more or less conscious reference to him. So with the central and comparatively unimpressive characters in many other plays—characters unimpressive on account of their facing the exciting and trying circumstances of the drama with the regard of pure reason, justice, and virtue. Each of these characters is a peaceful focus radiating the calm of moral solution throughout all the difficulties and disasters of surrounding fate; a vital centre, which, like that of a great wheel, has little motion in itself, but which at once transmits and controls the fierce revolution of the circumference.

Now in *Macbeth* Banquo supplies this Point of Rest. He is—though on an enlarged scale, having to stand beside the 'hero'—the Ordinary Man. Like Macbeth, he is a thane, a general, a gallant soldier. The two have fought side by side for the same liege-lord and, without jealousy, have helped one another to conquer. They are brought upon the stage together, two equal friends returning from victory. To Banquo as to Macbeth the witches' predictions are offered. Macbeth shall be King of Scotland: Banquo shall beget kings. But whereas Macbeth, taking evil for good and under persuasion of his wife as well as of the supernatural, grasps at the immediate means to the end, Banquo, like an ordinary, well-meaning, sensible fellow, *doesn't do it*, and

---

[1] But no: by Antonio surely.—A. Q.-C.

therefore on the fatal night can go like an honest man to his dreams.

This is not to say that Banquo did not feel the temptation.

To be sure he did: and Shakespeare would not have been Shakespeare if he had not made Banquo feel it. The point is that, feeling it (I do not say strongly—it may have been lethargically, as ordinary decent men *do* feel the spur to emprises which mean the casting-off of honour), Banquo did not yield to it: and (as it seems to me) Dr Bradley wastes a great deal of subtlety in trying to show him an accessory after the event, since he apparently acquiesces in Macbeth's attainment of the crown, while suspecting his guilt. For or against this I shall only quote Banquo's own words when the murder is discovered—

> 'Fears and scruples shake us:
> In the great hand of God I stand, and thence
> Against the undivulged pretence I fight
> Of treasonous malice'

—and leave the reader to determine. For what does it matter? What *does* matter is that, of the two soldiers, one is tempted and yields, the other is tempted but does not yield.

And it matters in this way: that from the moment Macbeth yields and apparently succeeds, Banquo, who has not yielded, becomes a living reproach to him. He is the shadowiest of *dangers*, but a very actual *reproach*: and therefore Macbeth's first instinct is by removing Banquo to obliterate the standard of decency, of loyalty—if that loyalty were partial only, why, then, the more credit for obeying it—which survives to accuse him. So Banquo becomes naturally the first sacrifice to be paid to a guilty conscience, and Banquo is murdered.

But now let us mark this: We are scarcely yet midway

in Act III: a half of the play has to come and we have done
away with the one man who, on the principle we have been
examining, is the touchstone to test the wrong from the
reasonably right. All the other characters are mere shadows
of men, painted on the flat. Macduff survives to be the
avenger, but he is to be the avenger by no strength of his
own, and he survives (as we have seen) by a pretty base
action; fleeing the country and leaving his wife and children
behind, unprotected.

The answer is that Banquo survives in his ghost: and that
the accusing sanity is still carried forward in the next victim,
little Macduff—one of those gallant, precocious, straight-
talking children in whom Shakespeare delighted—it may
be because he had lost such a son, at just such an age. Be
it noted how this boy is introduced close after Macbeth's
purposed visit to the Witches—*he* seeking *them*, this time.
(Another touch of insight: it is always the Devil who first
accosts, and the lost soul that later pays the visits, seeking
ways of escape.)

Straight upon that foul scene in the cavern light breaks,
for the last time in the drama, in the sunny wisdom of a
child. Good gospel, too, as I take it—

'Was my father a traitor, mother?'
'Ay, that he was.'
'What *is* a traitor?'

—and so on. 'Now God help thee, poor monkey!' says
his mother at length (irony again), even while the Murderer
is at the gate, being admitted.

'Where is your husband?...He's a traitor,' are the words
in the Murderer's mouth.

'Thou liest, thou shag-hair'd villain,' answers up the
proud, plucky boy, a moment before he is stabbed.

All these pretty ones end tragically in Shakespeare: but surely this one in this play lives his few moments not wholly in vain.

(5)

The wonderful counterpoise of will and character between Macbeth and his wife has been so often and on the whole so well discussed that I shall take leave to say very little about it, on the understanding that there, at any rate, the marvels of the workmanship are accepted. But this brief note I will make:

Looking into the matter historically, I cannot find that critics even began to do Lady Macbeth justice until Mrs Siddons taught them. Johnson, for example, wrote that 'Lady Macbeth is merely detested.' An amazing judgment, truly, to one who saw Ellen Terry rehearsing the part, and sat and watched John Sargent painting her, in her green robe of beetles' wings, as she stood in the act of lifting the crown to her brow!

Exquisitely chosen moment! For, reading the play carefully, let us observe how, for her, everything ends in that achievement. Up to it, hers has been the tiger nature, with every faculty glued, tense on the purpose, on the prey: her husband but a half-hearted accomplice. The end achieved, it would seem that the spring of action somehow breaks within her. It is Macbeth who, like a man, shoulders the weight of moral vengeance. *She* almost fades out. She is always the great lady; and while she can, she helps. They are both great: never one vulgar word of reproach or recrimination passes between them. But they drift apart. Macbeth no longer relies on her. Uncounselled by her he seeks the Witches again; solitary he pursues his way; and *her* mental anguish is left to be watched by a Doctor and a Gentlewoman. It is but reported to her husband. When the wail of the waiting-woman announces her death, he is busy arming himself for his doom. All he finds to say on the word 'dead' is:

> 'She should have died hereafter:
> *There* would have been a time for such a word.'

(6)

Through its strong simplicity of plot, its flattening of the stage as of all the subsidiary characters, its working out of vengeance by agents who are carefully kept as mere puppets in the hand of Heaven, *Macbeth* bears a resemblance unique among Shakespeare's writings to Greek Tragedy; nor can it by accident be full of that irony in which the Greek tragedians—say Sophocles—delighted.

But it is to be observed that the irony most prevalent in *Macbeth* is, if not an invention of Shakespeare's own, at least different from the usual tragic irony, that consists in making the protagonist utter words which, coming on the momentary occasion to his lips, convey to the audience (who know what he does not) a secondary, sinister, prophetic meaning.

There is, to be sure, some of this traditional tragic irony in *Macbeth*: but its *peculiar* irony is retrospective rather than prophetic. It does not prepare the spectator for what is to come; but rather, when it comes, reminds him as by an echo that it has been coming all the while. Thus, when Macbeth and Lady Macbeth stare—how differently!—at their bloodied fingers, *he* says

> 'Will all great Neptune's ocean wash this blood
> Clean from my hand?'

She says confidently,

> 'A little water clears us of this deed.'

The irony is not yet. It comes in after-echo, in the sleep-walking scene, when (*he* having passed beyond account of it) *she* says, 'Here's the smell of blood still! All the perfumes of Arabia will not sweeten this little hand.'

So when the ghost of Banquo seats itself at the feast, we catch, as by echo, the insistent invitation,

> 'Fail not at our feast,'

with the promise,

> 'My lord, I will not':

as, when Macbeth calls out on the same ghost,

> 'What man dares, I dare:
> Take any shape but that!'

we hear again,

> 'I dare do all that may become a man:
> Who dares do more is none.'

Again, when Birnam Wood comes to Dunsinane, do we not catch again the whisper,

> 'Stones have been known to move and trees to speak'?

The whole play, as it were a corridor of dark Inverness Castle, resounds with such echoes: and I know no other tragedy that so teems with these peculiar whispers (as I will call them) of reminiscent irony.

Macbeth (as I have said and as others have said before me) curiously resembles Greek tragedy in a dozen ways, of which I will mention but one more.

Though it is full of blood and images of blood, the important blood-shedding is hidden, removed from the spectator's sight. There is, to be sure, a set scene for Banquo's murder: but it can be omitted without detriment to the play, and, in fact, always is omitted. Duncan is murdered off the stage; Lady Macbeth dies off the stage; Macbeth makes his final exit fighting, to be killed off the stage. There is nothing here like the blood-boltered culmination of *Hamlet*.

Lastly—for there is no space left to argue it—I must proclaim my conviction that this tragedy, so curiously resembling classical tragedy, does, in fact, overpass in its bold workmanship any classical tragedy.

As we remember, Milton once proposed to rewrite *Macbeth*. The entry in his list of projects runs: '*Macbeth*, beginning at the arrival of Malcolm at Macduff. The matter of Duncan may be expressed by the appearing of his ghost.'

Milton, in effect, wished to cast *Macbeth* in the strict form of classical tragedy, as he afterwards cast *Samson Agonistes*. And another Cambridge man, Professor Richard Moulton, has actually taken Shakespeare's *Macbeth* and, by one of the most brilliant *tours de force* in modern criticism, recast it, with a Chorus and all, step by step back into a Greek tragedy.

Yes, and he uses scarcely anything that cannot be found in Shakespeare. It is an uncannily clever performance. But his permanent scene is, of course, Dunsinane Castle, not Inverness. That is to say, the play begins when all but the slow retribution—all that we first think of in *Macbeth*—is concluded.

'I have done the deed. Didst thou not hear a noise?'

'*Infirm of purpose,*
Give me the daggers.'

(*Knock, knock, knock.*)

And he begins with a Prologue spoken by Hecate. Hecate!—I have said nothing of her because (to be quite frank) I do not yet understand her. The commentators, ready as usual, surmise that Middleton, or somebody like Middleton, interpolated Hecate. I hesitate to accept this. It does *not* appear likely to me that a whole set of foolish men (though Middleton in itself seems a well-enough-invented name) were kept permanently employed to come in and write something whenever Shakespeare wanted it foolish.

But...Hecate!

It is permissible, I hope, to the meanest of us to think to himself, at one time or another, 'Now which in the world among masterpieces should I be proudest (God giving me grace) to have written?' My own choice would not be *Macbeth*, nor, indeed, any tragedy: nor the *Divina Commedia*, nor *Paradise Lost* (since, divine as are the accents of Dante and Milton, their religious systems, so diverse, yet both based on hatred rather than on charity, do not attract me). I think I would rather have written *The Tempest* or *Don Quixote*, and can never decide between them. Yes, in *The Tempest* the amazing craft which had imagined and designed *Macbeth* has beaten out of darkness to anchor in a fair haven of peace and sanity. But for an operation of genius and skill, beating through the dark and never losing one inch of a tack, I know nothing to equal this marvellous drama.

CHAPTER IV

A MIDSUMMER-NIGHT'S DREAM

Shakespeare's and Dickens's use of pet devices—Women in male disguise—Shipwrecks—Influence of Lyly and Plautus—Advance from stagecraft to characterisation—The stigmata of a court play—The value of inquiring *How was the thing done?*—The import of the fairies and the clowns—An ideal setting for the play.

(1)

Dr Jowett, famous Master of Balliol—

But in the manner of Sterne I must break off, here at the outset, to recall that figure, so familiar to me in youth, as every morning he crossed the quad beneath my bedroom window in a contiguous college for an early trot around its garden; a noticeable figure, too—small, rotund, fresh of face as a cherub, yet with its darting gait and in its swallow-tailed coat curiously suggestive of a belated Puck surprised by dawn and hurrying to

hang a pearl in every cowslip's ear.

—Dr Jowett used to maintain that after Shakespeare the next creative genius in our literature was Charles Dickens. As everybody knows, Dickens left an unfinished novel behind him; and a number of ingenious writers from time to time have essayed to finish the story of *Edwin Drood*, constructing the whole from the fragment—yet not from the fragment only, since in the process they are forced into

examining the plots of other novels of his: so into recognising
that his invention had certain trends—certain favourite
stage-tricks, artifices, *clichés*—which it took almost predic-
ably; and so to argue, from how he constructed by habit,
how he probably would have constructed this tale.

I do not propose, in a paper on *A Midsummer-Night's
Dream*, to attempt an ending for *Edwin Drood*, but I
suggest that if inventive criticism, driven up against such an
obstacle as *Drood*, turns perforce to examine Dickens's
habitual trends of invention, his favourite artifices and
clichés, the same process may be as serviceable in studying
the workmanship of the greater artist, Shakespeare.

For example, no careful reader of Dickens can fail to
note his predilection for what I will call dénouement by
masked battery. At the critical point in story after story, and
at a moment when he believes himself secure, the villain is
'rounded on' by a supposed confederate or a supposed dupe;
a concealed battery is opened, catches him unawares, levels
him with his machinations to the ground. Thus Monks
brings about the crisis of *Oliver Twist*; thus Ralph Nickleby
and Uriah Heep come to exposure; thus severally Jonas and
Mr Pecksniff in *Martin Chuzzlewit*; thus Quilp and Brass
in *The Old Curiosity Shop*. Thus Haredale forces the
conclusion of *Barnaby Rudge*; thus in *Bleak House* Lady
Dedlock (though she, to be sure, cannot be reckoned among
the villains) is hunted down. *Hunted Down*, in fact, the
name of one of Dickens's stories, might serve for any other
of a dozen. Sometimes the denouncer—old Chuzzlewit,
Mr Micawber, Mr Boffin—reaches his moment after a
quite incredibly long practice of dissimulation. But always
the pursuit is patient, hidden; always the *coup* sudden,
dramatic, enacted before witnesses; always the trick is
essentially the same—and the guilty one, after exposure,

usually goes off and in one way or another commits suicide.

I instance one only among Dickens's pet devices. But he had a number of them: and so had Shakespeare.

Take the trick of the woman disguised in man's apparel. It starts with Julia in *The Two Gentlemen of Verona*. It runs (and good reason why it should, when we consider that all women's parts were acted by boys) right through the comedies and into *Cymbeline*. Portia, Nerissa, Jessica (these three in one play); Rosalind, Viola, Imogen—each in turn masquerades thus, and in circumstances that, unless we take stage convention on its own terms, beggar credulity.

> The bridegroom may forget the bride
> Was made his wedded wife yestreen,

but not in the sense that Bassanio and Gratiano forget. Is it credible that Bassanio shall catch no accent, no vibration, to touch, awaken, thrill his memory during all that long scene in the Doge's court, or afterwards when challenged to part with his ring? Translated into actual life, is it even conceivable?

Let us take another device—that of working the plot upon a shipwreck, shown or reported. (There is perhaps no better way of starting romantic adventures, misadventures, meetings, recognitions; as there is no better way to strip men more dramatically of all trappings that cover their native nobility or baseness.) *The Comedy of Errors* and *Pericles* are pivoted on shipwreck; by shipwreck Perdita in *The Winter's Tale* is abandoned on the magical seacoast of Bohemia. *Twelfth Night* takes its intrigue from shipwreck, and, for acting purposes, opens with Viola's casting-ashore:

Viola.   What country, friends, is this?
Captain.   Illyria, lady.

Viola.   And what should I do in Illyria?
           My brother he is in Elysium.
           Perchance he is not drown'd—what think you,
           sailors?
Captain. It is perchance that you yourself were sav'd.

The Tempest opens in the midst of shipwreck. In *The Comedy of Errors* and in *Twelfth Night* shipwreck leads on to another trick—that of mistaken identity, as it is called. In *The Comedy of Errors* (again) and *Pericles* it leads on to the trick of a long-lost mother, supposed to have perished in shipwreck, revealed as living yet and loving. From shipwreck the fairy Prince lands to learn toil and through it to find his love, the delicate Princess to wear homespun and find her lover.

One might make a long list of these favourite themes; from Shakespeare's pet one of the jealous husband or lover and the woman foully misjudged (Hero, Desdemona, Hermione), to the trick of the potion which arrests life without slaying it (Juliet, Imogen), or the trick of the commanded murderer whose heart softens (Hubert, Leonine, Pisanio). But perhaps enough has been said to suggest an inquiry by which any reader may assure himself that Shakespeare, having once employed a stage device with some degree of success, had never the smallest scruple about using it again. Rather, I suppose that there was never a great author who repeated himself at once so lavishly and so economically, still husbanding his favourite themes while ever attempting new variations upon them. In the very wealth of this variation we find 'God's plenty,' of course. But so far as I dare to understand Shakespeare, I see him as a magnificently indolent man, not agonising to invent new plots, taking old ones as clay to his hands, breathing life into that clay; anon unmaking, remoulding, reinspiring it. We know for a fact that he worked upon old plays, old chronicles, other men's romances. We know, too, that men in his time made small account of what we call plagiarism, and even now define it as a misdemeanour quite loosely and almost capriciously.[1] Shakespeare, who borrowed other men's inventions so royally, delighted in repeating and improving his own.

(2)

It has been pretty well established by scholars that the earlier comedies of Shakespeare run in the following chronological order: *Love's Labour's Lost*, *The Comedy of Errors*, *The Two Gentlemen of Verona*, *A Midsummer-Night's Dream*. It may, indeed, be argued that *The Comedy of Errors* came before *Love's Labour's Lost*, but whether it did or did not matters very little to us. So let us take the four in the order generally assigned by conjecture.

In the 1598 Quarto of *Love's Labour's Lost* we are informed that it was presented before her Highness this last Christmas and is now 'newly corrected and augmented by W. Shakespeare.' It was a court play, then, and indeed it bears every mark of one. It is an imitative performance, after the fashionable model of John Lyly, but it imitates with a high sense of humour and burlesques its model audaciously.

All young artists in drama are preoccupied with plot or 'construction.' 'Character' comes later. The plot of *Love's Labour's Lost* turns on 'confusion of identity,' the Princess

---

[1] For instance, any poet or dramatist may take the story of Tristram and Iseult and make what he can of it; whereas if I use a plot of Mr Hall Caine's or of Mrs Humphry Ward's, I am a branded thief. The reader will find an amusing attempt to delimit the offence of plagiarism in an appendix to Charles Reade's novel *The Wandering Heir*.

and her ladies masking themselves to the perplexity of their masked lovers. For the rest, in its whole conception, as in its diction, the thing is consciously artificial and extravagant from first to last.

The Comedy of Errors is an experiment on a different model; not Lyly now, but Plautus, and Plautus out-Plautus'd. Again we have confusion of identity for the motive, but here confusion of identity does not merely turn the plot, as in *Love's Labour's Lost*; it means all the play, and the play means nothing else. Where Plautus had one pair of twin brothers so featured that they cannot be told apart, Shakespeare adds another pair, and the fun is drawn out with astonishing dexterity. Let four things, however, be observed: (1) The feat is achieved at a total sacrifice of character—and indeed he who starts out to confuse identity must, consciously or not, set himself the task of obliterating character. (2) Unless a convention of pasteboard be accepted as substitute for flesh and blood, the events are incredible. (3) On the stage of Plautus the convention of two men being like enough in feature to deceive even their wives might pass. It was *actually* a convention of pasteboard, since the players wore masks. Paint two masks alike, and (since masks muffle voices) the trick is done. But (4) Shakespeare, dispensing with the masks, doubled the confusion by tacking a pair of Dromios on to a pair of Antipholuses; and to double one situation so improbable is to multiply its improbability by the hundred.

It is all done, to be sure, with such amazing resource that, were ingenuity of stagecraft the test of great drama, we might say, 'Here is a man who has little or nothing to learn.' But ingenuity of stagecraft is not the test of great drama; and in fact Shakespeare had more than a vast deal to learn. He had a vast deal to unlearn.

A dramatic author must start by mastering certain stage mechanics. Having mastered them, he must—to be great—unlearn reliance on them, learn to cut them away as he grows to perceive that the secret of his art resides in playing human being against human being, man against woman, character against character, will against will—not in devising 'situations' or 'curtains' and operating puppets to produce these. His art touches climax when his 'situations' and 'curtains' so befall that we tell ourselves, 'It is wonderful—yet what else could have happened?' *Othello* is one of the cleverest stage plays ever written. What does it leave us to say but, in an awe of pity, 'This is most terrible, but it must have happened so'? In great art, as in life, character makes the bed it lies on, or dies on.

So in the next play, *The Two Gentlemen of Verona*, we find Shakespeare learning and, perhaps even more deliberately, unlearning. *The Two Gentlemen of Verona* is not a great play: but it is a curious one, and a very wardrobe of 'effects' in which Shakespeare afterwards dressed himself to better advantage.

In *The Two Gentlemen of Verona* Shakespeare is feeling for character, for real men and women. Tricks no longer satisfy him. Yet the old tricks haunt him. He must have again, as in *The Comedy of Errors*, two gentlemen with a servant apiece—though the opposition is discriminated and more cunningly weighted. For stage effect Proteus (supposed a friend and a gentleman) must suddenly behave with incredible baseness. For stage effect Valentine must surrender his true love to his false friend with mawkish generosity that deserves nothing so much as kicking:

All that was mine in Silvia I give thee.

And what about Silvia? Where does Silvia come in? That

devastating sentence may help the curtain. But it blows all character to the winds, and it leaves *no* gentlemen in Verona.

(3)

We come to *A Midsummer-Night's Dream*, and, with the three earlier comedies to guide us, will attempt to conjecture how the young playwright would face this new piece of work.

First we shall ask, 'What had he to *do*?'

Nobody knows precisely when, or precisely where, or precisely how *A Midsummer-Night's Dream* was first produced. But it is evident to me that, like *Love's Labour's Lost* and *The Tempest*, it was written for performance at court; and that its particular occasion, like the occasion of *The Tempest*, was a court wedding. It has all the stigmata of a court play. Like *Love's Labour's Lost* and *The Tempest*, it contains an interlude; and that interlude—Bully Bottom's *Pyramus and Thisbe*—is designed, rehearsed, enacted for a wedding. Can anyone read the opening scene, or the closing speech of Theseus, and doubt that the occasion was a wedding? Be it remembered, moreover, how the fairies dominate this play; and how constantly and intimately fairies are associated with weddings in Elizabethan poetry, their genial favours invoked, their malign caprices prayed against. I take a stanza from Spenser's great *Epithalamion*:

Let no deluding dreames, nor dreadfull sights
Make sudden sad affrights;
Ne let house-fyres, nor lightnings helpelesse harmes,
Ne let the Pouke nor other evill sprights,
Ne let mischivous witches with theyr charmes,
Ne let hob-Goblins, names whose sense we see not,
Fray us with things that be not:
Let not the shriech Oule nor the Storke be heard,

Nor the night Raven that still deadly yels;
Nor damnèd ghosts cald up with mighty spels,
Nor griesly Vultures, make us once afeard,
Ne let th' unpleasant Quyre of Frogs still croking
Make us to wish the'r choking.
Let none of these theyr drery accents sing;
Ne let the woods them answer, nor theyr eccho ring.

And I compare this with the fairies' last pattering ditty in
our play:

Now the wasted brands do glow,
    Whilst the screech-owl, screeching loud,
Puts the wretch that lies in woe
    In remembrance of a shroud.
Now it is the time of night
    That the graves, all gaping wide,
Every one lets forth his sprite,
    In the church-way paths to glide:
And we fairies, that do run
    By the triple Hecate's team,
From the presence of the sun,
    Following darkness like a dream,
Now are frolic; not a mouse
Shall disturb this hallow'd house;
I am sent, with broom, before,
To sweep the dust behind the door.

　　*　*　*　*　*　*

To the best bride-bed will we,
Which by us shall blessèd be....

　　*　*　*　*　*　*

And each several chamber bless,
Through this palace, with sweet peace.

Can anyone set these two passages together and doubt
A Midsummer-Night's Dream to be intended for a merry

κάθαρσις, a pretty purgation of those same goblin terrors which Spenser would exorcise from the bridal chamber? For my part, I make little doubt that Shakespeare had Spenser's very words in mind as he wrote.

Here, then, we have a young playwright commissioned to write a wedding play—a play to be presented at court. He is naturally anxious to shine; and, moreover, though his fellow-playwrights already pay him the compliment of being a little jealous, he still has his spurs to win.

As I read the play and seek to divine its process of construction, I seem—and the reader must take this for what it is worth—to see Shakespeare's mind working somewhat as follows:

He turns over his repertory of notions, and takes stock.

'Lyly's model has had its day, and the bloom is off it; I must not repeat the experiment of *Love's Labour's Lost*.... I have shown that I can do great things with mistaken identity, but I cannot possibly express the fun of that further than I did in *The Comedy of Errors*; and the fun there was clever, but a trifle hard, if not inhuman....But here is a wedding; a wedding should be human; a wedding calls for poetry— and I long to fill a play with poetry. (For I *can* write poetry—look at *Venus and Adonis*!)...Still, mistaken identity is a trick I know, a trick in which I am known to shine.... If I could only make it poetical!...A pair of lovers? For mistaken identity that means two pairs of lovers....Yet, steady! We must not make it farcical. It was all very well to make wives mistake their husbands. That has been funny ever since the world began; that is as ancient as cuckoldry, or almost. But this is a wedding play, and the sentiment must be fresh. Lovers are not so easily mistaken as wives and husbands—or ought not to be—in poetry.

'I like, too'—we fancy the young dramatist continuing—

—'that situation of the scorned lady following her sweetheart....I did not quite bring it off in *The Two Gentlemen of Verona*; but it is none the less a good situation, and I must use it again.[1]...Lovers mistaking one another...scorned lady following the scorner...wandering through a wood (that is poetical, anyhow)....Yes, and by night; this play has to be written for a bridal eve....A night for lovers—a summer's night—a midsummer's night—dewy thickets—the moon.... The moon? Why, of course, the moon! Pitch-darkness is for tragedy, moonlight for softer illusion. Lovers can be pardonably mistaken—under the moon....What besides happens on a summer's night, in a woodland, under the moon?

'Eh?...Oh, by Heaven! Fairies! Real Warwickshire fairies! Fairies full of mischief—Robin Goodfellow and the rest. Don't I know about *them*? Fairies full of mischief —and for a wedding, too! How does that verse of Spenser's go?

Ne let the Pouke—

'Fairies, artificers and ministers of all illusion...the fairy ointment, philters, pranks, "the little western flower"—

> Before milk-white, now purple with Love's wounds,
> And maidens call it Love-in-Idleness.

These and wandering lovers, a mistress scorned—why, we scarcely need the moon, after all!'

Then—for the man's fancy never started to work but it straightway teemed—we can watch it opening out new alleys of fun, weaving fresh delicacies upon this central invention. 'How, for a tangle, to get one of the fairies caught in the web they spin? Why not even the Fairy Queen

---

[1] And he did: not only here, but in *All's Well That Ends Well*, for instance.

herself?...Yes; but the mortal she falls in with? Shall he be one of the lovers?...Well, to say the truth, I haven't given any particular character to these lovers. The absolute jest would be to bring opposite extremes into the illusion, to make Queen Mab dote on a gross clown....All very well, but I *haven't any clowns*....The answer to that seems simple: if I haven't, I ought to have....Stay! I have been forgetting the Interlude all this while. We must have an Interlude; our Interlude in *Love's Labour's Lost* proved the making of the play....Now suppose we make a set of clowns perform the Interlude, as in *Love's Labour's Lost*, and get them chased by the fairies while they are rehearsing? Gross flesh and gossamer—that's an idea! If I cannot use it now, I certainly will some day.[1]...But I *can* use it now! What is that story in Ovid, about Midas and the ass's ear? Or am I confusing it with another story—which I read the other day, in that book about witches—of a man transformed into an ass?'

Enough! I am not, of course, suggesting that Shakespeare constructed *A Midsummer-Night's Dream* just in this way. (As the provincial mayor said to the eminent statesman, 'Aha, sir! that's more than you or me knows. That's *Latin*!') But I do suggest that we can immensely increase our delight in Shakespeare and strengthen our understanding of him if, as we read him again and again, we keep asking ourselves *how the thing was done*. I am sure that—hopeless as complete success must be—by this method we get far nearer to the $\tau\grave{o}$ $\tau\acute{i}$ $\mathring{\eta}\nu$ $\epsilon\mathring{i}\nu\alpha\iota$ of a given play than by searching among 'sources' and 'origins,' by debating how much Shakespeare took from Chaucer's *Knight's Tale*, or how much he borrowed from Golding's *Ovid*, or how much Latin he learned at Stratford Grammar School, or how far

[1] He did. See the last Act of *The Merry Wives of Windsor*.

he anticipated modern scientific discoveries, or why he gave the names 'Pease-blossom,' 'Cobweb,' 'Moth,' 'Mustard-Seed' to his fairies. I admit the idle fascination of some of these studies. A friend of mine—an old squire of Devon—used to demonstrate to me at great length that when Shakespeare wrote, in this play, of the moon looking 'with a watery eye'—

> And when she weeps, weeps every little flower,
> Lamenting some enforcèd chastity—

he anticipated our modern knowledge of plant-fertilisation. Good man, he took 'enforced' to mean 'compulsory'; and I never dared to dash his enthusiasm by hinting that, as Shakespeare would use the word 'enforced,' an 'enforcèd chastity' meant a chastity violated.

(4)

Let us note three or four things that promptly follow upon Shakespeare's discovering the fairies and pressing them into the service of this play.

(1) To begin with, Poetry follows. The springs of it in the author's *Venus and Adonis* are released, and for the first time he is able to pour it into drama:

> And never, since the middle summer's spring,
> Met we on hill, in dale, forest or mead,
> By pavèd fountain, or by rushy brook,
> Or in the beachèd margent of the sea
> To dance our ringlets to the whistling wind....

> I know a bank whereon the wild thyme blows,
> Where oxlips, and the nodding violet grows
> Quite over-canopied with luscious woodbine,
> With sweet musk-roses, and with eglantine:
> There sleeps Titania some time of the night,
> Lull'd in these flowers....

The honey-bags steal from the humble bees,
And for night-tapers crop their waxen thighs,
And light them at the fiery glow-worm's eyes
To have my love to bed, and to arise:
And pluck the wings from painted butterflies
To fan the moonbeams from his sleeping eyes.

Never so weary, never so in woe,
Bedabbled with the dew and torn with briers—[1]

The overstrained wit of *Love's Labour's Lost*, the hard
gymnastic wit of *The Comedy of Errors*, allowed no chance
for this sort of writing. But the plot of *A Midsummer-
Night's Dream* invites poetry, and poetry suffuses the play,
as with potable moonlight.

(2) The logic-chopping wit of *Love's Labour's Lost* had
almost excluded humour. Hard, dry wit had cased *The
Comedy of Errors* against it. With Launce in *The Two
Gentlemen of Verona* we have an incidental, tentative experiment in humour; but Launce is no part of the plot.
Now, with Bottom and his men, we have humour let loose
in a flood. In the last Act it ripples and dances over the
other flood of poetry, until demurely hushed by the elves.
The two greatest natural gifts of Shakespeare were poetry
and humour; and in this play he first, and simultaneously,
found scope for them.

(3) As I see it, this invention of the fairies—this trust in
an imaginative world which he understands—suddenly, in
A Midsummer-Night's Dream, eases and dissolves four-fifths
of the difficulties Shakespeare has been finding with his

---

[1] Echoed from *Venus and Adonis*:

                          The bushes in the way
Some catch her by the neck, some kiss her face,
Some twine about her thigh to make her stay.

plots. I remember reading, some years ago, a critique by Mr Max Beerbohm on a performance of this play, and I wish I could remember his exact words, for his words are always worth exact quotation. But he said in effect, 'Here we have the Master, confident in his art, at ease with it as a man in his dressing-gown, kicking up a loose slipper and catching it on his toe.' *A Midsummer-Night's Dream* is the first play of Shakespeare's to show a really careless grace— the best grace of the Graces. By taking fairyland for granted, he comes into his inheritance; by assuming that we take it for granted, he achieves just that easy probability he had missed in several plays before trusting his imagination and ours.

(4) Lastly, let the reader note how the fairy business and the business of the clowns take charge of the play as it proceeds, in proportion as both of them are more real— that is, more really imagined—than the business of Lysander and Hermia, Demetrius and Helena. The play has three plots interwoven: (*a*) the main sentimental plot of the four Athenian lovers; (*b*) the fairy plot which complicates (*a*); and (*c*) the grotesque plot which complicates (*b*). Now when we think of the play the main plot (*a*) comes last in our minds, for in (*b*) and (*c*) Shakespeare has found himself.

(5)

I once discussed with a friend how, if given our will, we would have *A Midsummer-Night's Dream* presented. We agreed at length on this:

The set scene should represent a large Elizabethan hall, panelled, having a lofty oak-timbered roof and an enormous staircase. The cavity under the staircase, occupying in breadth two-thirds of the stage, should be fronted with folding or sliding doors, which, being opened, should re-

veal the wood, recessed, moonlit, with its trees upon a flat
arras or tapestry. On this secondary remoter stage the lovers
should wander through their adventures, the fairies now
conspiring in the quiet hall under the lantern, anon with-
drawing into the woodland to befool the mortals straying
there. Then, for the last scene and the interlude of *Pyramus
and Thisbe,* the hall should be filled with lights and company. That over, the bridal couples go up the great staircase.
Last of all—and after a long pause, when the house is
quiet, the lantern all but extinguished, the hall looking vast
and eerie, lit only by a last flicker from the hearth—the
fairies, announced by Puck, should come tripping back,
swarming forth from cupboards and down curtains, somer-
saulting downstairs, sliding down the baluster rails; all
hushed as they fall to work with their brooms—hushed, save
for one little voice and a thin, small chorus scarcely more
audible than the last dropping embers:

> Through this house give glimmering light,
>   By the dead and drowsy fire;
> Every elf and fairy sprite
>   Hop as light as bird from brier....
> Hand in hand, with fairy grace,
> Will we sing and bless this place.
>
>   Trip away,
>   Make no stay,
> Meet me all by break of day.

CHAPTER V

THE MERCHANT OF VENICE

Its juvenile appeal—The difference between setting *and* atmosphere—*Unsympathetic characters—Bassanio and Antonio—Bad workmanship—A vital flaw—Two sides of the Renaissance—Three plots of intrigue—Plot* versus *character—The humanising of Shylock—Exaggerated estimate of the Trial Scene—An amateur stage-manager's tribute to the workmanship of the play—Johnson on the 'holy hermit'—The Fifth Act.*

(1)

SINCE in the end it taught me a good deal, and since the reader too may find it serviceable, let me start by shortly rehearsing my own experience with *The Merchant of Venice*.

I came first to it as a schoolboy, and though I got it by heart I could not love the play. I came to it (as I remember) straight from the woodland enchantments of *As You Like It*, and somehow this was not at all as I liked it. No fairly imaginative youngster could miss seeing that it was picturesque or, on the face of it, romantic enough for anyone, as on the face of it no adventure should have been more delightful than to come out of the green Forest of Arden into sudden view of Venice, spread in the wide sunshine, with all Vanity Fair, all the *Carnaval de Venise*, in full swing on her quays; severe merchants trafficking, porters sweating with bales, pitcher-bearers, flower-girls, gallants; vessels lading, discharging, repairing; and up the narrower waterways black gondolas shooting under high guarded windows, any gondola you please hooding a secret—of love, or assassination, or both—as any shutter in the line may open demurely, discreetly, giving just room enough, just time enough, for a hand to drop a rose; Venice again at night—lanterns on the water, masqued revellers taking charge of the quays with drums, hautboys, fifes, and general tipsiness; withdrawn from this riot into deep intricacies of shadow, the undertone of lutes complaining their love; and out beyond all this fever, far to southward, the stars swinging, keeping their circle—as Queen Elizabeth once danced—'high and disposedly' over Belmont, where on a turfed bank—

> Peace ho! the moon sleeps with Endymion,
> And would not be awak'd,

though the birds have already started to twitter in Portia's garden. Have we not here the very atmosphere of romance?

Well, no.... We have a perfect *setting* for romance; but setting and atmosphere are two very different things. I fear we all suffer temptation in later life to sophisticate the thoughts we had as children, often to make thoughts of them when they were scarcely thoughts at all. But fetching back as honestly as I can to the child's mind, I seem to see that he found the whole thing heartless, or (to be more accurate) that he failed to find any heart in it and was chilled: not understanding quite what he missed, but chilled, disappointed none the less.

Barring the Merchant himself, a merely static figure, and Shylock, who is meant to be cruel, everyone of the Venetian *dramatis personæ* is either a 'waster' or a 'rotter' or both, and cold-hearted at that. There is no need to expend ink upon such parasites as surround Antonio—upon Salarino and Salanio. Be it granted that in the hour of his extremity they have no means to save him. Yet they see it coming; they discuss it sympathetically, but always on the assumption that it is his affair not theirs—

> Let good Antonio look he keep his day,
> Or he shall pay for this,

and they take not so much trouble as to send Bassanio word of his friend's plight, though they know that for Bassanio's sake his deadly peril has been incurred! It is left to Antonio himself to tell the news in that very noble letter of farewell and release:

Sweet Bassanio: My ships have all miscarried, my creditors grow cruel, my estate is very low, my bond to the Jew is forfeit; and since in paying it it is impossible I should live, all debts are cleared between you and I, if I might but see you at my death. Notwithstanding, use your pleasure: if your love do not persuade you to come, let not my letter.

—a letter which, in good truth, Bassanio does not too extravagantly describe as 'a few of the unpleasant'st words that ever blotted paper.' Let us compare it with Salarino's account of how the friends had parted:

> I saw Bassanio and Antonio part:
> Bassanio told him he would make some speed
> Of his return: he answer'd, 'Do not so;
> Slubber not business for my sake, Bassanio,
> But stay the very riping of the time;
> And for the Jew's bond which he hath of me,
> Let it not enter in your mind of love:
> Be merry; and employ your chiefest thoughts
> To courtship, and such fair ostents of love
> As shall conveniently become you there':

And even there,[1] his eye being big with tears,
Turning his face, he put his hand behind him,
And with affection wondrous sensible
He wrung Bassanio's hand: and so they parted.

But let us consider this conquering hero, Bassanio. When we first meet him he is in debt, a condition on which—having to confess it because he wants to borrow more money—he expends some very choice diction.

'Tis not unknown to you, Antonio,

(No, it certainly was not!)

How much I have disabled mine estate
By something showing a more swelling port
Than my faint means would grant continuance.

That may be a mighty fine way of saying that you have chosen to live beyond your income; but, Shakespeare or no Shakespeare, if Shakespeare mean us to hold Bassanio for an honest fellow, it is mighty poor poetry. For poetry, like honest men, looks things in the face, and does not ransack its wardrobe to clothe what is naturally unpoetical. Bassanio, to do him justice, is not trying to wheedle Antonio by this sort of talk; he knows his friend too deeply for that. But he is deceiving *himself*, or rather is reproducing some of the trash with which he has already deceived himself.

He goes on to say that he is not repining; his chief anxiety is to pay everybody, and

To you, Antonio,
I owe the most, in money and in love;

and thereupon counts on more love to extract more money, starting (and upon an experienced man of business, be it

[1] Let the reader note this 'there,' so subtly repeated that we see the man turning on the spot and on the word together.

observed) with some windy nonsense about shooting a second arrow after a lost one.

> You know me well; and herein spend but time
> To wind about my love with circumstance;

says Antonio; and, indeed, his gentle impatience throughout this scene is well worth noting. He is friend enough already to give all; but to be preached at, and on a subject—money —of which he has forgotten, or chooses to forget, ten times more than Bassanio will ever learn, is a little beyond bearing. And what is Bassanio's project? To borrow three thousand ducats to equip himself to go off and hunt an heiress in Belmont. He has seen her; she is fair; and

> Sometimes from her eyes
> I did receive fair speechless messages....
> Nor is the wide world ignorant of her worth;
> For the four winds blow in from every coast
> Renowned suitors; and her sunny locks
> Hang on her temples like a golden fleece;
> Which makes her seat of Belmont Colchos' strand,
> And many Jasons come in quest of her.
> O my Antonio, had I but the means
> To hold a rival place with one of them,
> I have a mind presages me such thrift
> That I should questionless be fortunate!

Now this is bad workmanship and dishonouring to Bassanio. It suggests the obvious question, Why should he build anything on Portia's encouraging glances, as why should he 'questionless be fortunate,' seeing that—as he knows perfectly well, but does not choose to confide to the friend whose money he is borrowing—Portia's glances, encouraging or not, are nothing to the purpose, since all depends on his choosing the right one of three caskets—a two to one chance against him?

But he gets the money, of course, equips himself lavishly, arrives at Belmont; and here comes in worse workmanship. For I suppose that, while character weighs in drama, if one thing be more certain than another it is that a predatory young gentleman such as Bassanio would *not* have chosen the leaden casket. I do not know how his soliloquy while choosing affects the reader:

> The world is still deceiv'd with ornament,
> In law, what plea so tainted and corrupt,
> But, being season'd with a gracious voice,
> Obscures the show of evil? In religion,
> What damned error, but some sober brow
> Will bless it, and approve it with a text.

—but *I* feel moved to interrupt: 'Yes, yes—and what about yourself, my little fellow? What has altered you, that you, of all men, start talking as though you addressed a Young Men's Christian Association?'

And this flaw in characterisation goes right down through the workmanship of the play. For the evil opposed against these curious Christians is specific; it is Cruelty; and, yet again specifically, the peculiar cruelty of a Jew. To this cruelty an artist at the top of his art would surely have opposed mansuetude, clemency, charity, and, specifically, Christian charity. Shakespeare misses more than half the point when he makes the intended victims, as a class and by habit, just as heartless as Shylock without any of Shylock's passionate excuse. It is all very well for Portia to strike an attitude and tell the court and the world that

> The quality of mercy is not strain'd:
> It droppeth as the gentle rain from heaven....

But these high-professing words are words and no more to us, who find that, when it comes to her turn and the court's turn, Shylock gets but the 'mercy' of being allowed (1) to pay half his estate in fine, (2) to settle the other half on

> the gentleman
> That lately stole his daughter,

and (3) to turn Christian. (Being such Christians as the whole gang were, they might have spared him *that* ignominy!) Moreover, with such an issue set out squarely in open court, I do not think that any of us can be *satisfied* with Portia's victory, won by legal quibbles as fantastic as anything in *Alice in Wonderland*; since, after all, prosecution and defence have both been presented to us as in deadly earnest. And I have before now let fancy play on the learned Bellario's emotions when report reached him of what his impulsive niece had done with the notes and the garments he had lent to her. Indeed, a learned Doctor of another University than Padua scornfully summed up this famous scene to me, the other day, as a set-to between a Jew and a Suffragette.

Why are these Venetians so empty-hearted? I should like to believe—and the reader may believe it if he will—that Shakespeare was purposely making his Venice a picture of the hard, shallow side of the Renaissance, even as in *Richard III* he gives us a finished portrait of a Renaissance scoundrel ('I am determined to be a villain'), of the Italianate Englishman who was proverbially a devil incarnate. He certainly knew all about it; and in that other Venetian play, *Othello*, he gives us a real tragedy of two passionate, honest hearts entrapped in that same *milieu* of cold, practised, subtle malignity. I should like to believe, further, that against this Venice he consciously and deliberately opposed Belmont (the Hill Beautiful) as the residence of that better part of the Renaissance, its 'humanities,' its adoration of beauty, its wistful dream of a golden age. It is, at any rate, observable in the play that—whether under the spell of Portia or from some other cause—nobody arrives at Belmont who is not instantly and marvellously the better for it; and this is no less true of Bassanio than of Lorenzo and Jessica and Gratiano. All the suitors, be it remarked— Morocco and Aragon no less than Bassanio—address themselves nobly to the trial and take their fate nobly. If this be what Shakespeare meant by Belmont, we can read a great deal into Portia's first words to Nerissa in Act V as, reaching home again, she emerges on the edge of the dark shrubbery—

> That light we see is burning in my hall.
> How far that little candle throws his beams!
> So shines a good deed in a naughty world

—a *naughty* world; a world that is naught, having no heart.

It were pleasant (I say) to suppose this naughtiness, this moral emptiness of Venice, deliberately intended. But another consideration comes in.

(2)

Any school manual will recite for us the 'sources' of *The Merchant of Venice*. Briefly, we all know that it intertwists three plots of intrigue; and we need not vex ourselves here with their origins, because they are nothing to our purpose. We have:

Plot I. The story of the Jew and the pound of flesh.
Plot II. The story of the caskets.
Plot III. The intrigue of the exchanged rings.

To this summary I but append two remarks. The first,

obvious to anybody, is that Plots I and II, the pound of flesh and the caskets, are monstrous and incredible; the pound of flesh business starkly inhuman, the casket business scarcely more plausible when we examine it. Be it granted that, as Nerissa says, 'holy men at their death have good inspirations.' Yet this profound explanation scarcely covers Portia's father, since in point of fact his devise gave his daughter to a lucky fortune-hunter. Ulrici, like Portia's father, had a good inspiration; *he* divined that Shakespeare 'showed consummate art in introducing one improbability, that of the caskets, to balance and, as it were, excuse the other improbability, that of the pound of flesh'(!) The third intrigue—that of the exchanged rings—is mere light comedy.

For my other remark: In Stephen Gosson's *Schoole of Abuse*, an incentive against stage-plays by a playwright turned Puritan, published in 1579—when Shakespeare was a boy of fifteen and before he had written a line—there occurs an allusion to a play called *The Jew*, and described as 'representing the greediness of worldly chosers and bloody mind of usurers.' These coincident phrases—'The Jew,' 'the greediness of worldly chosers,' 'the bloody mind of usurers'—indicate a play on the very lines of *The Merchant of Venice*, and tell us, as well as such casual evidence can, (1) that Shakespeare was refurbishing an old play, (2) that the two themes of the pound of flesh and the caskets had already been combined in that play before Shakespeare ever took it in hand to improve it.

Reading this into Gosson's allusion, we see Shakespeare tackling, as a workman, an old piece of work which already included two monstrous, incredible stories. Even if we rule out Gosson, we see Shakespeare about to combine in one play these two monstrous, incredible stories, *plus* a third which is an intrigue of light comedy separate from both.

It does not matter to which alternative we incline. With either of them Shakespeare's first task as an artist was *to distract attention from the monstrosities and absurdities in the plot*. I shall return to this.

(3)

For the moment I postpone it, to consider another necessity. Every artist knows, and every critic from Aristotle down, that the more you complicate your plot—the more threads you tie together in your *nexus*—the less room you leave yourself for invention and play of character. That is ABC; and it is almost ABC that with three entanglements in hand—one inhuman, two incredible, one fantastic —and three hours to do your trick in—you almost exclude your chance of working seriously upon character.

Shakespeare had two outlets only, and he took full advantage of both. I rule out Antonio, who, as I said, is merely static. He is made, and rightly, the pivot of the action (and drama is by its very name dynamic). But the pivot is inert; he himself scarcely lifts a hand.

There remain Shylock and Portia, who do the work.

I am going to say very little upon Shylock, who, to my thinking, has been over-philosophised and yet more drearily over-sentimentalised. Charles Kean or Macklin began it. Irving completed (I hope) what they began. Heine, himself a Jew, tells how in a box at Drury Lane he sat next to 'a pale, fair Briton who at the end of the Fourth Act fell a-weeping passionately, several times exclaiming, "the poor man is wronged"'; and Heine goes on to return the compliment in better coin, with talk about 'a ripple of tears that were never wept by eyes…a sob that could come only from a breast that held in it the martyrdom endured for eighteen centuries by a whole tortured people.'

That is all very well. Few of us doubt that Shakespeare often wrote greater than he knew; that he is what we can read into him. But the point is that he started out to make Shylock such a cruel, crafty, villainous Hebrew as would appeal to an audience of Elizabethan Christians. The very structure of the plot shows that.

But every author knows how a character of his invention will sometimes take charge of him; as every reader must recognise and own in Shakespeare an imagination so warm, so large, so human, so catholic, that it could not, creating even a Caliban, help sympathising with Caliban's point of view. So it is with Falstaff; and so it is with Shylock. As I see Shylock, he takes charge of his creator, fenced in by intricacies of plot and finding outlets for his genius where he can. Shakespeare so far sympathises that, even in detail, the language of Shylock is perfect. I think it was Hazlitt who noted the fine Hebraism of his phrase when he hears that his runaway daughter has given in Genoa a ring to purchase a monkey:

Thou torturest me, Tubal! It was my turquoise: I had it of Leah when I was a bachelor: I would not have given it for *a wilderness of monkeys*.

Let us open our Bible for comparison, say, at the first chapter of Isaiah:

And the daughter of Zion is left as a cottage in a vineyard, a lodge in a garden of cucumbers, as a besieged city.

Supposing ourselves lodged in a garden of cucumbers, what could we more appropriately overlook, beyond its fence, than a wilderness of monkeys?

It is curious to reflect that Shakespeare most likely had never seen a Jew in his life.

(4)

Let us turn to Portia, the only other character on whom the pleached fence of the plot permits Shakespeare to expatiate. Hazlitt says, 'Portia is not a very great favourite with us....Portia has a certain degree of affectation and pedantry about her, which is very unusual in Shakespeare's women.' Pedantry, or a touch of it, she *must* have in the trial scene. It is a part of the plot. But—'affectation'? Let us for a moment dismiss that importunate trial scene from our minds and listen to these lovely lines, in which she gives herself, utterly, without low bargaining, as Shakespeare's adorable women always do, out of confessed weakness springing to invincibility:

> You see me, Lord Bassanio, where I stand,
> Such as I am: though for myself alone
> I would not be ambitious in my wish,
> To wish myself much better; yet, for you,
> I would be trebled twenty times myself;
> A thousand times more fair, ten thousand times
> More rich;
> That only to stand high in your account,
> I might in virtues, beauties, livings, friends,
> Exceed account; but the full sum of me
> Is sum of—something: which, to term in gross,
> Is an unlesson'd girl, unschool'd, unpractis'd;
> Happy in this, she is not yet so old
> But she may learn: happier than this,
> She is not bred so dull but she can learn;
> Happiest of all is that her gentle spirit
> Commits itself to yours to be directed
> As from her lord, her governor, her king.
> Myself and what is mine to you and yours
> Is now converted: but now I was the lord

> Of this fair mansion, master of my servants,
> Queen o'er myself: and even now, but now,
> This house, these servants, and this same myself
> Are yours, my lord; I give them with this ring—

This, by the way, is the first we hear of the ring; and we may observe how cunningly Shakespeare foists on us this new card, a moment after he has finished with the caskets. For though he runs three plots in *The Merchant of Venice*, he runs but two at a time. Indeed, he does not actually get to work on this plot of the ring (or, rather, of the rings) until Act IV, Scene 1, line 426, at the very moment again when the pound of flesh plot is played out and done with. But *here* we are prepared for it:

> I give them with this ring:
> Which when you part from, lose, or give away,
> Let it presage the ruin of your love,
> And be my vantage to exclaim on you.

'A girl's fancy?—a caprice?' we ask ourselves, noting a thought too much of emphasis laid on this trifle. Yet, after all, if Portia choose to make it a token of the much she is giving, why should she not? So we let it pass, to remember it later on.

But when we consider the body of this speech of Portia's (far more beautiful, with the reader's leave, than her more famous one on the quality of mercy, line by line flowing straight from a clean heart) and compare it with Bassanio's trash about his debts, surely our instinct discriminates between things that poetic language can, and things it cannot, dignify.

I regret to add that William Collins, author of the *Ode to Evening* (a poem which I worship 'on this side idolatry'), uttered, comparing him with Fletcher, the most fatuous observation pronounced upon Shakespeare by any critic, living or dead or German. In his Epistle to Sir Thomas Hanmer he actually wrote:

Of softer mould the gentle Fletcher came,
The next in order as the next in name.
With pleas'd attention 'midst his scenes we find
Each glowing thought that warms the female mind;
Each melting sigh, and every tended tear,
The lover's wishes and the virgin's fear,
His every strain the Smiles and Graces own:
But stronger Shakespeare felt for men alone.

A man who has said that deserves, on either side of the grave, the worst he can get, which is to have it repeated. Portia, indeed, is the earliest portrait in Shakespeare's long gallery of incomparable women. We can feel her charm at the full only if we get the Trial Scene back to its right focus. We then see what was amiss with Hazlitt, for instance, when he grumbled over 'a certain degree of affectation and pedantry about her...which perhaps was a proper qualification for the office of a civil doctor.' He had the Trial Scene in his eye. Now all star actors and actresses tend to exaggerate the significance of this scene, because it gives them an unrivalled occasion to exploit, as Portia or as Shylock, their personalities, their picturesqueness, their declamatory powers— Shylock whetting his knife on his boot, Portia publicly out-manning man, yet in garments decorously ample. Worse, far worse! it has become the happiest hunting-ground of the amateur.

There ought to be a close time for this scene. I grant it to be the crisis of the action. But it has been sentimentalised and sophisticated until we can scarcely see the rest of the play; and I, for one, long hated the rest of the play for its sake.

6-2

(5)

Here I take up and continue the personal confession. Some four or five years ago I had to stage-manage *The Merchant of Venice*. This meant that for two good months I lived in it and thought about little else. Having once achieved the difficult but necessary feat of getting the Trial Scene back into focus, I found a sense of the workmanship growing in me, and increasing to something like amazement: in the midst of which certain things new to me emerged and became clear.

Of these I beg to offer my report.

(1) To begin with, for purpose of the report—though in fact and in time it came about last of my little discoveries— Shakespeare was working upon that old play alluded to by Gosson, which combined the two incredible stories of the pound of flesh and the caskets. He started with his hands tied.

(2) He started, as in such hap every artist must, with one paramount object—*to distract our attention from the monstrous absurdity of the story*. Now let us mark with what ingenuity he does it. All artists know it for an axiom that *if you are setting out to tell the incredible, nothing will serve you so well as to open with absolute realism*. Then, with this axiom in mind, let us consider the first scene of this play. There is nothing about any pound of flesh in it. Still more astonishing, while the adventure to win Portia is propounded and discussed, there is not a word about caskets! By the end of the scene Shakespeare has impressed on our minds:—

(*a*) That we are dealing with people as real as ourselves;

(*b*) that Antonio, a rich merchant, has so deep an affection for young Bassanio that he will forget all business caution to help him;

and
> (*c*)—cunningest of all, when later we look back—
that this man of affairs, rather deeply involved, gets
very anxious without knowing quite why. The reader
goes on to note how it increases Antonio's hold on us
when he shakes off all his own melancholy at the first
hint of helping his friend.

As for the pound of flesh, we next observe how Shylock
in Scene III slides it in under cover of a jest. By this time
Shakespeare has us at his mercy; all the characters are so real
to us that we have no choice but to accept all the incredibilities to come. And meanwhile and moreover all the stage
for those incredibilities has been set in Antonio's opening
confession:

> In sooth I know not why I am so sad,

and Bassanio's other premonition, as with a start of fear—

> I like not fair terms and a villain's mind.

'Come on,' Antonio reassures him heartily—*he* is the cheer-
ful one now, forgetful of self and his own premonitions—

> Come on! in this there can be no dismay:
> My ships come home a month before the day.

(3) Launcelot Gobbo is patently own brother and twin
to Launce of *The Two Gentlemen of Verona*, and I think him
no improvement on Launce. But if we follow back that
hint and turn the pages of the earlier play, we soon begin to
rub our eyes. Inured as we are to Shakespeare's habit of
economising his material, of turning old plots, tricks, situations to new uses, his 'rifacciamenting' (if I may coin the
word) of *The Two Gentlemen of Verona* in *The Merchant of
Venice* is audacious. For a sample, compare the two early
scenes in which the two heroines discuss their lovers; while,
as for the main device of *The Two Gentlemen of Verona*—

the heroine in mannish disguise—in *The Merchant of Venice* there are but three female characters, and they *all* don man's clothes!

(4) 'This is a play,' wrote Hazlitt, 'that in spite of the change of manners still holds undisputed possession of the stage.' It does to-day; and yet on the stage, sophisticated by actors, it had always vexed me, until, coming to live with an acting version, I came to track the marvellous stage-cleverness of it all; when, in revulsion, I grew impatient with all judgments of Shakespeare passed on the mere reading of him. This had happened to me before with *The Taming of the Shrew*—a play noisier in the study than on the stage; strident, setting the teeth on edge; odious, until acted; when it straightway becomes not only tolerable, but pleasant, and not only pleasant, but straightforwardly effective. In particular, I had to own of *The Merchant of Venice* that the lines which really told on the stage were lines the reader passes by casually, not pausing to take their impression. It fairly surprised me, for an example, that Lorenzo's famous speech in the last Act—about the music and the moonlight and the stars—though well delivered, carried less weight than four little words of Portia's.

(5) And this brings me to the last Act, so often discussed. It became plain to me that Shakespeare had made at least one attempt at it before satisfying himself; as plain as that, if we resolutely hold the Trial Scene back to focus, this finish becomes the most delightful Act in the play.

That Shakespeare tried other ways is made evident by one line. Upon Lorenzo's and Jessica's lovely duet there breaks a footfall. Lorenzo, startled by it, demands—

Lorenzo. Who comes so fast in silence of the night?
Voice. A friend.

Lorenzo.   A friend? What friend? Your name, I pray you,
            Friend? [*Stephano enters.*]
Stephano. Stephano is my name; and I bring word
            My mistress will before the break of day
            Be here at Belmont; she doth stray about
            By holy crosses, where she kneels and prays
            For happy wedlock hours.
Lorenzo.   Who comes with her?
Stephano. None but a holy hermit, and her maid....

Nothing loose in literature—in play or in poem—ever caught Dr Johnson napping. 'I do not perceive,' says Johnson, in his unfaltering accent, 'the use of this hermit, of whom nothing is seen or heard afterwards. The Poet had first planned his fable some other way; and inadvertently, when he changed his scheme, retained something of the original design.'

But the Fifth Act, as Shakespeare finally gives it to us, is lovely past compare, even after professionals have done their worst on the Trial Scene. Nay, whatever they did or omitted, the atmosphere of the Doge's court was thunderous, heavily charged; after all, a good man's life was at stake, and we have hung on the lips of the pleaders. We have to be won back to a saner, happier acceptance of life; and so we are, by gracious, most playful comedy. It is all absurd, if we please. The unsealing of a letter telling Antonio, to make joy complete, that

> Three of your argosies
> Are richly come to harbour suddenly,

is unbelievable.

'You shall not know,' Portia adds—

> You shall not know by what strange accident
> I chancèd on this letter.

No; nor anyone else! It is absurd as the conclusion of *The Vicar of Wakefield*. Yet it is not more absurd than the ending of most fairy-tales.

And while all this has been passing, the moon has sunk and every thicket around Belmont has begun to thrill and sing of dawn. Portia lifts a hand.

> It is almost morning....

Let us go in.

CHAPTER VI

AS YOU LIKE IT

Lodge's *Rosalynde*, and *The Tale of Gamelyn*—The Forest of Arden—Its site on the Avon—A fantasy in colour—Jaques and Touchstone—A fantastic criticism of life—Playing at Robin Hood—Swinburne and George Sand—The influence of Lyly—An incongruous patch.

(1)

FOR the actual plot of *As You Like It* we have not to seek very far. Shakespeare took his story from a contemporary novel, *Rosalynde, Euphues' Golden Legacie*, written by Thomas Lodge and first published in 1590. Lodge derived a good part of his story from *The Tale of Gamelyn*, included in some MSS. of the *Canterbury Tales*, but certainly not written by Chaucer and probably packed by him among his papers as material for the *Yeoman's Tale* which he never wrote.[1]

[1] On this I cannot do better than quote Professor Skeat:
'Some have supposed, with great reason, that this tale occurs among the rest because it is one which Chaucer intended to recast, although, in fact, he did not live to rewrite a single line of it. This is the more likely because the tale is a capital one in itself, well worthy of being rewritten even by so great a poet; indeed, it is well known that the plot of the favourite play known to us all by the title of *As you Like It* was derived from it at second-hand. But I cannot but protest against the stupidity of the botcher whose hand wrote above it, "The Coke's Tale of Gamelyn." This was done because it happened to be found *next*

The Tale of Gamelyn (as the reader may remember) runs in this fashion:

> Litheth and lesteneth || and herkeneth aright,
> And ye schulle heere a talking || of a doughty knight;
> Sire Johan of Boundys || was his rightë name...

and he leaves three sons. The eldest, succeeding to the estate, misuses the youngest brother, who triumphs in a wrestling-bout and, escaping to the greenwood with an old retainer, Adam the Spencer, becomes an outlaw. The eldest brother, Johan, as sheriff, pursues him—just as the proud sheriff of Nottingham pursues Robin Hood. He is taken, and bailed; returns, in ballad-fashion (like the Heir of Linne, for example), just in time to save his bail, and the wicked Johan is sent to the gallows.

Upon this artless ballad Lodge tacked and embroidered a love-story—of an exiled King of France and of his daughter, Rosalind, who falls in love with the young wrestler, and escapes with the usurper's daughter Alieda (Celia) to the greenwood. As in the play, the usurper's daughter becomes 'Aliena' and Rosalind disguises herself as a page and calls herself 'Ganymede.' The name of the faithful old retainer, 'Adam,' persists down from *The Tale of Gamelyn* to *As You Like It*, and is the name of the character which (tradition says) Shakespeare as an actor personated in his own play.

after the "Coke's Tale."...The fitness of things ought to show at once that this "Tale of Gamelyn," a tale of the woods in true Robin Hood style, could only have been placed in the mouth of him "who bare a mighty bow," and who knew all the ways of wood-craft; in one word, of the Yeoman....And we get hence the additional hint, that the Yeoman's Tale was to have followed the Coke's Tale, a tale of fresh country life succeeding one of the close back-streets of the city. No better place could be found for it.'

(2)

So much for the source of the plot. But the plot of *As You Like It* is no great matter. Indeed, I would point out that by the end of Act I it is practically over and done with. With the opening of Act II we reach the Forest of Arden; and thenceforth, like the exiled Duke and his followers, we 'fleet the time carelessly, as they did in the golden world.' But let me quote the whole of Charles the Wrestler's answer to Oliver's question, 'Where will the old Duke live?' for in some five lines it gives us not only the Robin Hood and Gamelyn tradition of the story, but the atmosphere in which Shakespeare is to clothe it:

They say he is already in the forest of Arden, and a many merry men with him; and there they live like the old Robin Hood of England: they say many young gentlemen flock to him every day, and fleet the time carelessly, as they did in the golden world.

'They say...they say'—I note those two *they says*, to return to them anon. For the moment let us be content to mark that no sooner do we arrive at the fringe of this forest with the other fugitives (and I break off to remark that they all in turn reach it dead-beat. Sighs Rosalind, 'O Jupiter, how weary are my spirits!' invoking Jupiter as a Ganymede should. Touchstone retorts, 'I care not for my spirits, if my legs were not weary'; and Celia entreats, 'I pray you, bear with me; I cannot go further': as, later on, old Adam echoes, 'Dear master, I can go no further'; and again, we remember, Oliver arrives footsore, in rags, and stretches himself to sleep, so dog-tired that even a snake, coiling about his throat, fails to awaken him. It is only the young athlete Orlando who bears the journey well)—I say that the fugitives, and we too, no sooner win to the forest than life is found to have

changed its values for us, as it has awhile already for the
Duke and his followers. Henceforth we hear next to nothing
of the usurping Duke Ferdinand and his court, and we care
less. We have left him behind. He is not suffered again to
obtrude his person, and in the last Act we learn of his
repentance but by report:

> Duke Frederick, hearing how that every day
> Men of great worth resorted to this forest,
> Address'd a mighty power; which were on foot,
> In his own conduct, purposely to take
> His brother here and put him to the sword:
> And to the skirts of this wild wood he came;
> Where meeting with an old religious man,
> After some question with him, was converted
> Both from his enterprise and from the world;
> His crown bequeathing to his banish'd brother,
> And all their lands restor'd to them again
> That were with him exil'd.

'I do not perceive the use of this hermit,' says Dr Johnson
of the holy man introduced with very similar abruptness
into the last Act of *The Merchant of Venice*. I venture to echo
it of this intruder upon the last Act of *As You Like It*. Whoso
lists may believe in him. But who cares?

The wicked brother Oliver is even more violently converted to a right frame of mind, by means of a snake and a
lion. We are not shown it. We don't want to see it. We
take his word for it, and quite cheerfully, in spite of its
monstrous improbability. For, again, who cares? We are
fleeting the time carelessly; we are 'not at home' to him, but
engaged with Rosalind's wooing, Touchstone's amorous
vagaries with his Audrey, the pure pastoral of Silvius and
Phebe, Jaques' moralising, the killing of the deer, food and
song beneath the bough.

(3)

Some years ago, in hope to get a better understanding of Shakespeare, a friend and I tracked the Warwickshire Avon together, from its source on Naseby battlefield down to Tewkesbury, where, by a yet more ancient battlefield, it is gathered to the greater Severn. From Naseby, where we found its source among the 'good cabbage' of an inn-garden, we followed it afoot through 'wide-skirted meads,' past 'poor pelting villages, sheep-cotes and farms,' to Rugby. This upper region of Avon undulates in long ridge and furrow divided by stiff ox-fences (the 'bull-finches' of the fox-hunter—for this is the famous Pytchley country); and in Shakespeare's time these same ridges and furrows were mainly planted with rye. We went down through this pastoral heart of England, where yet (as Avon draws the line between her north and her south) so many of her bloody internal battles have been decided—Bosworth and Naseby by her headwaters, Evesham and Tewkesbury by her lower fords—and at Rugby we took ship: that is to say, we launched a canoe—a 'canader.'

I am pretty sure she was the first[1] ever launched upon Avon from Rugby. A small curious crowd bore murmured testimony to this. The Avon is not—or was not in those days —a pleasure stream. You might meet a few boats above Warwick, a few at Stratford. Far lower down, below Stratford, the river was made navigable in 1637. But the locks are decayed, and the waterway disused. I suppose that along its extent, half the few houses by this most lonely river resolutely turn their back gardens on it.

[1] The first Canadian canoe. I learn that in the dim past, early in the second half of the nineteenth century, two 'Rob Roys' might have been observed threading the Avon below Rugby.

On the second day, after much pulling through reed beds and following for many miles Avon's always leisurely meanders, we came to the upper bridge of Stoneleigh Deer Park.

A line of swinging deer-fences hung from the arches of the bridge, the river trailing through their bars. We, having permission, pushed cautiously under these—which in a canoe was not easy. Beyond the barrier we looked to right and left, amazed. We had passed from a sluggish brook, twisting among water-plants and willows, to a pleasant, expanded river, flowing between wide lawns, by slopes of bracken, by the roots of gigantic trees—oaks, Spanish oaks, wych-elms, stately firs, sweet chestnuts, backed by filmy larch coppices.

This was Arden, the forest of Arden, actually Stoneleigh-in-Arden, and Shakespeare's very Arden.

Actually, as we rested on our paddles, down to a shallow ahead—their accustomed ford, no doubt—a herd of deer tripped daintily and charged across, splashing; first the bucks, in single file, then the does in a body. The very bed of Avon changes just here: the river now brawling by a shallow, now deepening, and anon sliding over slabs of sandstone.

This (I repeat) is verily and historically Arden. We know that Arden—a lovely word in itself—was endeared to Shakespeare by scores of boyish memories; Arden was his mother's maiden name. I think it arguable of the greatest creative artists that, however they learn and improve, they are always trading on the stored memories of childhood. I am sure that, as Shakespeare turned the pages of Lodge's *Rosalynde*—as sure as if my ears heard him—he cried to himself, 'Arden? This made to happen in a Forest of Arden, in France? But I have wandered in a Forest of Arden ten times lovelier; and, translated thither, ten times lovelier shall be the tale!'

And he is in such a hurry to get to it!

The opening Act of *As You Like It* (we shall find) abounds in small carelessness of detail. Rosalind is taller than Celia in one passage, shorter in another. A name, 'Jaques,' is bestowed on an unimportant character, forgotten, and later used again for an important one. In one passage there is either confusion in the name of the two Dukes, exiled and regnant, or the words are given to the wrong speaker. Orlando's protasis is a mere stage trick. The persiflage between Rosalind and Celia has a false sparkle. Actually it is dull, level, chop-logic, repetitive in the rhythm of its sentences. In fact, the whole of the language of this Act, when we weigh it carefully, is curiously monotonous. It affects to be sprightly, but lacks true wit. Until he gets to Arden, Touchstone never finds himself. All goes to show that Shakespeare, while laying out his plot, was impatient of it and ardent for Arden.

Now, in Stoneleigh Deer Park, in Arden, I saw the whole thing, as though Corin's crook moved above the ferns and Orlando's ballads fluttered on the boles. There was the very oak beneath which Jaques moralised on the deer—a monster oak, thirty-nine feet around (for I measured it)—not far above the ford across which the herd had splashed, its 'antique roots' writhing over the red sandstone rock down to the water's brim. And I saw the whole thing for what the four important Acts of it really are—not as a drama, but as a dream, or rather a dreamy delicious fantasy, and especially a fantasy in colour.

(4)

I want to make this plain: and that the play, not my criticism, is fanciful. I had always thought of *As You Like It*—most adorable play of boyhood, in those days not second even to *The Tempest*—in terms of colour, if I may so put it. Shakespeare, improving on Lodge, invented Jaques and Touchstone. Both are eminently piquant figures under the forest boughs; both piquantly out of place, while most picturesquely in place; both critics, and contrasted critics, of the artificial-natural life ('the simple life' is our term now-adays) in which the exiled Duke and his courtiers profess themselves to revel. Hazlitt says of Jaques that 'he is the only purely contemplative character in Shakespeare.' Well, with much more going on about him, Horatio, in *Hamlet*, is just as inactive—the static, philosophical man, the *punctum indifferens* set in the midst of tragic aberrations. This function of the critic amid the comic aberrations of *As You Like It*, Jaques and Touchstone share between them. Jaques moralises; Touchstone comments and plays the fool, his commentary enlightening common sense, his folly doing common sense no less service by consciously caricaturing all prevalent folly around it.

As contrast of character indicated by colour, can we conceive anything better than Jaques' sad-coloured habit opposed to Touchstone's gay motley? With what a whoop of delight the one critic happens on the other!—

> *Jaques.* A fool—a fool! I met a fool i' the forest,
> A motley fool; a miserable world!
> As I do live by food, I met a fool.

Well then, to pass from Jaques' to our own appreciation of motley, can we not see Touchstone's suit—scarlet, we will say, down one side, and green down the other—illustrating his own contrast of wit and conduct, in speech after speech! Take, for example, his answer to Corin's query, 'And how like you this shepherd's life, Master Touchstone?' and see him exhibiting one side of himself, then the other:

Truly, shepherd, in respect of itself, it is a good life; but in respect that it is a shepherd's life, it is naught. In respect that it is solitary, I like it very well; but in respect that it is private, it is a very vile life. Now, in respect it is in the fields, it pleaseth me well; but in respect it is not in the court, it is tedious. As it is a spare life, look you, it fits my humour well; but as there is no more plenty in it, it goes much against my stomach.

(5)

The comedy, then, is less a comedy of dramatic event than a playful fantastic criticism of life: wherein a courtly society being removed to the greenwood, to picnic there, the Duke Senior can gently moralise on the artificiality he has left at home, and his courtiers—being courtiers still, albeit loyal ones—must ape his humours. But this in turn, being less than sincere, needs salutary mockery: wherefore Shakespeare invents Jaques and Touchstone, critics so skilfully opposed, to supply it. But yet again, Jaques' cynicism being something of a pose, he must be mocked at by the Fool; while the Fool, being professionally a fool, must be laughed at by Jaques, and, being betrayed to real folly by human weakness, laughed at by himself. Even Rosalind, being in love, must play with love. Even honest Orlando, being in love, must write ballads and pin them on trees; but he writes them so very ill that we must allow him honest. Otherwise I should maintain his ancient servant Adam (whose part Shakespeare himself enacted) to be the one really serious figure on the stage. It is at any rate observable that while, as we should expect, the play contains an extraordinary number of fanciful and more or less rhetorical moralisings——such as the Duke's praise of a country life, Jaques' often-quoted sermon on the wounded deer and his 'All the world's a stage,' Rosalind's lecture on the marks of a lover, Touchstone's on the virtue in an 'If,' on the Lie Circumstantial, and on horns (to name but a few), it is Orlando who speaks out from the heart such poetry as:

> ...whate'er you are
> That in this desert inaccessible,
> Under the shade of melancholy boughs,
> Lose and neglect the creeping hours of time;
> If ever you have look'd on better days,
> If ever been where bells have knoll'd to church,
> If ever sat at any good man's feast,
> If ever from your eyelids wip'd a tear
> And know what 'tis to pity and be pitied,
> Let gentleness my strong enforcement be...

while to Adam it falls to utter the sincerest, most poignant, line in the play:

> And unregarded age in corners thrown.

An exquisite instance of Shakespeare's habitual stroke!—with which the general idea, 'unregarded age,' is no sooner presented than (as it were) he stabs the concrete into it, drawing blood: 'unregarded age *in corners thrown.*'

But in truth all the rest of our bright characters are not in earnest. They do but *play* at life in Arden. As Touchstone knew, 'cat will after kind'; and, as Shakespeare knew, the world is the world as man made it for man to live in. These courtiers are not *real* Robin Hoods. When the *ducdame, ducdame* has been played out, yet not so as to over-weary,

Shakespeare gathers up his 'fashionables'—as afterwards in *The Tempest* he gathers up the Neapolitan courtiers—and restores them, like so many fish, to their proper element; even as he himself, after living with shows and making himself a motley to the view, returned to his native Stratford, bought land, and lived doucely. The Duke regains his dukedom, his followers are restored to their estates. By a pretty turn of workmanship, Orlando, who started with a patrimony of 'poor a thousand crowns,' dependent on an unjust brother, returns as heir-apparent and that brother's prospective liege-lord. By an equally pretty turn of irony, the one man—the usurping Duke—who reaches Arden on his own impulse, moved by a ferocious idea to kill somebody, is the only one left there in the end, when the sentimental moralists have done with the Forest, to use it as a school of religious contemplation.

Some critics have held it for a blot on the play that Oliver, his brotherly crime condoned, is allowed to marry Celia. Shakespeare merely neglects the excuse found for it in Lodge's story, where the repentant elder brother helps to rescue Aliena (Celia) from a band of robbers. It *is* unsatisfactory, if we will. The play, according to Swinburne, would be perfect 'were it not for that one unlucky slip of the brush which has left so ugly a little smear in one corner of the canvas as the betrothal of Oliver to Celia.' And George Sand, in her French adaptation, like the bold woman she was, married Celia to—Jaques!

(6)

But 'perfect,' after all, is a word we should keep in hand for perfection: and full though *As You Like It* is of life and gaiety and exquisite merriment, on other points than Oliver's betrothal (I have instanced the mechanical introduction, and the rather pointless chop-logic of the First Act), it does not quite reach perfection. And, after all, a fantasy is a fantasy, and forgiveness Christian. I cannot feel my soul greatly perturbed over the mercy shown to Oliver; and I will give Celia to him, any day of the week, to save her from Jaques. The only possible wife for Jaques was one that Shakespeare omitted to provide. She would have to be an arrant shrew, to talk him dumb: and so he and Touchstone might have expiated their criticism together on a fair balance of folly. Rosalind herself would have cured him; but Rosalind, of course, is by miles too good for Jaques. She is reserved to be loved by an honest man his life through; and, like many another dear woman, to nag him his life through.

Rosalind herself is not perfect; but she is in a way the better for it, being adorable: at once honest and wayward, 'true brow and fair maid,' and infinitely tantalising. She means to be the Nut Brown Maid of the Greenwood, as the whole play seems trying, over and over again, to be a Robin Hood play. She means this, I repeat; but being courtly bred she has to play with it before admitting it. Yet she is honest, and confesses her love almost from the first, to herself and to Celia. She does not, as Imogen does, lift the heart out of us, ready to break for her: but she bewitches us, and hardly the less because all the while she allows us to know that the witchery is conscious and intentional.

The play is—'as you like it'—a woodland play treated courtly-wise, or a courtly play treated woodland-wise. It plainly derives, through *Love's Labour's Lost*, from John Lyly; whose polite comedies, highly artificial, but in one way or another a wonderful artistic advance, held the ear of Court and of City at the moment when Shakespeare set up as a playwright: and I hold that Mr Warwick Bond, Lyly's learned and devoted editor, makes out unanswerably Shakespeare's debt to Lyly during his apprenticeship in dramatic architecture. Mr Bond says:

That Shakespeare was his (Lyly's) disciple in this respect is beyond a doubt....To the fundamental brainwork which Lyly put into his plays, the greater poet and the Shakespearean stage in general are almost as much indebted as they are to his introduction of a lively, witty and coherent dialogue.

Lyly's notion of a lively and witty dialogue, though begotten (I make no doubt) of an instinct for reform, resulted—like many another innovation—in a tyranny of its own making; and to my taste the dreariest passages in Shakespeare are those in which his ladies and courtiers exchange 'wit.' But it remains true that if we would understand Shakespeare's workmanship in the early Comedies, and trace how *Love's Labour's Lost* grew into *As You Like It*, we must study Lyly's *Campaspe*, his *Endymion*, and his *Galatea*. The main point to grasp is that *As You Like It*, however much improved by genius, belongs to the Lyly line of descent and to the order of the court-pastoral.

The 'pastoral' being granted, we may recognise excellent workmanship in the Silvius and Phebe episode. To have garbed Rosalind as a boy without making a girl fall in love with him would have been to miss a plain opportunity— almost as plain a one as the sight of the bloody cloth at which Rosalind faints. It doubles the intrigue, and it provides with due irony one of the most charming chiming quartets in all Comedy:

Phebe. Good shepherd, tell this youth what 'tis to love.
Silvius. It is to be all made of sighs and tears;
And so am I for Phebe.
Phebe. And I for Ganymede.
Orlando. And I for Rosalind.
Rosalind. And I for no woman.

And so on, and so on. The *genre* and the convention of it granted, nothing could be prettier than the inter-chime and the counter-chime. It is Lyly carried to the *n*th power.

Having said this in praise of a piece of good workmanship, I must in fairness mention a piece of sheer botchwork. I mean the introduction of Hymen in the last Act. To explain away this botch as an imposition upon Shakespeare by another hand—to conjecture it as some hasty alternative to satisfy the public censor, who objected to Church rites of marriage on the stage—would be as easy as it were accordant with the nice distinctions of critical hypocrisy. were it not that Shakespeare, almost if not quite to the end of his days, was capable of similar ineptitudes, such as the vision of Posthumus and the scroll dropped into his lap. You can explain away one such lapse by an accident; but two scarcely, and three or four not at all. That kind of artistic improbability runs almost in harmonical progression. Hymen in *As You Like It* is worse than Hecate in *Macbeth.*

CHAPTER VII

THE STORY OF FALSTAFF

An innovation—A permanent artistic principle in the treatment
of history by fiction—An Aristotelian induction—A tetralogy
and a pageant—Its unity of theme and treatment—The tradition of Chaucer—Falstaff and the *Interludes*—Meaning of
Interlude—Falstaff in *The Merry Wives*—Prince Hal and
Henry V—Characters and their creators—*David Copperfield*—
Johnson on Falstaff—The dismissal of Falstaff—Why Shakespeare killed him—The scenes at the Boar's Head—The apo-
theosis of good-fellowship.

(1)

ANYONE coming to the two parts of *King Henry IV*
—which in fact make one—can see that here is something new. Though his acquaintance with other history
plays of the time be slight; even though it be confined to the
other history plays of Shakespeare, he cannot miss to perceive, in the mixture and blend of high political intrigue, of
royalties, proud nobles and rebellious wars, with footpads,
tapsters, bawds and all the fun of the fair on Gad's Hill and
in Eastcheap, an innovation upon the old method of
chronicle drama. I am not pretending, of course, that the
innovation has come at a stroke; that, as Pallas Athene from
the head of Zeus, the invention sprang upon the world fully
armed and complete out of Shakespeare's brain. For (1)
as a matter of history, when a new and strong idea, such as
Elizabethan drama, starts fermenting, all manner of men
bring their grapes to the vat: (2) as a matter of history, the

germ of the Gad's Hill frolic is to be found in an old play, *The Famous Victories of King Henry the Fifth*, on which Shakespeare undoubtedly worked; and (3) again as a matter of history, Prince Hal's youthful follies were a tradition so fixed in men's minds that no play about him could dispense with them.

But when all this has been granted, when we note how Falstaff is no sooner introduced than he takes charge and establishes himself as the real hero of the play; how he compels everyone into his grand circumference; what a globe this earthy carnal man is, and how like a globe of earth he rolls; how, from his first merry encounter with Henry to his last sorrowful one, he is and remains (as Hazlitt said) the better man of the two; why, then, as we go on to read Scott, Dumas, Thackeray or any great historical novelist, we cannot miss to observe how powerful an innovation Shakespeare made of it. *It has set up a permanent artistic principle in the treatment of history by fiction;* the principle that, in drama or novel of this kind, your best protagonists, and the minor characters you can best treat with liveliness as with philosophy, are not those concerning whose sayings and doings you are circumscribed by known fact and documentary evidence, but rather some invented men or women—pawns in the game—upon whose actions and destinies you can make the great events play at will. Thus not only does Falstaff give Scott the trick of Dugald Dalgetty, Dumas the trick of The Three Musketeers, Charles Reade the trick of Denis the Burgundian; not only is Mistress Quickly the artistic mother of Madame Sans Gêne; but if we take almost any historical novel of the first class—*Esmond*, or *L'Homme Qui Rit*, or *The Cloister and the Hearth*, or *La Chartreuse de Parme*, or *The Tale of Two Cities*, or Tolstoy's *War and Peace*—we shall find the protagonists of the story to be figures evoked from the vaguest shadows of history, when they are not (as more often happens) pure figments of the author's brain.

I touched upon this principle in my first paper, on *Macbeth*. It was Aristotle, of course, who first laid hold of the secret, when he asserted that 'poetry is a more philosophical and a higher thing than history; for poetry occupies itself in expressing the universal, history the particular. The particular is, for example, what Alcibiades did or suffered.' And this (let me say) was a very remarkable discovery for Aristotle to make by induction from the Greek dramatists, who concerned themselves mainly with the dooms of kings and royal houses—

> Sometime let gorgeous tragedy
> In scepter'd pall come sweeping by,
> Presenting Thebes' or Pelops' line....

But these, to be sure, were mythical, or, at most, legendary, allowing Æschylus or Sophocles to choose a great deal and to invent no little. So with Shakespeare—There had, once upon a time, been an actual Lear, an actual Cymbeline, and both were kings; an actual Hamlet, Prince of Denmark; an actual Macbeth, who made himself king. These, however, are legendary figures, evoked from the penumbra of Holinshed or Saxo Grammaticus; and Shakespeare calls them up almost in what shape he wills, to be reinspired with life and played with as his genius may choose. Obviously he could not play thus with the houses of York and Lancaster, whose rivalries were not only documented but fresh in men's memories. Red, or white, or parti-coloured—if I may adapt Cowper—

> The rose was just washed, just washed by the shower,
> Which Henry to Edward conveyed—

and Richard to another Henry, and a third Henry to another Edward, to Mary, and to Elizabeth. The blood and the tears that had washed it alternate red and white were too recent. The Elizabethan audience *knew* these champions of York and Lancaster—these cousins, making young men bleed for their sordid domestic quarrel.—

And Abner said to Joab, 'Let the young men now arise and play before us.' And Joab said, 'Let them arise.' Then there arose and went over by number twelve of the servants of Benjamin, which pertaineth to Ishbosheth the son of Saul, and twelve of the servants of David.

And they caught everyone his fellow by the head, and thrust his sword into his fellow's side: so they fell down together, wherefore that place was called Helkathhazzurim (or the Field of Strong Men) unto this day.

> The many men so beautiful!
> And they all dead did lie....

An Elizabethan audience, at any rate, knew all about Civil War, or their fathers had told them. Let the reader recall the two little vignettes that Shakespeare introduced into the Third Part of *King Henry VI*, '*Enter a Son that hath killed his Father, with the dead body,*' and its pendant, '*Enter a Father, that hath killed his Son, with the body in his arms.*' How poignant they are, for all their conventionality! I confess that to me the sad but yet selfish comment of Henry VI—

> Sad-hearted men, much overgone with care,
> Here sits a king more woeful than you are,

seems little if at all less hollow, as it holds far less sophistry, than the famous but sentimental, selfish, sophistical meditations of Henry V after the honest soldier Williams has floored him in argument. But this is a matter of opinion touching, in these times, upon politics: I will not press it.

(2)

Coming back to our business, which is Shakespeare's workmanship, I will ask the reader to peruse *King Richard II*, *King Henry IV* (both parts), and *King Henry V*, *in succession*, and note—

(1) that, as a pageant, they follow in straight and almost undivided succession—as all the evidence of data goes to show they were composed in fairly rapid succession;

(2) that they carry the house of Lancaster from its usurpation to its highest point of prosperity;

(3) that the progress of this climb to the greatest fortune is dogged throughout by a sense of fate, an apprehension that what has been evilly won cannot endure, a tedium upon each success and an incapacity for joy in it. 'Vaulting Bolingbroke' has no sooner won the crown than we see him a care-weary man, fearful of the future, haunted by the past.

> So shaken as we are, so wan with care.

That is the first line of the play: and at the back of his mind plays a notion to make it all right with God in some other way than by straight restitution. He will (when his enemies at home give him leisure) raise an English Crusade—

> To chase these pagans in those holy fields
> Over whose acres walk'd those blessèd feet
> Which fourteen hundred years ago were nail'd
> For our advantage on the bitter cross.

But 'now' will never come: for this service to Christ must wait till Henry's own kingdom is secure. He does not greatly care for himself: for himself royalty has lost savour as soon as tasted: but alas! the heir-apparent is a madcap, and cannot be trusted to secure and enjoy the precious Dead Sea fruit. This fear poisons him: at the opening of Part 2 we see him a broken man and a dying one. He dies unhappy. He has never known joy. Prince Henry, who *has* known joy, succeeds him, to renounce joy, to become an ingrate to those who taught him joy; to be a soldier and fight Agincourt, yet still to know that he in his turn is but fending off retribution—

> Not to-day, O Lord!
> O! not to-day, think not upon the fault
> My father made in compassing the crown.

Yes, we must take the four plays as a tetralogy, not as separate pageants. So taken, they carry a single sense of doom; not insisted upon, as it is in the *Oresteia*, but scarcely the less haunting because intermittent, recurrent, a sense of a doom that is delayed but for a while.

Into this procession of doom, then, of stately, somewhat wooden personages following high selfish ambitions, Shakespeare thrusts the jollity of common folk; real irresponsible wantoning of flesh and blood, and all as English as Chaucer —for he who cannot read the racy tradition of Chaucer into Falstaff must be blind as a bat.

Now just how did that happen?

(3)

I have spent some time in presenting Falstaff as an innovation. Let us consider him for a while on the reverse side, as an archaism.

If we turn to the end of *King Henry IV*, Part 2, we shall find there an Epilogue, 'spoken by a Dancer.' It closes thus:

One word more, I beseech you. If you be not too much cloyed with fat meat, our humble author will continue the story, with Sir John in it, and make you merry with fair

Katharine of France; where, for anything I know, Falstaff shall
die of a sweat, unless already 'a be killed with your hard
opinions: for Oldcastle died a martyr, and this is not the man.
My tongue is weary: when my legs are too, I will bid you good-
night: and so kneel down before you; but, indeed, to pray for
the Queen.

Now I will wager the reader supposes me to be on the
point of telling him how Sir John Oldcastle became converted into Sir John Falstaff; which is what every one of our
little text-books will laboriously explain, saving me the
trouble. I am going to do nothing of the sort. I merely
direct attention to those last very simple words—

My tongue is weary; when my legs are too, I will bid you
good-night: and so kneel down before you; but, indeed, to pray
for the Queen.

Why do I lay stress on words so simple? Because, while
the old miracle plays and moralities are sometimes ended
with a general prayer for the spiritual welfare of 'sofereyns,'
'lordings,' and the rest of the audience,[1] this particular
prayer for the reigning sovereign and sometimes the estates
of the realm is a particular characteristic, or *stigma*, of a
particular kind of play called *Interlude*. In dealing with the
text of one of these Interludes we may often get the date of
its first presentation from the prayer at the close.

What, precisely, was an Interlude? Well, the Interlude
passed through several phases. Moreover the outlines of
these phases were not distinct in their sequence, but inter-
fused and blurred: so that at no given date can we say 'the
Interlude was just *this*' or 'just *that*.' Therefore I must be
understood, in what follows, to pretend no more than rough-
and-ready accuracy.

The *New English Dictionary* defines 'Interlude' as 'a

[1] E. K. Chambers. *The Mediæval Stage*, vol. II, p. 189.

dramatic or mimic presentation, usually of a light or humorous character, such as was commonly introduced between the acts of the long mystery-plays or moralities, or exhibited as part of an elaborate entertainment.' Sir Adolphus Ward gives a somewhat different account. The name, says he, 'seems to have been applied to plays performed by professional actors from the time of Edward IV onwards. Its origin is doubtless to be found in the fact that such plays were occasionally performed in the intervals of banquets and entertainments.' Mr Chambers in his *Mediæval Stage* gives reasons for holding neither one nor the other of these explanations to be satisfactory: and my own hypothesis (with the grounds of which I will not here interrupt my argument) is that 'Interlude' meant, or came to mean, a play of a sort commonly presented indoors, in banqueting-halls, in the *interval* between the theatrical seasons—that is, during the winter; or, in other words, the sort of play to amuse a Christmas or Twelfth Night audience.

Whichever of us be right matters very little in comparison with these points, which can be established—

(1) It was brief.

(2) It aimed to amuse, and was traditionally comic. The *Interludium de Clerico et Puella*, for instance, is (as its name suggests) mere farce.

(3) It started by borrowing abstract vices from the Moralities—vices such as gluttony, lechery, avarice—and personifying them so as to exhibit their comic side. Now, to do this (it is a rule of art), you must turn the abstractions into real people. Here I quote Mr Chambers again:

From the Moral the Interlude drew abstractions; from the farce, social types. The possibility of vital drama lay in *an advance to the portraiture of individuals.*

(4) In the course of this progress the Interlude took a queer turn. Its patrons—the great nobles who invited it to amuse them in their banqueting-halls—were, as we all know, sharply and hotly divided over the Old and Reformed Religions. The actors took their cues. Soon, for its patrons' delectation after dinner, the Interlude became a farcical presentment of venal priests or of sour puritans, as this or that lordly midriff demanded to be tickled. We may follow this queer development in any history of the drama. *And now can we not see the point of Sir John Oldcastle, the Lollard, and how he came to be mixed up in this affair, and why Shakespeare, adapting the play for a mixed audience, had to change the name to Falstaff and apologise?*

(5) —and lastly—the Interlude ended by custom with a prayer for the reigning Sovereign; to send its audience away, no doubt, with the assurance that its loyalty was in the right place, and that, in spite of appearances, it had not gone too far.

Now let us apply all this to *King Henry IV*, and we shall see, past all that has been so wonderfully changed in the process, back to the original device of it. I am occupied for the moment less with the fertility of Shakespeare's genius in *execution* (I shall come to that by-and-by) than with the genius that *originated* the design, that devised the anatomy of a new thing in art by taking the stiff conventional bones of the old chronicle play and articulating them into the minor but equally conventional bones of the Interlude. I defer for the moment to consider how Shakespeare superinduced the live flesh and infused the live blood. For the moment I am concerned only with the anatomy of the thing and how he made it flexible.

(4)

I must pursue this convention of the Interlude for a while, because it leads us on to another discovery.

Everyone knows the tradition that Shakespeare wrote *The Merry Wives of Windsor* because Queen Elizabeth expressed a desire to see Falstaff in love. Well, I believe in that tradition. It combines all one might expect of a royal command in general with all one might expect in particular of a command by a Virgin Queen. We know also that Shakespeare is reputed to have, obeying it, written *The Merry Wives of Windsor* in a fortnight. That again is easily credible. I have the author's word for it that one of the most brilliant plays of our time—*The Admirable Crichton*—was written in about that time. The evidence that Shakespeare was a rapid writer—an extremely rapid writer—cannot be contested.

But I suggest that the real reason why we are troubled in reading *The Merry Wives* is that we cannot recognise Falstaff as the same man. He has obvious similarities with the Falstaff of *King Henry IV*: but he is somehow not our Falstaff. For an instance (and it lies at the root), the Falstaff that we know was easy enough with Doll Tearsheet: he would simply not have troubled to intrigue with Mistress Ford or with Mistress Page. He is too English, moreover, to be at home in an Italian comedy (and the plot of the *Merry Wives* is pure Italian). Again, though Bardolph, Pistol, Nym, wear their old names, they are not quite the same people; while Dame Quickly, but for tricks of resemblance in her chatter, is a different Dame Quickly altogether; and Master Silence has become Master Slender without a word to tell us why.

Now, in *King Henry IV* these characters had become so

individual to us that we cannot understand what has happened. Again I suggest that we shall understand better by casting back and remembering that, to the playwright, these figures—all of them—were, first of all, types; types of the old Interlude: the Clown, the Pantaloon, Harlequin, Columbine; Pierrot, Pierrette, Punch, Judy; Falstaff (Gluttony) with a fat paunch; Bardolph (Drunkenness) with a red nose; Mistress Quickly the conventional Hostess, Shallow the conventional Country Justice, Slender—or Silence —the conventional awkward country Booby—all types— 'Here we are again!' in fine. Shakespeare's mind is working; but the whole Elizabethan drama is in ferment too, yeasting up from type to individual; to Iago from Richard III, who is 'determinèd to be a villain'; to Shylock from Judas with a red beard; from 'the old Vice with his dagger of lath' to tragedy in which passion spins the plot and

We are betrayed by what is false within.

(5)

I return to *King Henry IV*, and to the question which ever recurs in these pages—'What was Shakespeare trying to do?'

Well, that for once has an answer staring us in the face. Prince Hal has to become King Harry; since (as Dr Johnson puts it) 'Shakespeare has apparently designed a regular connection of these dramatic histories from Richard the Second to Henry the Fifth.'

Prince Hal has to become King Harry: to start, as a matter of history, by being a scapegrace, and be converted into the ideal warrior-king.

We observe then how deftly from the beginning he is poised on the balance. In the one scale is Hotspur, challenging him to honour with a provocation purposely made exorbitant: in the other, packed into Falstaff, all that is sensual—this also exorbitant, the very bulk of the man helping our impression of the weight that would drag the Prince down. Each challenge is extreme. We have only to oppose Hotspur's high rant about honour with Falstaff's low appraisement of it, and we have two cross-lights that illumine the whole play. Here are the two in sample:

> *Hotspur.* By heaven, methinks it were an easy leap
> To pluck bright honour from the pale-fac'd moon,
> Or dive into the bottom of the deep
> Where fathom-line could never touch the ground,
> And pluck up drownèd honour by the locks,
> So he that doth redeem her thence might wear
> Without corrival all her dignities.

> *Falstaff.* Honour!...Can honour set to a leg? No. Or an arm? No. Or take away the grief of a wound? No. Honour hath no skill in surgery, then? No. What is honour? a word. What is that word 'honour'? air....Who hath it? he that died o' Wednesday. Doth he feel it? No. Doth he hear it? No. 'Tis insensible, then? Yea, to the dead. But will it not live with the living? No. Why? Detraction will not suffer it. Therefore I'll none of it. Honour is a mere scutcheon: and so ends my catechism.

That leaves no more to be said.

Scarcely less obvious, as master-strokes, are the two great shocks by which Shakespeare works conversion on the Prince's character—(1) the call to arms for the Shrewsbury campaign (2) the scene of the crown, with the reconciliation that follows, in the dying King's bed-chamber.

These patent strokes have been applauded by critic after

critic. It remains for one mainly intent upon workmanship to point out how the whole of the business is built on the old Morality structure imported through the Interlude. Why, it might almost be labelled, after the style of a Morality title, *Contentio inter Virtutem et Vitium de anima Principis.*

(6)

But 'Falstaff!' it will be said. 'Could Shakespeare have fashioned and developed such an individual, total, full-bodied, full-blooded, teeming and gigantic man as this Falstaff out of a mere figure in an interlude?'

I begin my answer with a request of the reader. Let him get out of his mind all the solemn discussions of all the commentators who never created a play or a novel or a scene or a character in their lives, and no more know how it happens than how a child comes to birth. *No true artist develops or fashions a real character, once brought to birth, any more than a mother thenceforth develops or fashions a child.* It has a separate life: it takes charge; the older it grows the more it takes charge. Which are we to suppose? —that, delivered of his *partus masculus,* Shakespeare took charge of Falstaff, or that Falstaff ran away with Shakespeare?

I think we may say of Falstaff and Shakespeare precisely what Maurice Morgann (who published a Study of Falstaff in 1777) says of Shakespeare and us:

'Him we may profess rather to feel than to understand; and it is safer to say on many occasions that we are possest by him than that we possess him.'[1]

[1] An Essay on the Dramatic Character of Sir John Falstaff: London. Printed for T. Davies, in Russel-street, Covent Garden: MDCCLXXVII.

Artists do not develop or fashion these characters to any extent of which those verbs are descriptive. It is not the process: it is not how the thing happens. Searching to convince of this, I hit on an illustration. Many women nowadays are daily parting with sons, brothers, lovers, husbands, bound for the War. Shakespeare has to write down the words of many a woman at such a parting. Let us hear now what Volumnia says to Coriolanus:

> Thou hast never in thy life
> Show'd thy dear mother any courtesy:
> When she, poor hen, fond of no second brood,
> Hath cluck'd thee to the wars, and safely home
> Laden with honour.

Now let us to Lady Percy, clinging on Hotspur's strong hand:

> But if you go—
> Come, come, you paraquito, answer me
> Directly unto this question that I ask:—
> In faith, I'll break thy little finger, Harry,
> An if thou wilt not tell me all things true.

And lastly let us hear how poor Doll Tearsheet puts it, seated on Falstaff's knee:

> Come, I'll be friends with thee, Jack: thou art going to the wars; and whether I shall ever see thee again or no, there is nobody cares.

These three speeches will suffice; all so different, each so appropriate, and so poignant on the lips of the speaker. Surely we cannot conceive of Shakespeare, that rapid writer, as seated, with the end of a quill in his mouth, *thinking out* these differences! It simply does not happen like that. Volumnia, Lady Percy, Doll Tearsheet—though two of the three are minor characters—each in her turn has charge of Shakespeare: and as she dictates, he writes.

If this seem an arbitrary pronouncement, let us take evidence for it, and from an artist of genius, Charles Dickens; just pausing to remind ourselves how the incomparable Mr Pickwick grew out of an engagement to provide 'letterpress' for a series of comic sporting prints. This is how Dickens commended another masterpiece—*David Copperfield*—to the world:

It would concern the reader little, perhaps, to know how sorrowfully the pen is laid down at the end of a two-years' imaginative task; or how an Author feels as if he were dismissing some portion of himself into the shadowy world, when a crowd of the creatures of his brain are going from him for ever. Yet I had nothing else to tell, unless indeed I were to confess (which might be of less moment still) that no one can ever believe this Narrative in the reading more than I believed it in the writing.

That is how a great character in fiction—be he Pickwick or Don Quixote or my Uncle Toby or Falstaff—grows: grows as a plant, its creator tending it and watching, as it puts forth its own leaf, flower, fruit. If I may apply the words reverently, 'that which thou sowest is bare grain, *it may chance of wheat*, or of some other grain.'

(7)

In this short study I shall not indulge in any panegyric upon Falstaff: and I ask the reader to credit this to a Roman fortitude, since they say that all who write about Falstaff, loving him, write well. The performance I like best is Dr Johnson's singular outburst beginning, 'But Falstaff—unimitated, inimitable Falstaff—how shall I describe thee?'

because it breaks from the heart of a moralist who, being human, could not help himself. Let us, to set beside it, recall that passage in Boswell which relates how his two rowdy young friends, Topham Beauclerk and Bennet Langton, knocked up the Doctor at dead of night:—

One night when Beauclerk and Langton had supped at a tavern in London, and sat till about three in the morning, it came into their heads to go and knock up Johnson, and see if they could prevail on him to join them in a ramble. They rapped violently at the door of his chambers in the Temple, till at last he appeared in his shirt, with his little black wig on the top of his head, instead of a nightcap, and a poker in his hand, imagining probably that some ruffians were coming to attack him. When he discovered who they were, and was told their errand, he smiled and with great good humour agreed to their proposal. 'What, is it you, you dogs? I'll have a frisk with you.' He was soon drest and they sallied forth together into Covent Garden where the greengrocers and fruiterers were beginning to arrange their hampers, just come in from the country. Johnson made some attempts to help them: but the honest gardeners stared so at his figure and manner and odd interference that he soon saw that his services were not relished. They then repaired to one of the neighbouring taverns and made a bowl of that liquor called *Bishop*, which Johnson had always liked; while in joyous contempt of sleep, from which he had been roused, he repeated the festive lines—

> Short, O short then be thy reign
> And give us to the world again!

They did not stay long, but walked down to the Thames, took a boat, and rowed to Billingsgate. Beauclerk and Johnson were so well pleased with their amusement that they resolved to persevere in dissipation for the rest of the day: but Langton deserted them, being engaged to breakfast with some young ladies. Johnson scolded him for 'leaving his social friends to go and sit with a set of wretched *unidea'd* girls.' Garrick, being told of this ramble, said to him smartly, 'I heard of your frolic t'other night. You'll be in *The Chronicle*.' Upon which Johnson afterwards observed, '*He* durst not do such a thing. His wife would not le. him.'

I think this passage explains why Johnson could not help loving Falstaff. They were both men of extravagant bulk, too, and both good Londoners.

(8)

The story of Falstaff can be extricated from the chronicle portion of the three plays and presented in a play by itself. In fact I have visited the Cambridge University Library, and seeking out a volume of Miscellaneous Plays marked Q, 28, 58, found it done (and not badly done, though sadly Bowdlerised) in 1822 by an author, unknown to me, who signs himself C. S. It will, at any rate, reward curiosity in a spare hour: but I do not want to see it ont he stage; because in proportion as Falstaff dominates all the scene and makes himself the hero, with no historical pageantry to divert us, the end of the story works out into pathos, with 'Put not your trust in princes' for its moral. I grant the artistry of Scenes 4 and 5 of the last Act of *King Henry IV*, Part 2.... *Enter Beadle dragging in Mistress Quickly and Doll Tearsheet*, this little scene ironically preparing us for the next, wherein Falstaff, who knows nothing of what has befallen the women, appears hot-foot from Gloucestershire, with Justice Shallow, just in time for the Coronation show as it returns from the Abbey:

Stand here by me, Master Robert Shallow: I will make the King do you grace; I will leer upon him as 'a comes by; and do but mark the countenance that he will give me.

Now for the event:—

Shouts within and the trumpets sound. Enter the King and his train, the Lord Chief Justice among them.

Fal. God save thy grace, King Hal! my royal Hal!

Pist. The heavens thee guard and keep, most royal imp of fame!

Fal. God save thee, my sweet boy!

King. (*recognising him*) My Lord Chief Justice, speak to that vain man.

Ch. J. Have you your wits? Know you what 'tis you speak?

Fal. My King! my Jove! I speak to thee, my heart!

King. I know thee not, old man. Fall to thy prayers.
How ill white hairs become a fool and jester!
I have long dream'd of such a kind of man,
So surfeit-swell'd, so old, and so profane;
But, being awake, I do despise my dream.

—and so forth. I have not the stomach to follow the rest of that speech. White hairs may not become a fool and a jester, but no more does a growing beard excuse a cold prig. There is an obvious error in the stage directions, which the Cambridge editors have omitted to correct. Henry V was not crowned at Westminster Abbey; the ceremony took place at Exeter Hall.

When the King has done, Falstaff turns to Master Shallow with a wrung face:—

Master Shallow, I owe you a thousand pound.

And—the mischief of it—there cracks a great heart.

(9)

I have often tried to make excuses for this scene. To be sure, no excuses are needed: for a king must be a king, and no decent king can have a Falstaff about him. And yet...

it is curious to observe that just at this time—almost, as accurately as one can fix it, when he handed Doll Tearsheet over to the beadles and dismissed Falstaff to the Fleet— Shakespeare was preparing to leave London, buying property in Stratford, applying for a coat-of-arms, and generally (as they say) turning respectable. It may be no more than a coincidence: I hope that it is.

But anyhow I would see him relieved of the most damnable piece of workmanship to be found in any of his plays. I mean Prince Hal's soliloquy at the close of the second Scene of *The First Part of King Henry IV*. 'I know you all,' says he, when Falstaff, Poins, and the rest have gone out—

> I know you all, and will a while uphold
> The unyok'd humour of your idleness:
> Yet herein will I imitate the sun,
> Who doth permit the base contagious clouds
> To smother up his beauty from the world,
> That, when he please again to be himself,
> Being wanted, he may be more wonder'd at.

This, if we accept it, poisons what follows, poisons the madcap Prince in our imagination for good and all. Most of us can forgive youth, hot blood, riot: but a prig of a rake, rioting on a calculated scale, confessing that he does it coldly, intellectually, and that he proposes to desert his comrades at the right moment to better his own repute— *that* kind of rake surely all honest men abhor.

Yet the lines are pretty obviously written by Shakespeare. I should like to think—as I have brought myself to feel sure—that Shakespeare wrote the play without them, and with no idea of them: that by and by Burbage (or whoever it was) came to him with a 'Look here! We have later on, you know, to turn Prince Hal to respectability: and our fool of an audience always wants that sort of thing to be made

$a \times b = ab$ to it from the first': and that *so* Shakespeare obediently inserted those lines in his opening Act.

(10)

We cannot keep them and keep any opinion of Henry as a decent fellow. But even if we omit them his conduct is cruel enough; which brings me to my last consideration— 'Why did Shakespeare kill Falstaff?'

Well, he had to. He had made the King kill Falstaff's heart. The heart broken, the man dies, and there's an end.

But let us wait a moment, and go a little deeper. Shakespeare killed Falstaff because he couldn't help it. He tells us of his death, but he could not bring him upon the stage in *King Henry V, because he dared not.*

How? Why? Because, as between two mortal men of this world, Henry was the wronger, Falstaff the wronged. Falstaff had never consciously hurt Henry, had never—so far from unkindness—thought of him but kindly. Wisely or not—wisely, if we will—Henry had hurt Falstaff to death: and not for any *new* default, sin or crime; but for continuing to be, in fault and foible, the very same man in whose faults and foibles he had delighted as a friend.

Then, if the object of the new play be—as all will admit —to present King Harry as our patriotic darling, henceforth Bates and Williams are good enough for him to practise his talk upon, and he may rant about St Crispin's Day until the lowing herd winds slowly o'er the lea. But he must not be allowed to meet Falstaff. As he once very prettily said of Hotspur—

Two stars keep not their motion in one sphere

and therefore he must not be allowed to meet Falstaff. *For Falstaff can kill him with a look.*

(11)

In their daily life, in business, in affairs of State, men constantly do wrong and are able as constantly to justify the wrong in their own eyes—nay, boldly to justify it before the world—with excuses. As I write this, I see the reader's mind fly off to such things as 'scraps of paper,' to the man who pleaded 'necessity' for murdering Belgium—

> So spake the Fiend, and with *necessity*,
> The tyrant's plea, excused his devilish deeds.

But I have known an Archbishop from a University pulpit excuse a war with a weaker nation *not* because our cause was just (which, though quite arguable, he made no attempt to argue), but because we were a greater, more enlightened, more progressive race than they, with a great literature, too —for in his fervour the preacher even dragged in literature —and therefore (argued he) God, who encourages and presides over the evolution of mankind, *must* be on our side! At the time I thought this a blasphemous argument, and that if a true word of the Gospel had dropped from Heaven like a bomb, interrupting it, there would not, as Thoreau once said, have been left one stone of that meeting-house upon another.

For of course you cannot righteously kill or maim a man or swindle him, on the ground that you are godlier than he, or cleanlier, or better. *The whole point rests on the justice of the particular quarrel.* 'Are you, or is he, in the right?' Even if you be in the right, there still remain the questions of patience, charity, elementary forgiveness. 'Do these not rest on you as a duty towards your neighbour by your very claim to be better than he?'

Poetry—which I suspect *therefore*, as well as for other

reasons, to be divine—will have nothing to do with such ointments of conscience. In Poetry, if one man wrong another, that other becomes *ipso facto* the better man. It was Henry (plead what excuses of State you will) who wronged Falstaff and killed his heart: Falstaff had never a thought of hurting Henry: and therefore, or ever you can present Harry of Agincourt as your *beau idéal* of a warrior king, you must kill Falstaff somehow and get his poor old body behind the arras: for, as Hazlitt said, he is the better man of the two.

(12)

I have (as I promised) left myself no space for the customary panegyric on Falstaff. I am sorrier that I have left myself no space to show how wonderfully in these Eastcheap scenes Shakespeare, to give an old Interlude life, sought back, recaptured the very spirit of Chaucer and improved it. In all the great sweep of the plays there is nothing so racy, so English.

But, for a last word:—Falstaff—with all his imperfections on his head and all his offences rank—has, and has to the nth degree, what we mean when we call So-and-so 'a good fellow.' He may have led Prince Hal astray: but Shakespeare invented him some two hundred years later, since when, for three hundred years, he has been doing nothing but good to man, woman, or child. His laugh at its grossest is salutary, refreshing; and, as for us, we laugh with him or at him, but we usually do both together.

CHAPTER VIII

HAMLET

I

A factitious mystery—A masterpiece, not a problem—The evidence of its perennial popularity—Every 'star' his own Hamlet—Highest art never unintelligible—Some imperfect diagnoses of Hamlet—A masterly opening—Superbness of diction—A flaw of construction.

(1)

SO much has been written upon *Hamlet*, that one can hardly descry the play through the rolling cloud of witness. The critical guns detonate with such uproar, and, exploding, diffuse such quantities of gas, as to impose on us that moral stupor which I understand to be one of the calculated effects of heavy artillery in warfare. The poor infantryman—if I may press the similitude—discerns not, in the din, that half of these missiles are flying in one direction, half in another, still less how large a proportion of both hit no mark at all. He can scarcely command nerve for a steady look at the thing itself. This loud authority confuses us all. It *starts* us thinking of *Hamlet* not as an acted play but as a mystery, a psychological study, an effort of genius so grandiose, vast, vague, amorphous, nebulous, that other men of admitted genius—even such men as Coleridge and Goethe—tracking it, have lost their way in the profound obscure.

(2)

Now, with all the courage of humility, I say that this is, nine-tenths of it, rubbish.

I insist that we take Shakespeare first and before any of these imposing fellows. At all events he wrote the play, and they did not.

Moreover, he wrote it as a play—to be acted on a stage, before an audience.

Moreover, he wrote it, not for an audience of Goethes and Coleridges, but for an audience of ordinary men and women.

And yet further, if pressed, I am ready to maintain that *any* work of art which is shapeless, nebulous; any work of art which from its artistic purpose naturally falls to be the prey of pedants and philosophers, to that extent lies suspect as a piece of art. And I hope to demonstrate that *Hamlet* is no such thing, but a masterpiece.

All this may seem brazenly bold: but having gone so far I will go yet one more step further and say that while, to understand *Hamlet*, the best way is to see it acted on a stage, a second-best way is to read it by ourselves, surrendering ourselves to it as a new thing, as childishly as anyone pleases. As Emerson wrote, 'All that Shakespeare says of the king, yonder slip of a boy that reads in a corner feels to be true of himself.' In this chapter I shall ask the reader to take *Hamlet* by itself, as a new thing. Let us renew our courage from a sentence of Bacon's: '*Regnum Scientiæ ut regnum Coeli non nisi sub persona infantis intratur*—Into the Kingdom of Knowledge, as into the Kingdom of Heaven, whoso would enter must become as a little child.'

(3)

The earliest printed copy of *Hamlet*, known to us, was discovered in 1823—a little, horribly cropped quarto bearing date 1603, and entitled:

The | Tragicall Historie of Hamlet | Prince of Denmark | By William Shake-speare. | As it hath beene diverse times acted by his Highnesse ser | vants in the Cittie of London: as also in the two U | niversities of Cambridge and Oxford, and elsewhere | At London printed for N.L., and John Trundell | 1603.

It was a *drama,* then; written by a real playwright, whose name was Shakespeare: and not by Hegel nor by Werder. 'As it hathe beene diverse times acted by his Highnesse servants in the Cittie of London: as also in the two Universities of Cambridge and Oxford....' It would seem from that to have been a popular play. Can we suppose that it would have been a popular play had it been a mystery, a problem, or anything like the psychological enigma that Coleridge and Goethe and their followers have chosen to make of it? Let us ask ourselves as men—Does that sort of thing happen?

But I will tell what *does* happen. To this day a travelling company of actors, thrown on their beam-ends for lack of money, having acted this or that to empty houses, always as a last resort advertise *Hamlet*. It can be counted upon, above any other play, to fill the treasury. Again, when an actor takes a benefit, what is the piece most commonly chosen?— *Hamlet*. Why? 'Because,' it may be answered, 'Hamlet himself is notoriously a "star" part, with plenty of soliloquies, with plenty of what I believe is called "fat" in the Profession; and moreover because the part has become consecrated somehow, invested by tradition with a certain aura of greatness and crowned as with a halo.' I applaud the answer: it is an excellent one so far as it goes. But why does the gentleman who enacts the First Gravedigger also choose *Hamlet* for his 'benefit night'? Now that question happens to be more searching than for a moment it may seem. I was once assisting at a dress rehearsal of *Hamlet*, when the First Gravedigger came off the stage in a passion. In the green-room it exploded. 'Why,' he wished to know, 'should I be treated like a dog by that conceited fool?'— meaning our Hamlet, of course. 'His temper gets viler at every rehearsal. Surely, after airing his vanity through four Acts, he might be quiet while I have *my* little say!' 'Bless you, sir,' answered an old dresser, 'it's always like that. In these forty years, I've helped dress (I dare say) all that number of Hamlets: and Hamlet and the First Gravedigger always fall out. It's a regular thing. I've known 'em come to blows.' The old man allowed that he could not account for it at all. *Hamlet*, he said, was a great play—a wonderful play—and there it just was. 'Hamlet and First Grave-digger: when you've said that, you've said oil and vinegar.' Well, while engaged in denying that *Hamlet* is a mystery in the sense in which Coleridge, Goethe, and the rest would make it a mystery, I fairly admit there *are* mysteries about it. But why the First Gravedigger should choose for *his* benefit night the great and wonderful drama which gives his hated rival such opportunity for display is neither beyond con-jecture nor even a puzzling question. It fills the cash-box.

Let me illustrate my argument from another side, using another tradition of the theatre. We all know that to play Hamlet, and play him successfully, is the crown of every young actor's ambition. But here comes in another mystery —which yet is no mystery at all, unless the critics have fogged us. *When he comes to it, he always plays it success-fully*. An actor, about to play Hamlet for the first time, once assured me (and from boyhood he had known the theatre, as we say, 'from the inside')—'If I make a mess of this, I shall be either a complete fool or too good to live; and I am neither.' Well, he did not make a mess of it, and so I escaped choosing between those dismal alte.natives. But when reading the play I have often pondered his words, and it is not in any love of paradox that I suggest this question.

It is the fashion, and was the fashion before we were born, so that we may call it the custom—it is the custom to talk of So-and so's Hamlet: of Garrick's Hamlet, Kemble's Hamlet, Kean's Hamlet; Macready's, Salvini's, Phelps's, Irving's Hamlets; Sir Herbert Tree's Hamlet, Mr Forbes Robertson's Hamlet. This custom of speech, if it mean anything, would seem to imply that each of these gifted interpreters has given the world a different resolution of that mystery; and that each has made an individual success of it: which, when we come to think of it, approaches the miraculous, if not the absurd. By various paths they all arrive at the core of the great secret: and yet there would seem to be some mystery about a mystery which turns out to be a different one every time it is explained.

(4)

Now I suggest that all these fine fellows in their turn have made a success in *Hamlet* simply because it was *there all the time*: ready-made by a man who had been beforehand with them, and, having a capital interest in the play, had unconsciously taken care that their self-conscious displays should never attain to spoiling it. I suggest that all those critics, too (Coleridge, Goethe, Klein, Werder, and the rest), have been plucking different hearts out of the mystery and exhibiting them, simply because there was never any mystery in *Hamlet*, and consequently no secret heart to pluck out.

I know that this is a bold thing to say. But I say it and shall support it (1) with a monumental principle of all great art and (2) with an ordinary piece of evidence, as common as our daily *Times* and *Morning Post*.

(1) For the principle.—It is never a test of the highest art that it is unintelligible. It is rather the last triumph of a masterpiece—the triumph definitely passing it for a classic—that all men in their degree can understand and enjoy it. Of course they will understand and enjoy in varying degrees according to their intelligence and sensibility. But all the great masterpieces we rank in the first class have this essential note—a noble and naked simplicity. The *Odyssey*, the Venus of Milo, a passage of Virgil, or of Dante, or of Milton, Botticelli's *Prima Vera*, Velasquez' *Surrender of Breda*, *Othello*, *The Tempest*, a lyric of Hugo's, Lincoln's peroration on the dead of Gettysburg, a preface of Plato's, or a parable of Christ's—all these hold you with a wonder at what they *show*, not of what they may perchance *hide*. To be sure, we come to them again and again, to discover fresh beauties. But our delight is to have our eyes unsealed; to feel ourselves alive in a world where this thing has been shown us. It is your stained-glass window critics that great art has no use for.

Do we, knowing Shakespeare, suppose that he wrote the longest of his plays to hide what he meant? If so, on every ground of presupposition, 'the less Shakespeare he!'

(2) For my piece of ordinary evidence—I have already given it. *Hamlet* is the most popular of his plays. The man we pass in the street eagerly pays his money to see it. Can we suppose that he pays to see something he cannot

understand? Is that the way of men who make up an audience?

I, for my part, believe that he goes to it because it is an amazingly fine play.

(5)

In a later chapter I propose to examine some theories about *Hamlet* put forward by men whose names compel one to treat whatever they may preach with respect. But it is permissible here, as it is convenient, to enter a plea that, although I may prove foolish in attempting to analyse it as a simple, straightforward piece of workmanship, at any rate I have been precedently matched—if not overmatched—in folly by the extreme mystifiers. A certain Mr Edward P. Vinting, in the *Mystery of Hamlet* (Philadelphia, 1881), has demonstrated that the Prince of Denmark was a woman in disguise, and in love with Horatio!—another injustice to Ophelia! A previous American researcher had found the key in the line 'He's fat and scant of breath.'[1] A German critic, Loening (as quoted by Tolman), thinks that the evidence points to an internal fatness, fatness of the heart; and he believes that this physical infirmity helps to explain the inactivity of the hero!

(6)

Let us dismiss these and far more respectable theories from our minds for a while, and suppose that we are seated in a theatre, expectant but knowing no more of what is to come than the play-bill promises: that his Highness's servants are to enact *The Tragical History of Hamlet, Prince of Denmark*, written by William Shakespeare, an author in

---

[1] *Popular Science Monthly*, May, 1860—article entitled *The Impediment of Adipose—a Celebrated Case* ('case' being Hamlet).

whom we have some confidence. I know that this is to ask
a great deal: since, as Hazlitt says, 'we have been so used to
this tragedy that we hardly know how to criticise it any
more than we should know how to describe our own faces'
—and Hazlitt had the luck to be a good-looking man. I
know that this is to risk a good deal. The reader will
pardonably think to himself, recalling the sentence I quoted
just now, that in practice the effort to become as children is
apt to result in being merely childish. Well, let us take that
risk!

It shall suffice me here to lay the scene and indicate some
of the characters as they are first presented to us: figures of
men and women that we see with our eyes and hear talking,
but men and women of whose business in life up to this
point we know nothing, as we must listen to learn what
thoughts and emotions are at work within them, as we must
watch to discover how, in the space of three hours or so,
they will work out their dooms.

(7)

The scene opens upon the battlements before the Castle
of Elsinore. It is night—midnight—and freezing hard; the
air still as it is cold. The stars are out. Under them, on the
terrace—the wash of the waves just audible far below—a
single sentry keeps guard. To him enters the relief guard,
but so noiselessly, whether because of the snow on the platform or by his own stealth along it, that it is this new-comer
who anticipates the challenge.

Bernardo. Who's there?
Francisco. Nay, answer me: stand and unfold yourself.
Bern. Long live the King!
Fran. Bernardo?
Bern. He.

Fran. You come most carefully upon your hour.

Bern. 'Tis now struck twelve: get thee to bed, Francisco.

Fran. For this relief much thanks: 'tis bitter cold,
And I am sick at heart.

Bern.   Have you had quiet guard?

Fran. Not a mouse stirring.

Bern.   Well, good-night...
              (*then as Francisco begins to move off*)
If you do meet Horatio and Marcellus,
The rivals of my watch, bid them make haste.

Fran. (*halting and listening*).
      I think I hear them. (*In the act of changing guard,*
           having stepped a little forward, he challenges)
               Stand ho! Who is there?

Now here already, in fifteen broken lines (or eleven, as we choose to count), we have conveyed to us (the hushed voices helping) the place, the freezing cold, the night, the very hour of the night, and withal a kind of creeping expectancy. We are on the watch: the mere figure of the sentinel—stiff, in his armour, under the stars—means *that*. But we are on the watch against something unusual, something fearful. This is not the usual relief of guard: the inverted challenge proves it. And the men know something.

Bern.   Have you had quiet guard?

Fran. Not a mouse stirring.

What is it they know, or suspect? Why is Bernardo, eager and prompt on time, at once so anxious that Horatio and Marcellus shall not be late? Doubtless we shall know in a moment....

But already we, seated in the audience—we, fairly familiar with William Shakespeare as a playwright—know, if we can think of it above this wonderful arrest of our attention, that he is bringing off his opening scene magnifi-

cently. He is sometimes a little careless with these openings.
We are not old enough to have witnessed the opening—but
for this, unparalleled—of *The Tempest*. That is a marvel to
come. But the quarrel which started *Romeo and Juliet* was
brisk and went with a swing: as the first Scene of *King
Henry IV*, Part I, and the first Scene of *A Midsummer-
Night's Dream*, both courtly and noble, led us exquisitely up
to the plunge, with Scenes II, into Mistress Quickly's
tavern, Peter Quince's back shop. *The Merchant of Venice*
—not bad: *Henry V*, if we allow prologues, good enough:
The Merry Wives, admirable chatter: *The Taming of the
Shrew*, original and first-class—original, that is, to us, who
don't happen to have read the *Arabian Nights' Entertainments*. But *As You Like It*, as poor as could be...'As I
remember, Adam, it was in this fashion bequeathed me by
will, etc.'—somebody telling somebody else, for the
audience's instruction, something which somebody else had
known perfectly well for years. In *Macbeth*, to be sure, the
other day, he scarified us with those three hags on a desert
heath—

> When shall we three meet again—
> In thunder, lightning, or in rain?

But this promises to be still better. What is the dread *something* that makes these men—soldiers too—talk so hoarsely,
breathe so tensely, their breath a vapour on the night air?

> *Mar.* What, has this—*thing*—appear'd again to-night?
> *Bern.* I have seen nothing.
> *Mar.* Horatio says 'tis but our phantasy,
> And will not let belief take hold of him
> Touching this dreaded sight, twice seen of us
> Therefore I have entreated him along
> With us to watch the minutes of this night,
> That if again this apparition come,

He may approve our eyes and speak to it.
Hor.   Tush, tush, 'twill not appear.

We begin to keep our eyes for this Horatio, this sane,
sceptical man: for in truth we, who by report know something less about it than he, turn with a certain trust to one
who refuses to take seriously that which we are coming
gradually to dread: that which, in less than thirty lines, has
been successively insinuated into our fears as 'this thing,'
'this dreaded sight,' 'this apparition.'...
Says Bernardo,

> Last night of all,
> When yond same star that's westward from the pole
> Had made his course to illume that part of heaven
> Where now it burns, Marcellus and myself,
> The bell then beating one,—
>
> (*The Ghost enters*)
>
> *Mar.*   Peace!...break thee off!
> Look where it comes again!

There is our opening, and it closes on that unforgettable
note of the half line—

> The bell then beating one,—

closes and reopens upon this apparition which, awfully
lambent out of darkness, chokes Bernardo's tale and in the
same moment tells it out, answering the expectancy up to
which—though the play is as yet but forty lines old—we
have been gradually strung since midnight was.

> The bell then beating one.

Now we know why Bernardo, relieving guard at twelve,
would have word carried to the others to make haste.
It—the thing—is a ghost crossing the terrace, tall, pale,

majestical, with frosty glints on its eyes, beard, armour: as Bernardo whispers, quavering back,

> In the same figure like the King that's *dead*.

The two soldiers, as the apparition stalks by, turn to Horatio and beg him to question it. Their dependence helps our steadily growing respect for him as he pulls his wits together and challenges. This sceptical fellow has courage. But the Ghost passes on. It will have none of *his* challenge.

Now let us mark how the men take it:

Mar.   **Is it not like the King?**
Hor. (*musing*). As thou art to thyself:
       Such was the very armour he had on
       When he the ambitious Norway combated;
       So frown'd he once, when, in an angry parle,
       He smote the sledded Polacks on the ice.
       'Tis strange....
Mar. (*the inferior man, still eager—as inferior men always are*
       —to constate the unimportant evidence).
       Thus twice before, and jump at this dead hour,
       With martial stalk hath he gone by our watch....

I shall hereafter spare to worry the reader with details: but here at the beginning will ask him to note the superb diction already closing us in its grip—

> He smote the sledded Polacks on the ice

—the ice—that picture at once recalled by the silvery glitter shed about the spectre—

> Thus twice before, and *jump* at this dead hour.

Your second-rate man would have written 'prompt,' or 'right,' or 'pat,' or 'lo! at this dead hour,' even if he had the

wit to make the hour dead. But 'jump at this dead hour'—
whose stroke was that ever but a Shakespeare's?

The rest of the scene, even the Ghost's return, I find
inferior. There is too much about Fortinbras, of whom we
are thus led to expect that he will have great effect upon
what is to follow. Actually he has next to none, though the
dramatist seems to start by intending that he should. Moreover some thirty lines are wasted on the old protasis trick I
mentioned just now: Horatio, with an eye on the audience,
informing Marcellus of what Marcellus must be supposed
to know beforehand.

(8)

But in Scene II we come to the real protasis, and to a
great feat of artistry which (although we are not for the
moment supposed to know it) Shakespeare was to bring to
perfection in *The Tempest*: the feat, having opened with an
astounding shock, of making his second scene quietly and
naturally explain it, unravelling a knot so that all the threads
reach out separately, intelligibly, ready for the predestined
new ravel.

If we except Ophelia, all the main characters are gathered
in the state-room: King Claudius, the Queen, Hamlet
himself, Polonius, Laertes, Horatio, Marcellus. Bernardo
enters before the scene is done.

The King acquaints us with the main situation in a speech
which, as a public one, addressed to full Court, is not re-
capitulatory beyond reason. Recital of things known to
everybody is generally allowed in a public speech, else
where should many of us be? The situation, as explained by
King Claudius, comes to this:

The late King, his brother, is dead (how, it is not
suggested), and his memory yet green. But there is no use

crying over spilt milk; it is bad for the commonwealth; and meanwhile, and moreover, he, Claudius, has somewhat hastily married his brother's widow.

[What he does not explain, by the way—and what the commentators conspire with him and with Shakespeare to overlook—is the small difficulty that, Hamlet's father deceased, Hamlet should *ipso facto* have inherited the throne. From the commentators, discreetly silent over this hitch in workmanship, I turn to Charles Lamb, who, of course, has noted it, but slides it over; telling us in his tale of the play merely that Claudius took the crown 'to the exclusion of young Hamlet, the son of the buried king and lawful successor to the throne.' But this will not quite do. Hamlet is not 'young Hamlet': for in the graveyard scene his age is accurately made out to be thirty. Unless some strange law of succession be hinted at in the line describing Hamlet's mother as

The imperial jointress of this warlike state,

there is a flaw of construction here.]

But, Shakespeare overlooking this trifle, Hamlet does not seem to mind or indeed to think about it first or last. We turn our eyes to him. He—a man of thirty, or nearly thirty—a student, but a paragon of youth when he has ever asserted himself—is not thinking of himself, or of title and royalty. He is occupied with something very much more human and essential—the awful haste with which his mother has married again, with her husband's brother, too. He loves his mother: but he has *adored* his father; and how his mother can have so quickly shifted from such a man to this Claudius ...O, most horrible, this lust in a woman, and that woman his own mother! He idolises his father's memory, and amid the factitious rejoicings wears black, in a Court he loathes

He craves leave to be dismissed from it, to go back to his old
University, Wittenberg. This being denied him, he con-
sents, but when the Court has withdrawn, he breaks out—

> That it should come to this!
> But two months dead! Nay, not so much, not two:
> So excellent a king; that was, to this,
> Hyperion to a satyr: so loving to my mother,
> That he might not beteem the winds of heaven
> Visit her face too roughly. Heaven and earth!
> Must I remember?

Now let us mark that at this point Hamlet suspects not at
all any foul play in the manner of his father's taking-off.
But the very scurf of what he knows is so loathsome that he
cannot help suspecting a putridity deeper still.

On the acute moment of this suspicion comes Horatio—
the sound, sane, sceptical friend Horatio—to report (two
solid soldiers, Bernardo and Marcellus, confirming) the
vision seen haunting the Castle platform.

So we leave him on the eve of discovery.

CHAPTER IX

HAMLET

II

Polonius and Laertes—A family failing—The loneliness of Ophelia—The cause of Hamlet's horror—The two keys to Hamlet's soul—Criticism divorced from knowledge of life—Beatrice Cenci—Hamlet's 'madness' and hesitancy—The Queen's insight into Hamlet—Shakespeare's passing misogyny—Hamlet's affected madness before fools—His moral scrupulousness—A self-explanatory soliloquy.

(1)

IN Scene III we improve our small acquaintance with Laertes, who has leave to return to France after the coronation and is now on the eve of sailing. In bidding farewell to his sister Ophelia, to whom Prince Hamlet has made certain protestations of love, he takes occasion to give her a quantity of advice touching the regulation of her conduct. We soon begin to suspect this sententious young man of being a fairly accomplished prig, and, when he has done, applaud the gentle irony and the spirit in his sister's retort.

> I shall the effect of this good lesson keep
> As watchman to my heart. But, good my brother
> Do not, as some ungracious pastors do,
> Show me the steep and thorny way to heaven,
> Whiles, like a puff'd and reckless libertine,
> Himself the primrose path of dalliance treads
> And recks not his own rede.

'O, fear *me* not!' Laertes assures her complacently. But he is to get back a deal more than this of what he has been giving: for at this moment his father Polonius enters, and after chiding him for his delay in getting aboard, proceeds to delay him yet further and unconscionably, treating him to a homily on the Whole Duty of a Young Man; and ending, when Laertes craves leave to be gone, with a glance at the clock, and

> The time invites you: go, your servants 'tend.

We perceive that Laertes takes after his father, that the males of this family are addicted to longwindedness; and surmise that Lady Polonius (as I must call her) has died of it, some while before. From the first we have a sense of a most pathetic orphaned loneliness about Ophelia. Throughout, she has no one to turn to, no woman to give her advice. (For let us note that, unlike many another heroine of Shakespeare's, she is not even allowed a waiting-maid. Save the Queen, there is no other woman in the play-bill. And what kind of help or advice could such a woman as the Queen give?) On the other hand, of male admonition—of advice which is precisely the kind of advice she does not want—the poor child gets enough and to spare. Her brother is no sooner gone than her father turns on her and reads her another lecture—reams of worldly counsel, all withered, conventional. Poor Ophelia!

> There is enough of wither'd everywhere
> To make her bower, and enough of gloom;
> There is enough of sadness to invite,
> If only for the rose that died, whose doom
> Is Beauty's...
> There is enough of sorrowing, and quite
> Enough of bitter fruits the earth doth bear.

If this scene vex us a little, halting our impatience and procrastinating on the edge of Hamlet's terrible enlightenment, let us do justice to that check and suspense as a piece of artistry.

If Laertes and Polonius seem (and are) tedious as well as conventional, may we not recognise that Shakespeare deliberately made them so? In this Court of Denmark an abyss of horror has been half-opened to us. Earth has parted, and for a moment given up its dead; has shut again, not yet surrendering the secret. But enough has been revealed to seize our minds, and Hamlet's mind, with suspicion deep as hell. On the stage, which is for the moment a crust thinly closed over damnation, these two courtiers, father and son, prate saws on the proper conduct of life, meaningless as they are worldly-wise; batter them on the brain of a helpless girl whose heart, we divine (though as yet we know not how it will come to pass), has fatally engaged her in the tragedy of which, as she has set no spring in motion, her will can control no spring. She, a helpless victim, is being prated to her doom by brother and father, the only two beings in the world she might naturally have counted on for help.

It is too pitiful: and at the same time, if our impatience allow leisure for it, the subtlest of comedy: high comedy, upon the very edge of all most tragic. Let us, when the play is over, revert our minds to this scene which at the time we thought dull.

(2)

Of the fourth Scene, wherein Hamlet awaits his father's spirit upon the terrace: and of the famous fifth Scene, wherein he encounters it alone and the horrible secret is revealed to him, I shall say very little. They speak for themselves. They conclude the First Act.

But, since so many of the commentators seem to make wholly insufficient allowance for it, I must recur to the extreme horror of the shock inflicted on Hamlet. I have already tried to show that he had positively adored his father and still adores his father's memory. His words, as Dr Bradley quite justly says, 'melt into music whenever he speaks of him.'

I have tried to illustrate, by the passage beginning 'That it should come to this...' with what a violence of loathing his soul is affected—even before he suspects murder—by his mother's foul haste in mating so swiftly with her husband's brother; by the scent of lust in it, nay of incest; for again and again (though this is often overlooked) Hamlet and the Ghost insist upon the marriage as incestuous. That thought is preying on Hamlet's mind before ever he hears of the Ghost.

It may be shown further, by many quotations, that he is a man naturally well-conditioned; which means, apt and eager to accept folk at their best, and to see good rather than evil in them.[1] I shall not labour this, for this again Dr Bradley has sufficiently shown, and quite incontrovertibly.

Now let us hear and attend the effect of the full disclosure:

> *Hamlet.* O all you host of heaven! O earth! what else?
> And shall I couple hell? O fie! hold, hold, my
> heart!
> And you, my sinews, grow not instant old,
> But bear me stiffly up! Remember thee!
> Ay, thou poor ghost, while memory holds a seat
> In this distracted globe. Remember thee!
> Yea, from the table of my memory
> I'll wipe away all trivial fond records,

[1] Let the reader note—for it is highly significant—how often the word 'noble' occurs in this play.

All saws of books, all forms, all pressures past,
That youth and observation copied there;
And thy commandment all alone shall live
Within the book and volume of my brain,
Unmix'd with baser matter: yes, by heaven!
A most pernicious woman!
O villain, villain, smiling, damnèd villain!
My tables,—meet it is I set it down,
That one may smile, and smile, and be a villain;
At least, I'm sure it may be so in Denmark.

I have quoted the passage because it is the key of the action, as the famous soliloquy is the key to the inaction of the drama: and without both keys we cannot unlock the awful perturbation of Hamlet's soul. Reading the commentators one would think that to discover your father had been murdered and your mother to be an incestuous adulteress were all in the day's work. So they fall to discovering it to be strange, nay even a little absurd, that a man after such a shock should call for his tablets. Can they not see that under such a shock a decent man must dread that his mind is going? 'Remember thee!...Remember thee!' 'Remember' is the word tolling above all the chaos in his brain; and as a drowning man at a straw he snatches the tablets. Men in such extremity always snatch on some concrete, some trivial thing. Why will not these scholars start with a little practice in learning about men and women? Has none of them heard, perchance, of sailors who, when their ship was going down and the last hope had perished, have slipped quietly below and started—to shave? What are these commentators made of? What crisis have they ever dared in their lives—if they do not know, if they cannot even surmise, that when this solid world seems breaking under the feet of any sound man in health and strength, it is always some such small solid trifle that he grips?—Ay, and woman, too! Let us recall Beatrice Cenci, as she goes to her death.

> Give yourself no unnecessary pain,
> My dear Lord Cardinal. Here, mother, tie
> My girdle for me, and bind up this hair
> In any simple knot: ay, that does well.
> And yours, I see, is coming down. How often
> Have we done this for one another; now
> We shall not do it any more. My Lord,
> We are quite ready.

So it is with that letting down of hysteria in which Hamlet, hearing the voice of the ghost underfoot as he swears Horatio and Marcellus to secrecy, the two touching the cross of his sword-hilt, breaks into wild scoffing—all the while facing it out before them:

> *Ghost* (*beneath*). Swear.
> *Hamlet.* Aha, boy! say'st thou so? art thou there, true-
>   penny?
>   Come on: you hear this fellow in the cellarage;
>   Consent to swear.

The critics who object to this are the very critics, of course, who cannot abide that knocking on the gate in *Macbeth* and that vulgar porter.

(3)

But we will suppose the First Act ended. In the interval those of the audience not entirely occupied with nuts and oranges fall to chattering and chatting, their hubbub breaking forth sudden as one's own sob of the breath now that the long tension is for a while relaxed. An intelligent stranger seated next to me on my right breaks the ice by remarking that the First Act has gone very well. 'Very well indeed,' I answer. 'And indeed,' says he, 'the old play of *Hamlet's*

Revenge, though it has amused me once or twice, was never a patch on this.' 'I have heard of it, of course,' say I, 'but as it happens, I never saw the thing.' 'And now you never will,' he promises me; 'for this will drive it clean off the boards. Yet the story itself is the same, so far, and comes (I believe) straight out of an old chronicle. In the next Act we shall see how this Hamlet feigns madness, the better to execute his revenge.'

Well, sure enough, in Act II this business is developed. And here, with the reader's leave, I shall deal compendiously with much talk about Hamlet's 'madness,' closing with, as I hope shortly to have done with, that dwindling band of critics who would persuade us that Hamlet is actually 'mad.'

What is 'madness'? Surely we have only to think for a moment to know that up to a point it is a purely relative term, like 'drunkenness.' When is a man 'drunk'? On the one hand we have the fanatic teetotaller who cannot speak of a glass of claret save as 'alcohol' or 'intoxicating liquor'; and so *he* darkens counsel. At the other end of the critical scale we have the indignant witness upon oath: 'What? Bill *drunk*? Why, I seen him close, as the Police was carryin' him past on the stretcher, and he distinctly opened an eye!'

So again with 'mental deficiency'—another relative term. I remember once, as Chairman of an Elementary Schools Committee, having to attempt, under orders from the Board of Education, a census of the mentally defective children in a certain county area. That area was divided, for executive purposes, into eight districts, and we set their several clerks to work. Their reports ranged from ·8 per cent. in one fortunate district to 15 or more in its all-but-next-door neighbour: these extremes, of course, yielding us no more than the not immediately useful information that two men can employ widely different standards upon a relative term.

And so with madness. Very few of us are without some little kink of the brain, some tendency to estimate this or that out of its due proportion in what the most of us allow to be an ordered universe. Still fewer of us perhaps—fewer indeed of strong passions and affections—shall never on our way through this transitory life be thrown off our balance by distress of mind or the shock of calamity. We have seen Hamlet, a man of strong affections, reeling under such a shock, most terribly accumulated. Now, Shakespeare, of course—it is the dramatist's first function—invites each of us to put himself in Hamlet's place. The point of *every* tragedy is its demand on our several assent—'There, but for the grace of God, go I'—A or B or C or D. Cannot any one of us, imagining such a shock to fall upon him as fell upon Hamlet, conceive it as rocking his mind in violent oscillation on its pivot? Can we easily conceive it as doing less?

Then may we not go on to own that the evidence of this oscillation at least partly explains the apparent hesitancy of Hamlet's purpose? But he is never thrown off the pivot—never; though his own mind, now and again, may doubt it.

Here I would call attention to two points:

(1) It is as certain as can be that an exhibition of real madness would not evoke in the breasts of an Elizabethan audience the compassionate pity it evokes from ours, or anything like it. Our rude forefathers treated lunacy as a subject for brutal mirth, and behaved to it much as the boys who pelt a village idiot. Let us read our *Twelfth Night*, and ponder what happened to Malvolio.

(2) It is now provided by English law that no one,

whatever the doctors may say, shall be declared a lunatic
and removed to a madhouse unless the necessity for it be
certified by a magistrate, who must personally examine the
patient. Now if you, my reader, were a magistrate and
Polonius, no doubt you would give that certificate without
a qualm, and Hamlet would be shut up—while you would
remain Polonius.

The Queen (who, after all, is his mother) guesses, as a
mother will, more swiftly and accurately than any one else,
what is amiss with Hamlet. When, after idle reports from
the other courtiers, Polonius comes with *his* explanation—
fatuously wrong, I need not say—and the King is comforted
by it—

> He tells me, my dear Gertrude, he hath found
> The head and source of all your son's distemper—

she pierces to the root of it in a flash:

> I doubt it is no other but the main;
> His father's death and our o'erhasty marriage.

She never deems him mad, save for that moment in her
room, when he sees the ghost which she does not see.[1] Then,
observing him (as she puts it) to bend his eye on vacancy and
with the incorporal air to hold discourse, for one moment

---

[1] Let me here interpose a word on the Ghost. Up to this
scene between Hamlet and his mother he has been the most positive ghost in all Shakespeare. He is not like Macbeth's floating
spectral dagger, which Macbeth sees, but we do not: he differs
from Banquo's ghost, which Macbeth sees, and *we* see, but the
guests about the tables do not. Up to this scene the ghost of
Hamlet's father, though he will *speak* to none but Hamlet, is
visible to every person whose path he crosses. In this scene he
is visible to one person alone, Hamlet, and not to another, the
Queen.

she surmises excusably that the tale has been truer than she
has deemed it, and Hamlet cries:

> Why, look you there! look, how it steals away!
> My father, in his habit as he lived!
> Look, where he goes, even now, out at the portal!
> [*Exit Ghost.*

Queen. This is the very coinage of your brain,
> This bodiless creation ecstasy
> Is very cunning in.

Hamlet turns on her:

> Ecstasy!
> My pulse, as yours, doth temperately keep time,
> And makes as healthful music. It is not madness
> That I have utter'd. Bring me to the test
> And I the matter will re-word, which madness
> Would gambol from. Mother, for love of grace,
> Lay not that flattering unction to your soul,
> That not your trespass but my madness speaks.

Yet, though Hamlet seems to her to be staring at vacancy,
addressing vacancy—in spite of this, though it follows on the
swift careless stroke which kills old Polonius, hiding behind
the arras—his mother knows that he is not mad, and his
accusing words tear through her, not as any ravings of
lunacy, but as the direct impeachment of moral right,
stripping bare her crime. I shall return upon this; but I
wish here to establish the point that his mother, the first to
divine, here and throughout thoroughly understands.

Yet, let us mark, she thoroughly understands at the point
where Hamlet is nearest to insanity, if by insanity we mean
that a man is 'possessed,' ridden by an idea which throws
the rest of life into disproportion. If you press this, Hamlet
was beside himself—ridden by furious disgust of the lechery
that can inhabit woman. Nor can I, reading and comparing

the plays he wrote about this time, deny that Shakespeare himself (whatever his story) was possessed, tormented, maddened by some revelation of the lust possible in woman. This man, who has joyfully created Beatrice, Rosalind, Viola—this man who is to create Imogen, Perdita, Miranda —this man for the nonce is a mad dog, biting upon all that is vilest in sex—let a hundred filthy comparisons in *Troilus, Othello, Lear* be witness—and constantly and hideously referring this lust back to the most sacred name of 'mother.' Says Troilus, shuddering, to Ulysses:

> Think, we had mothers!
>
> *Ulysses.* What hath she done, Prince, that can soil our mothers?
>
> *Troilus.* Nothing at all, unless that this were she.

I dwell on this because it is the central explication of Hamlet's behaviour towards Ophelia. I cannot excuse that behaviour, and my explication here will need some enforcement which I hope to give by-and-by. For the present I content myself with this:

Hamlet loves Ophelia. But the discovery of his mother's lust drives him—and it is as nigh as he ever gets to positive madness—into a loathing perversion of mind against *all* women and *especially towards this single maid of his choice.* Even as in the recoil from Cressida's perfidy Troilus swings round upon the holiest memory of woman—'Think! we had mothers!'—so, in the recoil from a mother's lust, Hamlet swings round, rends the veil down from that other altar of love, scatters the sacred fire, stamps black the live coal.

We note in Act II, Scene 1, it is Ophelia who first brings word of Hamlet's derangement; and we note how her old dotard of a father jumps at each piece of evidence, accepting with fresh glee whatever confirms his wrong conclusion, until he can hold his delighted folly no longer.

> Come, go with me: I will go seek the King.
> This is the very ecstasy of love!...

We note, moreover, that in dealing with all such complacent fools—not only Polonius, but Rosencrantz and Guildenstern—Hamlet deliberately and with relish *enacts* the madman. We watch him tucking his arm under Polonius's and drawing him aside:

Polonius (*entering with his message*). My lord, the queen would speak with you, and presently.

Hamlet. Do you see yonder cloud that's almost in shape of a camel?

Pol. By the mass, and 'tis like a camel indeed.

Ham. Methinks 'tis like a weasel.

Pol. It is backed like a weasel.

Ham. Or like a whale?

Pol. Very like a whale.

Ham. (*dropping his arm suddenly*). Then I will come to my mother by and by. (*Aside*) They fool me to the top of my bent. (*Aloud*) I will come by and by.

We mark the absurd discomposing questions with which Hamlet staggers Rosencrantz and Guildenstern in the midst of their fashionable chatter about the players.—

Ros. Faith, there has been much to do on both sides....There was for a while no money bid for argument unless the poet and the player went to cuffs in the question.

Ham. Is it possible?

Guil. O, there has been much throwing about of brains.

Ham. Do the boys carry it away?

But he never talks like that to the sane man, Horatio.

Horatio knows: Gertrude, his mother, knows too. For a moment, in the great scene closing the Third Act, she is shaken: but that is only because he stares at a Ghost which she cannot see. His awful arraignment—surely the most awful ever spoken by son to mother—has turned her eyes into her very soul. She bows her head on her beautiful arms, the arms that have nursed him:

> O Hamlet, thou hast cleft my heart in twain!
> *Hamlet.* O, throw away the worser part of it
> And live the purer with the other half....

No: Hamlet is sane. Considering the shock he has undergone, we may almost say there was never man saner.

(4)

The commentators want to know why Hamlet, having discovered his uncle's guilt, did not make an end of him at once. It appears that this is what *they* would have done.... So, you see, one never knows. One meets them going to the University Sermon or shuffling along upon some other blameless errand, and—can we believe it?—any one of these Harry Hotspurs will have killed him some six or seven dozen Scots at a breakfast, washed his hands, and said to his wife, 'Fie upon this quiet life! I want work.' O yes; and that is the sort of men they *are*, if only you believe what they write just now, about War, to the newspapers.

But, about this pusillanimous Hamlet, what answer can we give them? I think we can give them half a dozen, and any one good enough.

Shall we answer (and truly I think it should suffice for them) that had Hamlet been like them and slain his uncle at the beginning of Act II, there would have been no more play, or at any rate the rest of the tragedy would have been transferred to the box-office?

Or shall we tell them that, as we see him, Hamlet is a man of gentle, scrupulous nature, and of an exceedingly active intellect? Now all the *positive* evidence Hamlet has, when all is said and done, is the word of a Ghost: and if, as in a famous trial Mr Justice Stareleigh informed the court, 'what the soldier said is not evidence,' still less is the word of a Ghost. Men in this world do not post off to stab other men on the affidavit of a Ghost.

The worst of taking such a common-sense view as this is that you always find some German Professor waiting to expound your common-sense with a pestle until he has brayed it down to a solemn theory, and you are tempted to curse the day on which you ever ventured the observation that two and two make four. Professor Werder, of Berlin, in this solemn way proves that, being unable to call the Ghost into a witness-box, Hamlet *has* to deal circuitously, or the Court of Denmark will interpret his revenge as based upon insufficient evidence. But the Court of Denmark has nothing to do with it. Hamlet's responsibility rests with his own conscience. As Sir Walter Raleigh says—

A curiously business-like vein of criticism runs through essays and remarks on Hamlet. There is much talk of failure and success. 'A ghost has told him to avenge the murder of his father; why does he not do his obvious duty, and do it at once, so that everything may be put in order?' His delay, it has sometimes been replied, is justified by his desire to do his duty in a more effective and workmanlike fashion. The melan-choly Prince has certainly not been able to infect all who read his story with his own habit of thought.

If the government of the State of Denmark were one of the issues of the play, there would be a better foothold for these practical moralists. But the State of Denmark is not regarded at all, except as a topical and picturesque setting for the main interest. The tragedy is a tragedy of private life, made conspicuous by the royal station of the chief actors in it.

I repeat, Hamlet's responsibility is to his own conscience. That is why, being a grown and thoughtful man, he cannot strike in the way these commentators demand. He is scrupulous. That is why (as he tells us) he designs the play-scene, to entrap the king's conscience and get better proof. That is why (as he tells us) he cannot kill Claudius pat, while he is praying. And let us note how Shakespeare prepares us for his leniency as we listen to Claudius's agony:

> O bosom black as death!
> O limèd soul, that struggling to be free
> Art more engag'd!

Nay, Hamlet himself at times is moved by a doubt of the Ghost, if it be authentic or no:

> The spirit that I have seen
> *May* be the devil; and the devil hath power
> To assume a pleasing shape; yea, and perhaps
> Out of my weakness and my melancholy,
> As he is very potent with such spirits,
> Abuses me to damn me. I'll have grounds
> More relative than this. The play's the thing
> Wherein I'll catch the conscience of the King.

(5)

And yet, and after all, and although, if we reckon up the time covered by the action of the play, we find it but a month or two, Hamlet *does* reproach himself with his

irresolution, and the Ghost *does* reappear to remind him of
its impatience. Hamlet has *not* swept to his revenge

> with wings as swift
> As meditation or the thoughts of love.

Yes: and why should a man like Hamlet, noble of nature,
gentle, thoughtful, scrupulous, eager to believe the best of
his fellows—why should such a man *not* shrink from the
deed and cast about for new incentives? The charge, let us
remind ourselves, is imposed upon him. He has done
nothing to invite it. In itself he loathes it:

> The time is out of joint. O cursèd spite
> That ever I was born to set it right.

At first he finds the thought of it so intolerable that he
meditates suicide. I contend that the famous soliloquy, and
the scene with Ophelia that immediately follows, explain
themselves.

And after them—let us mark the anguish of the irony—
it is Ophelia that is to know *real* madness and die of it: as—
let us mark the master-stroke—in her babblings this clean
maid, of a mind unhinged, pours forth the pretty sad simple
bawdry of

> To-morrow is Saint Valentine's day.

Who save Shakespeare could ever have wrung our ears
with *that*?

CHAPTER X

HAMLET

III

The simple secret of the critics—Coleridge and another—'It is
we who are Hamlet': the key is in every man's breast—An
old play furbished and refurbished—How this explains Ophelia
in Hamlet's brutality—Blank verse as a vehicle for drama—
Dryden's examination examined—Milton and the cæsura—
Dryden's own practice *versus* his theory—How blank verse
helps the actor.

(1)

I HAD intended to conclude these notes on *Hamlet* with
a discussion of the principal commentators and their
theories, and to be as dull as the subject demanded. But
in the process of wading through so much of their out-
pourings as fills 300 pages of the second volume of the late
Mr Furness's Variorum edition of the play I made, or
seemed to make, a discovery warning me not to pursue an
inquest foredoomed to be idle.

Indeed, the discovery had lain under my hand since, in
the first few pages of this book, when dealing with *Macbeth*,
I had insisted that the most necessary aim of a tragic poet, of
a dramatist, was to make his hero sympathetic (ὅμοιος is
Aristotle's term, and Aristotle is strenuous on this point): to
present him as a man, however much higher in rank and
station than we, however circumstantially exalted, still

recognisable as of like passions with ourselves: so that, as the drama goes on, we enter completely into his feelings, hang upon what is happening to him, hold our breath with a sense that all this is happening to *us*. The reader will certainly remember this; for I have recurred to it more than once or twice. Without it, of course, we cannot understand Macbeth or Lady Macbeth, Othello or Desdemona.

(2)

Now let us listen to this from Coleridge—perhaps the richest critical genius that ever spent its powers on Shakespeare:

Hamlet's character is the prevalence of the abstracting and generalizing habit over the practical. He does not want courage, skill, will, or opportunity; but every incident sets him thinking; and it is curious, and at the same time strictly natural, that Hamlet, who all the play seems reason itself, should be impelled at last by mere accident to effect his object.

He [Shakespeare] intended to portray a person in whose view the external world, and all its incidents and objects, were comparatively dim, and of no interest in themselves, and which began to interest only when they were reflected in the mirror of his mind....The poet places him in the most stimulating circumstances that a human being can be placed in. He is the heir-apparent of a throne; his father dies suspiciously; his mother excludes her son from his throne by marrying his uncle. This is not enough: but the ghost of the murdered father is introduced to assure the son that he was put to death by his own brother. What is the effect upon the son?—instant action and pursuit of revenge? No; endless reasoning and hesitating —constant urging and solicitation of the mind to act, and as constant an escape from action; ceaseless reproaches of himself for sloth and negligence, while the whole energy of his resolution evaporates in these reproaches....

He is full of purpose, but void of that quality of mind which accomplishes purpose. Anything finer than this conception and working out of a great character is merely impossible. Shakespeare wishes to impress on us the truth that action is the chief end of existence—that no faculties of intellect, however brilliant, can be considered valuable, or indeed otherwise than as misfortunes, if they withdraw us from, or render us repugnant to, action, and lead us to think and think of doing, until the time has elapsed when we can *do* anything effectually. In enforcing this moral truth Shakespeare has shown the fulness and force of his powers: all that is amiable and excellent in nature is combined in Hamlet, with the exception of one quality. He is a man living in meditation, called upon by every motive human and divine, but the great object of his life is defeated by continually resolving to do, yet doing nothing but resolve.

Now, with all respect to the memory of Coleridge, I call this fluffy writing. I have combed out whole paragraphs of fluff, but fluff is still the residue—a continual saying of the same thing over and over again, helping nothing, elaborately beating a bush for minutes after the hare has been started. But I have omitted one sentence which, to my mind, knits up the whole rigmarole. Into the middle of his criticism Coleridge drops the artless remark, 'I have a smack of Hamlet myself, if I may say so.'

(3)

That small confession gives the secret. What would Samuel Taylor Coleridge have done if *his* murdered father had arisen to him from the grave and enjoined revenge? Intelligent readers of the late Mr J. Dykes Campbell's life of him must know perfectly well what Coleridge would have done. First of all he would have searched in his pockets for his tablets, which were not there; next, to advance his fell purpose, he would have borrowed five pounds at least off Horatio; and thereupon he would have wandered off to live with somebody else at Highgate (or whatever might be the corresponding suburb of Elsinore) and talked about what he was going to do, until—at the end of twenty years or so—he discussed it with equal prolixity as an accomplished fact.

Coleridge was a great critic and a genius: but as Shakespeare imposes Hamlet on us, upon the stage, so he imposes Hamlet on the critic in the library. I have quoted a critic of genius: now let me plunge and quote one Carl Karpf, a German:

The Myths used by the poet as the foundation of *Hamlet* we interpret in reference to the different activities personified in Hamlet and Laertes, the speculative and the active, the theoretic and the practical, the intensive and the extensive (reason and fear). In reference to *Hamlet*—the First Myth, which may relate to the divine Thought, founded upon the One, the First being—from the union of one god Odin and the giantess Jordh, the union of Spirit and Matter, sprang Thor. Thor carries Orvandill in a basket upon his back, wading through the wintry ice streams. One of Orvandill's toes, sticking out of the basket, is frozen, and thrown by Thor at the heavens, where it is made a star, which is now called Orvandill's Toe....Orvandill (the Frozen Toe, the chilblain), (*Frostbeule*), is, as the lighting-spark, the hypostasis of Thor....That the poet was acquainted with this myth, and had special reference to it, appears from a very significant remark of Hamlet, in the graveyard, in relation to the tragic singer, the first clown, and to his ambiguity and equivocation. After recognising the absolute, revealed in the tragic figure, and after emphasising the equivocation (*Doppelsinnigheit*) which points to annihilation, Hamlet says, 'By the Lord, Horatio, these three years I have taken note of it, the age is grown so picked[1] that the toe of the peasant comes so near the heel of the courtier, he galls his kibe (*Frostbeule*).'

To resume and conclude:

In the relation in which the star (the Frozen Toe, the chilblain) Orvandill stands to Thor as hypostasis, Hamlet may be regarded as standing to the Time-Idea and destructive moment of the force imminent in nature, 'nature' (comp. Sonnet 126) personified in the First Grave-digger (Chronos or Æon), and Hamlet appears to intend to say that the tragical personified activity, its own hypostasis, seeks to injure and annihilate himself.

And, after that, he proceeds to dispute whether or no Hamlet was mad.

(4)

These two criticisms, the subtle and the frantic, yield us the key to unlock, not *Hamlet*, but all the criticism that ever has been written on Hamlet. I repeat that just as Shakespeare in the theatre draws out each individual soul of the audience and so incarnates it in Hamlet, Prince of Denmark, that each feels 'This is I,' even so he exerts that illusion upon the several critics in their libraries and in such strength that each, seizing a pen, starts (as he thinks) to interpret Hamlet: whereas, beguiled man! he is all the while unconsciously revealing and appraising himself. Now, every one knows (or at any rate the older among us know) what tricks memory can play us, as everyone knows how what we call Accident has a trick of letting us down of a sudden, at a moment when we are in best conceit of our-

[1] Steevens here remarks that this word is taken from the preening of birds, and *we* think that there is here also some allusion to self-evolution for the purpose of purification. [Karpf's note.]

selves. I honestly reckoned to have made the above small discovery for myself, when pat upon it came the discovery that my discovery was no discovery at all: for I found myself staring at these words of Hazlitt's, which I must have read twice or thrice at one time or another, but hitherto carelessly:

Hamlet is a name: his speeches and sayings but the idle coinage of the poet's brain. What, then?—are they not real? They are as real as our own thoughts. Their reality is the reader's mind. It is *we* who are Hamlet.

And, as though this had not been enough, again pat upon it I opened a page of Victor Hugo and translated this:

Aloof from men, Hamlet has yet within him a something undefined which represents them all. *Agnosco fratrem.* If sometimes we felt our own pulse we should be conscious of *his* fever. His uncanny reality is our reality, after all. He is the sad man we all are, in certain situations. Morbid, if you will, Hamlet expresses a permanent condition of man.

There we have, yielded by one of the few worthy in Elysium to walk beside our poet as a peer, the key by which we may read all criticism of Hamlet.

But I insist that for *Hamlet* itself, the play, there is no key but what each one of us will find in his own breast.

If the world have not so far warped or shrivelled us but that our hearts respond to the appeal of a noble nature; if they can sympathize with one, noble and nobly scrupulous, faced suddenly with a sin clamouring for revenge, a sin contaminating his own mother; all the responsibility to answer murder with murder solemnly, by a voice from the grave, charged upon this delicate, sensitive, and *innocent* soul; why, then (I say), we can read *Hamlet* with understanding, and may leave the commentators alone. That is my advice: and I propose to do here what is not always done with one's own advice. I propose to follow it.

(5)

But I will add one note on the history of the play (for this directly bears on Shakespeare's workmanship); and another on a particular detail in its history which throws some illumination on a point which has puzzled many readers and spectators.

Every one knows that *Hamlet* did not spring full-armed from the head of Shakespeare: that it was an old play built upon, taken down, rebuilt, and again pulled to pieces and rebuilt, before it reached the *Hamlet* of the 1623 Folio, the form in which we are familiar with it. There is nothing to surprise us in this: it is just what happened with plays in the Elizabethan theatre (as we call it), and, in fact, something very like it often happens with a play in our own days. But about *Hamlet* there is evidence that makes it manifest. In 1603—that is, twenty years before the First Folio—we find, printed in Quarto, a play which is obviously our *Hamlet*, is assigned on the title-page to William Shakespeare, and yet is amazingly different. Omitting a German version, and travelling back by clue of various contemporary hints (allusions to *Hamlet's Revenge* and *The Ghost*), we pretty solidly establish that a play on the subject, named after Hamlet, took the boards as early as 1589 (thirty-four years before we get the First Folio version), and almost as solidly that its author was Kyd, author of *The Spanish Tragedie*— which, by the way, *Hamlet* in some points of plot and structure curiously resembles. But it concerns us not here whether Kyd or Tom or Dick or Harry was the original author. The important point is that for thirty-odd years at least, from one form to another (in all its phrases apparently popular), this play *grew*, grew at the back of the theatre; until at some point Shakespeare took a hand in its gardening and raised it to the miracle we know.

So much for the *play*. But the *story*, with Hamlet's deliberate pretence of madness, was told by Saxo Grammaticus, a Danish chronicler, in the thirteenth century; was turned into a sort of 'historical novel' in French by one Francis de Belleforest in 1570; and was published soon after this date. It was next translated into English and entitled *The Historie of Hamblet*. I now quote Capell:

> There can be no doubt made, by persons who are acquainted with these things, that the translation is not much younger than the French original; though the only edition of it that is yet come to my knowledge is no earlier than 1608; that Shakespeare took his play from it there can be likewise little doubt.

Now, why do I lay this stress upon Belleforest's story upon which Shakespeare, and may be his precursor, pretty certainly wrought? Because I find explained in it, clear as daylight, one puzzle of detail which, when I read the play, had beaten me again and again. Or, rather, there was a double puzzle. I could never quite understand (or forgive) that Ophelia, being Ophelia, should so readily lend herself, in Act III, Scene 1, to entrap Hamlet to confession, with the King and her father for eavesdroppers; as far less could I forgive Hamlet, a gentleman, for speaking to her (in the play-scene, for example) so vilely as he does. My instinct all through prompts me to say, 'Yes, yes, you are driven. But for God's sake, need you speak to this child as to a strumpet? O man, leave *her*, at least, alone!' Allowing the most for Hamlet's perverted recoil against all women on fathoming his mother's guilt, I think we must all feel this. But I turn to Belleforest and I find that in the original

Ophelia *was* a courtezan, though a kind-hearted one. Here
is the text. The King's advisers are puzzled by Hamlet's
pretended madness.

...esteeming that under that kinde of folly there lay hidden a
greate and rare subtility...for which cause they counselled the
king to try and know, if possible, how to discover the intent
and meaning of the young prince; and they could find no better
nor more fit invention to intrap him than to set some faire and
beautifull woman in a secret place, that with flattering speeches
and all the craftiest meanes she could use, should purposely seek
to allure his mind to have his pleasure of her....To this end
certaine courtiers were appointed to lead Hamblet into a
solitary place within the woods, whither they brought the
woman.

The story goes on that a gentleman who had been 'nourished
with Hamlet' (obviously Horatio)

by certain signes gave Hamblet intelligence in what danger he
was like to fall...if he obeyed the wanton toyes and vicious
provocations of the gentlewoman....But by *her* he was like-
wise informed of the treason, as being one that from her in-
fancy loved and favoured him and would have been exceedingly
sorrowful for his misfortune.

Here was a strong dramatic situation ready to Shakespeare's hand. But he, in his great wisdom, preferred to
replace this experienced lady by the innocent Ophelia—

> Nymph, in thy orisons
> Be all my sins remembered!

This (I say) he did very wisely; but I hold that, being an
indolent man, he failed to remove or to recast some sentences
which, cruel enough even when spoken to a woman of easy
virtue, are intolerable when cast at Ophelia.

(6)

I will conclude these notes of *Hamlet* with an observation on Shakespeare's use of the blank verse line. It is late in the day. But it may come in here as well as anywhere: and after saying much about structure, plot, stage-setting, the interplay and development and handling of character, I cannot fairly let the reader go under the impression that Shakespeare's actual versification is a small part of his dramatic technique.

I assume him to know something of the invention of English blank verse, and how Marlowe, if he did not invent it, made it the vehicle of Elizabethan drama. I assume him to know, in a general way, how Shakespeare used it from *Love's Labour's Lost* up (let us say) to *Antony and Cleopatra*, to *The Tempest*. I assume him to know, further, what Milton claimed for it, in the famous prefatory note to *Paradise Lost*, as a vehicle for Epic.

But we are concerned with Drama—with English Drama. Now, if we turn to Dryden's *Prefaces*, and particularly to the Epistle Dedicatory to his play of *The Rival Ladies*, to his *Essay of Dramatic Poesy* and his *Defence* of that Essay, we shall find that there is no question whatever about the true English dramatic line being in hendecasyllables. No critic doubts this. But Dryden and others doubt whether we do better for dramatic purposes by rhyming our hendecasyllables in heroics or by giving them the open play (call it 'freedom' or 'licence') of blank verse. When Shakespeare began to write, blank verse was a comparatively new invention, and we know that he—that his genius—steadily explored and perfected it for his dramatic vehicle, more and deliberately ridding his plays of rhyme. *Love's Labour's Lost* contains but 579 lines of blank verse, 1028 rhymes.

When we reach *A Winter's Tale* we find 1825 lines of blank verse to no rhymes at all, and *The Tempest* (apart, of course, from the songs and the Masque of Iris) has but two rhymes to 1458 blank verse lines. But then came a change of fashion, if not of considered opinion. About the middle of the next century, or a little later, Waller and others took up the rhymed heroic couplet and set about improving it; and at last Davenant boldly reintroduced it as the sole and proper vehicle for the drama. In Dryden's words, 'if we owe the invention of it to Mr Waller, we are acknowledging the noblest use of it to Sir William Davenant, who at once brought it upon the stage and made it perfect, in *The Siege of Rhodes.*'

The attempt—which had its origin, of course, in emulation of the great French playwrights of that time, with their rhymed alexandrines—powerfully engaged Dryden; and we may follow his apology for it through various prefaces; notably those which I have mentioned above. Now Dryden was a great man, a great artist, and (in all that concerned his art) a great gentleman. To borrow a phrase from Newman's famous description of a gentleman, 'he may be right or wrong in his opinions; but he is too clear sighted to be unjust.' So Dryden, together with his plea for the heroic couplet in drama, as fairly as he can sets forth and opposes the contra-account. I shall presently give reason for holding that he missed, though narrowly, the essential point: but his argument is moderate, fair, and patently that of a workman who has tried both ways and brings in his report of them.

Let us schedule some of the advantages he claims for rhyme over blank verse.

(1) He observes (quoting Sidney's *Defence of Poesie* in support) that rhyme is a help to memory: which it

'so knits up by affinity of sounds that, by remembering the last word in one line we often call to mind both the verses.'

I will say at once that I think little of this argument, though he calls it 'in my opinion not the least considerable.' Whose memory is helped? If the actors', then let them take more trouble to learn their parts. If ours, then if we cannot remember and carry away such lines as

> Canst thou not minister to a mind diseased?
> Pluck from the memory a rooted sorrow?

without help of the mind diseased being eased, or the rooted sorrow being uprooted to-morrow, then (without more words about it) we ought to be ashamed of ourselves.

(2) 'Then,' he goes on, 'in the quickness of repartees (which in discoursive scenes fall very often) it has so particular a grace, and is so aptly suited to them, that the sudden smartness of the answer, and the beauty of the rhyme, set off the beauty of each other.'

I am spared the trouble of answering this, because Dryden himself in his *Essay on Dramatic Poesy* has put the answer into the mouth of his supposed interlocutor Crites. 'They say the quickness of repartees in argumentative scenes receives an ornament from the verse. Now what is more unreasonable than to imagine that a man should not only light upon the *wit*, but the *rhyme*, too, upon the sudden?... The hand of art will be too visible in it, against that maxim of all professions, *Ars est celare artem....*'

(3) 'But that benefit which I consider most in it,' says Dryden, 'because I have not seldom found it, is that it bounds and circumscribes the fancy....The great easiness of blank verse renders the poet too luxuriant.'

'The great easiness of blank verse'? O Dryden! great

man! You wrote those words in 1664, and *Paradise Lost* was not published until three years later. And if I could summon you from the dead, a great awe would tie my tongue. But I should want to read you this:

> Far within
> And in their own dimensions like themselves,
> The great Seraphic Lords and Cherubim
> In close recess and secret conclave sat,
> A thousand demi-gods on golden seats,
> Frequent and full.

Or this:

> Yet not the more
> Cease I to wander where the Muses haunt
> Clear spring, or shadie grove, or sunny hill,
> Smit with the love of sacred song: but chief
> Thee, Sion! and the flow'ry brooks beneath
> That wash thy hallow'd feet and warbling flow,
> Nightly I visit; nor sometimes forget
> Those other two, equall'd with me in fate
> (So were I equall'd with them in renown!),
> Blind Thamyris, and blind Mæonides,
> And Tiresias and Phineus, prophets old:
> Then feed on thoughts that, voluntary, move
> Harmonious numbers—as the wakeful bird
> Sings darkling, and, in shadiest covert hid,
> Tunes her nocturnal note. Thus with the year
> Seasons return, but not to me returns
> Day, or the sweet approach of Even or Morn,
> Or sight of vernal bloom, or summer's rose,
> Or flocks, or herds, or human face divine...

Read it, ponder it: read it twenty, fifty, a hundred times, and while not insensible to the noble diction, mark—mark all the while the exquisite slide and pause and balance of the

cæsura (so much more difficult to compass than any rhyme)
as it moves under Milton's hand:

> Thus with the year
> Seasons return, but not to me returns
> Day, or the sweet approach of Even or Morn,
> Or sight of vernal bloom, or summer's rose,
> Or flocks, or herds, or human face divine.

'Easy'? *That* 'easy'? Why, it is fit to make one weep over
the unattainable, and this man's mastery of it!

(7)

But let me appeal from Dryden's theory to his own
practice. I choose, quite at random, half-a-dozen heroic
couplets of his, from *The Indian Emperor* (Act II, Scene III).

Cydaria. Your gallants, sure, have little eloquence;
     Failing to move the soul, they court the sense.
     With pomp and trains and in a crowd they woo,
     When true felicity is but in two.
     But can such toys your women's passions move?
     This is but noise and tumult, 'tis not love.
Cortez. I have no reason, madam, to excuse
     Those ways of gallantry I did not use:
     My love was true, and on a nobler score.
Cydaria. 'Your love,' alas! Then have you loved before?

Let us set against this a blank verse passage from Dryden's
Don Sebastian, where the hero counsels the captive queen
Almeyda against self-destruction.

> Death may be called in vain, and cannot come;
> Tyrants can tie him up from your relief;
> Nor has a Christian privilege to die.
> Alas! thou art too young in thy new faith!
> Brutus and Cato might discharge their souls,
> And give them furloughs for another world;

> But we, like sentries, are condemned to stand
> In starless night, and wait the appointed hour.[1]

It is easy to see that these two passages differ in dramatic feeling: and almost as easy to see what ails the one first quoted. At the close of each distich, of each rhymed couplet, it 'shuts up.' The stuff is good; but we get it in short monotonous doses.

> With pomp and trains and in a crowd they woo,
> When true felicity is but in two.
>> (Selah)
> But can such toys your women's passions move?
> This is but noise and tumult, 'tis not love.
>> (Selah)

Now this conclusive stroke of the distich is excellent when closing a Shakespearian sonnet—as—

> If this be error, and upon me proved,
> I never writ, nor no man ever loved.

It is excellent as rounding off, containing, completing an epigram of Pope's—

> Good nature and good sense must ever join:
> To err is human, to forgive divine.

[1] Dryden, bold thief, stole this idea out of Spenser (*Faerie Qyeene. Book I, Canto* 9); as Blair, author of the much admired poem *The Grave*, afterwards lifted words and idea together out of *Don Sebastian*, and spoiled them hopelessly:

Spenser.   The terme of life is limited,
       Ne may a man prolong nor shorten it;
       The souldier may not move from watchfull sted,
       Nor leave his stand until his captain bid.

Blair.   Our time is fix'd, and all our days are number'd
       How long, how short, we know not:—This we know,
       Duty requires we calmly wait the summons,
       Nor dare to stir till Heav'n shall give permission:
       Like sentries that must keep their destin'd stand,
       And wait th' appointed hour till they're reliev'd.

Or

    Whoever thinks a faultless piece to see,
    Thinks what ne'er was, nor is, nor e'er shall be.

Or

    Words are like leaves; and, where they most abound,
    Much fruit of sense beneath is rarely found.

But the rhyme of drama, of action, of life, is and should be nothing like that clue of a sonnet, this accomplished turn of an epigram. Life is not like a maxim of La Rochefoucauld's: it goes on and on and on. The 'snap of the snuff-box' may be used in drama—Shakespeare often used it to round off an Act, a signal to the man in the wings to drop the curtain. In *Hamlet*, for example:

              The play's the thing
    Wherein I'll catch the conscience of the king.

Here it makes a temporary conclusion. At the very end of the tragedy we get it with a broken close—

    Take up the bodies: such a sight as this
    Becomes the field, but here shows much amiss
    Go, bid the soldiers shoot.

But for the play itself—for drama, which is action—to convey the multitudinous rhythm of life, broken yet harmonious, continuous, various, out of itself unfolding, in a moment responding to sudden thoughts, interruptions, gusts of passion, changings of mind, ardours, repentings, dejections, interchange of eyes, quick embraces of the young, slow deathbeds of the old: for all this the artist must have something infinitely more free, pliant, and subtle than the rhymed heroic couplet ever was or ever could be: something infinitely more free, pliant, supple than the French alexandrine. Though by their exquisite intonation French actors disguise the sameness and tameness of the French alexandrine, yet the point is that their art lies in disguising, all the while: they are doing it *in spite* of the monotonous verse But all the while, as Shakespeare mastered it, the English unrhymed iambic line, with its freedom and play of cæsura, is *helping* the actor.

The following famous passage, carefully read aloud, will support, better than argument, my claim for this pliant capacity of blank verse, when blank verse is written by a Shakespeare:

> O, what a rogue and peasant slave am I!
> Is it not monstrous that this player here,
> But in a fiction, in a dream of passion,
> Could force his soul so to his own conceit
> That from her working all his visage wann'd;
> Tears in his eyes, distraction in 's aspect,
> A broken voice, and his whole function suiting
> With forms to his conceit? and all for nothing!
> For Hecuba!
> What's Hecuba to him, or he to Hecuba,
> That he should weep for her? What would he do,
> Had he the motive and the cue for passion
> That I have? He would drown the stage with tears
> And cleave the general ear with horrid speech,
> Make mad the guilty and appal the free,
> Confound the ignorant, and amaze indeed
> The very faculties of eyes and ears.
> Yet I,
> A dull and muddy-mettled rascal, peak
> Like John-a-dreams, unpregnant of my cause,
> And can say nothing; no, not for a king,
> Upon whose property and most dear life
> A damn'd defeat was made. Am I a coward?
> Who calls me villain? breaks my pate across?

Plucks off my beard, and blows it in my face?
Tweaks me by the nose? gives me the lie i' the throat,
As deep as to the lungs? who does me this?
Ha!
'Swounds, I should take it: for it cannot be
But I am pigeon-liver'd and lack gall
To make oppression bitter, or ere this
I should have fatted all the region kites
With this slave's offal: bloody, bawdy villain!
Remorseless, treacherous, lecherous, kindless villain!
O, vengeance!
Why, what an ass am I! This is most brave!
That I, the son of a dear father murder'd,
Prompted to my revenge by heaven and hell,
Must, like a whore, unpack my heart with words,
And fall a-cursing, like a very drab,
A scullion!
Fie upon 't! foh! About, my brain! I have heard
That guilty creatures, sitting at a play,
Have by the very cunning of the scene
Been struck so to the soul that presently
They have proclaim'd their malefactions;
For murder, though it have no tongue, will speak
With most miraculous organ. I'll have these players
Play something like the murder of my father
Before mine uncle: I'll observe his looks;
I'll tent him to the quick: if he but blench,
I know my course. The spirit that I have seen
May be the devil; and the devil hath power
To assume a pleasing shape; yea, and perhaps
Out of my weakness and my melancholy,
As he is very potent with such spirits,
Abuses me to damn me. I'll have grounds
More relative than this. The play's the thing
Wherein I'll catch the conscience of the king.

[Exit.

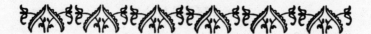

CHAPTER XI

SHAKESPEARE'S LATER
WORKMANSHIP

The last group of plays—General characteristics—Some striking resemblances—One common theme, a woman wrongfully
used—Unity of Time not to be compassed at first—Alleged
decline in power—The agony of Imogen—The reconciliation
of man with man—The artist's last infirmity—Shakespeare's
theme and stage limitations—Probable development of scenic
resources in the Elizabethan stage—Influence of the masque—
Sea-scenes—Reconciliation through the young and for the
young—Blending of tragedy and comedy.

(1)

I PROPOSE in this paper to offer some general observations on Shakespeare's later workmanship, and hereafter
to deal in detail with *Pericles, King Henry VIII, Cymbeline,
The Winter's Tale, The Tempest,* as exemplifying it. I
choose these five plays because almost all scholars and critics
agree to include them, as they do not agree to include others,
among the last heirs of Shakespeare's invention. Scholars
and critics, to be sure, have their individual caprices, their
wayward and often amusing crotchets. Gervinus, for
example, chose to polarise *Pericles* with *Titus Andronicus*:
Dr Courthope will have *The Tempest* to be an early play:
and I have even heard *All's Well That Ends Well* plausibly
upheld to be one of the last. But these are truancies from the

broad road of consent, and to follow them here would be a waste of time. For I believe that, as the reader goes along with me, we shall casually collect evidence that each of the five belongs, as we possess it, to the last years of Shakespeare's life, as the five together will be sufficient for our enquiry, What in those last years was he trying to do, and how was he doing it?

(2)

Quite apart from external evidence many critics have noted a temperament or 'atmosphere' common to these plays (or to all but *King Henry VIII*, which stands apart for many reasons): an atmosphere quite unlike that which pervades the great agonising tragedies of *Macbeth, Hamlet, Othello, King Lear*; although in structure and motive *Cymbeline* reminds us of *Lear* and *Othello, The Winter's Tale* of *Othello*, a scene in *Pericles* of a scene in *Macbeth*. Even further are we removed in these plays from the hot passion of *Antony and Cleopatra*, the coarse fierce cynicism of *Troilus and Cressida*, the cold opposition of character in *Coriolanus*, the turgid misanthropy of *Timon of Athens*.

Of a sudden, as the critics agree in pointing out, the hard shadows melt. Consummate tragic intensity has already weakened; there are to be no more *Othellos*, no more *Macbeths*. Passion, cynicism, fierce judgment, fade into a benign permeating charitable sunset.

> The soul's dark cottage, batter'd and decay'd,
> Lets in new light through chinks that time has made

—and the light is not earthly. Even the fairies, who were such positive Warwickshire imps, have turned to angels, influences. Robin Goodfellow has 'followed darkness like a dream' and become Ariel. Man, whom Shakespeare no more feared to depict as brutal than as godlike, goes brutally as ever to shipwreck in the first scene of *The Tempest*, is cast through

the foam
Of perilous seas in fäery lands forlorn

and emerges upon an elfin shore where spirits harp on dying gales; where one shipwrecked courtier notes 'The air breathes upon us here most sweetly,' and another, rubbing his eyes—

How lush and lusty the grass looks! how green!...But the rarity of it is...that our garments, being as they were drenched in the sea, hold notwithstanding their freshness and glosses, being rather new-dyed than stained with salt water...as fresh as when we put them on first in Afric, at the marriage of the King's fair daughter Claribel to the King of Tunis.

As I say, many critics have noted this mellowly romantic atmosphere; that it pervades all Shakespeare's last work and is, in fact, as truly characteristic of it as any of the date-marks we detect in phrasing or in versification. We shall (I hope) take full account of it before we have done. But let us start with resemblances more definite: threads that we can touch and follow as clues connecting, this way and that, one with another of our five plays, or two with a third, or three with a fourth. The fifth—*King Henry VIII*—we must let stand somewhat apart; not only for some special reasons to be given, but for the broad and general reason that, being a historical play, it differs from the other four in scheme and purpose, and the limits imposed on invention. A dramatist may, indeed, play tricks with history: but he cannot play with it as with pure fiction. History, as Aristotle puts it, tells us what a certain known man, Alcibiades, did or suffered. To be sure, if our particular Alcibiades be as far removed out of men's memory or written record as (say)

King Lear or King Cymbeline of the Caliph Haroun Alraschid, we can melt him almost into a pure creature of fiction. But Shakespeare, who could do this with Lear and Cymbeline, obviously could not do it with Henry the Eighth. And even to-day, after a lapse of four hundred years, a cautious playwright would avoid choosing Henry the Eighth as a hero of a drama that either turned on celibate renunciation or called itself *All for Love*, or *The World Well Lost*.

(3)

For a start, then, upon our list of curious resemblances, we observe that—

Every one of these plays—including even *Henry VIII*, which has no business to do anything of the kind—ends happily. *Cymbeline* happens to be labelled 'A Tragedy,' but in fact is no more tragic than *The Winter's Tale*, labelled 'A Comedy.' Both alike work upon cruel passions, to end in a general reconcilement. To put the converse— *The Winter's Tale*, built on a motive of cruel passion, has no more right to be called a comedy than the other to be called a tragedy. You will find it hard to invent any two categories separating the pair. *The Winter's Tale*, 'a Comedy,' turns on the wrong done to a good woman, a wife cruelly suspected, afterwards for a while supposed to be lost, in the end restored to the arms of her repentant husband. But so does *Cymbeline*, 'a Tragedy,' with quite as happy a result. And if it be urged that Shakespeare had once already, in *Much Ado about Nothing*, built a comedy on this plot, I shall answer that he did it by cleverly distracting our interest, upon Beatrice and Benedick; that *Much Ado* was a comedy in spite of its main plot; and finally that angry suspicion of an innocent feeling woman, driving to the issue (whether happy or not) through the torture of her soul, is no proper motive of Comedy, however we define Comedy.

Let us not then waste time in setting up between Tragedy and Comedy nice boundaries which these five plays remarkably ignore. However he treats it, we can see that Shakespeare's mind is playing with variations upon a theme that in one way or another keeps vexing his mind—that of a woman wrongfully used. We see this in *King Henry VIII* as well as in *The Winter's Tale* and *Cymbeline*.

We see, further, how constantly forgiving the woman is. She always is so in Shakespeare. Hermione and Imogen do but repeat the wrongs and forgiveness of Hero and Helena.

Yet further we observe how constantly, in these later plays, the wronged woman is righted. Shakespeare's great tragedies (as we call them) have no room for such charity. Ophelia is thrust aside and goes under. The entirely innocent Desdemona is led relentlessly to her bed and her death. But Imogen is Desdemona rejudged and tenderly vindicated.

(4)

To come to a more technical point, all these last plays (all but *The Tempest*) show, whether wilfully or of necessity, a common disobedience to what is called 'Unity of Time.' I pass by *King Henry VIII*, which neglects or overrides this, as every pageant must. But *Pericles, Cymbeline, The Winter's Tale* cover whole lifetimes of their *dramatis personæ*. Between one Act and another twenty years or more may be supposed to be dropped. The dramatist has many devices for carrying us over the intervals. In *Pericles*, for example, he introduces between each separate Act the old poet Gower as prologue and artificial scene-shifter, saying in effect, 'So far we have conducted our story. Now transfer your minds, if you please, to Tyre or Mitylene, suppose that so many years have elapsed, and give your kind attention to the next scene on the film.' In *The Winter's Tale*, having to skip sixteen years after Act III, he boldly hales in Father Time with an hour-glass, and not only makes him apologise for sliding over the interval, but uses him as prologue to a second intrigue.

> Imagine me,
> Gentle spectators, that I now may be
> In fair Bohemia; and remember well,
> I mentioned a son o' the King's, which Florizel
> I now name to you; and with speed so pace
> To speak of Perdita.

Now that is a pure 'fake.' Shakespeare, having proposed to himself a drama in which a wronged woman has to bear a child, who has to be lost for years and restored to her as a grown girl, simply did not know how to do it, save by invoking some such device.

His difficulty lay in the nature of things. In the nature of things, any engagement of human will or passion comes naturally to a point of issue; the conflict or explosion, as exhibited in drama, may be as sharp as you please: but just as naturally the process of cooling, of appeasement, of repentance, of forgiveness is patient and slow. This, too, may be brought dramatically to a point, but it takes time.

We should bear this constantly in mind when we are tempted, contrasting Shakespeare's later work with the great tragic masterpieces—*Macbeth, Hamlet, Othello, Lear*—to say that it betrays a decline in mental power. A loss of mastery there is, an apparent relaxation of grip on the means to the end. But these do not prove any slackening of mental power. It may more likely be that, having triumphed in the possible, this magnificent workman has grown discontented with it and started out to conquer the impossible, or the all but impossible. Sharp sudden retribution upon crime—'God's Revenge against Murder,' as the old book has it—the awful awakening of Œdipus, the swift slaughter that in the last scene of *Hamlet* wipes out score after score and leaves the stage piled with corpses—these effects have always lain within the range of drama. 'O proud death!' gasps Fortinbras on the threshold—

> What feast is toward in thine eternal cell?—

and Horatio, the sane, sad man, answers him—

> Give order that these bodies
> High on a stage be placèd to the view;
> And let me speak to the yet-unknowing world
> How these things came about; so shall you hear
> Of carnal, bloody and unnatural acts,
> Of accidental judgments, casual slaughters,
> Of deaths put on by cunning and forc'd cause,
> And, in this upshot, purposes mistook
> Fall'n on th' inventors' heads.

If I may say it reverently, human forgiveness for the wrong that men do to us—such forgiveness, for example, as Imogen extends—has something nobler in it than any revenge, even than God's revenge against murder. I shall not argue this as a theologian, since Shakespeare did not write plays for an audience of theologians. I simply place myself alongside of the reader, both of us as spectators in the Globe Theatre, Blackfriars. Do we not *feel*, that though we may talk of God's being injured, insulted, wounded by our sins, He cannot (being so great and above rivalry and enormously magnanimous) be injured by Posthumus's cruel wrong as Imogen is injured? It costs Him so much less! It cost Imogen all she had in the world. It is not for her life she pleads, but for death, as she stands 'the elected deer' before Pisanio:

> Prithee, despatch:
> The lamb entreats the butcher; where's thy knife?
> Thou art too slow to do thy master's bidding
> When I desire it too!

Hear her, a half-minute later, utter the soul of her reproach:

> Talk thy tongue weary; speak;
> I have heard I am a strumpet; and mine ear,
> Therein false struck, can take no greater wound,
> Nor tent to bottom *that!*

Hear her, lastly, with what bitter desperate contempt she answers Pisanio when he—soft, honest man—proposes that she shall escape death and hide. You can feel her sad gaze searching—searching—into his stupid brain:

> Why, good fellow,
> What shall I do the while? Where bide? how live?
> Or in my life what comfort, when I am
> Dead to my husband?

What can any Deity suffer comparable with *that*? How can any God of our conception vie for our pity against this woman? God has so many things to fall back upon! Imogen, losing this, has lost all: she that was infinitely rich in one little thing, deprived of it is infinitely ruined. The very frailty of the wronged one makes the act of forgiveness the more heroic. The reader and I are—let me repeat and insist—seated in a theatre, watching a play. There a deadly hurt done upon a Deity, who can take care of himself, awakes small resentment in comparison with a deadly hurt done upon a woman. Nay—and further—the best of our emotion springs directly from our sense that she *is* a woman, and weak: and, further yet, when such weakness, persecuted back upon the soul's last innermost citadels of love, finds the great reinforcement there and in due time marches out victorious, to forgive, we witness something which accords with the noblest we ask of human life.

If my argument, so far, be sound, it follows that Shakespeare in his later plays, which (by consent) deal with human forgiveness, atonement, reconciliation, was not necessarily a weaker workman than the Shakespeare who triumphed in *Macbeth* and *Othello*; but, likely enough, the same excellent workman passing on to attempt a far more difficult thing than any justification, by a stroke, of the ways of God to man; passing on to attempt the reconciliation, by slow process, under God, of man with man.

(5)

I break off here, to advance three propositions.

(1) My first is, that every artist of the first class—and I will instance Shakespeare, Molière, Dickens—tires of repeating his successes, but never of repeating his experiments. A Wordsworth will do amazing things for three or four years, and thenceforward will content himself with fiddling on the same string until he has frayed it into utter tenuity. But your inventive master never cares for a success but as a step to something further. What he tries may be worse; what he achieves may be (as the saying goes) unworthy of his powers: but he is still trying; from one height which we applaud as consummate he springs for another which is (if you will) impossible; and to miss it is to land in a pit. But he has the divinest of discontent, a discontent with achievement. He is still a learner. Of our English creative writers I have quoted Jowett's opinion that Dickens comes

next, in fulness of genius, after Shakespeare; and here is
what William Ernest Henley has to say upon Dickens:

The freshness and fun of *Pickwick*...seem mainly due to high
spirits; and perhaps that immortal book should be described
as a first improvisation by a young man of genius not yet sure
of either expression or ambition, and with only vague and
momentary ideas about the duties and necessities of art. But
from *Pickwick* onwards to *Edwin Drood* the effort after improvement is manifest. What are *Dombey* and *Dorrit* themselves
but the failures of a great and serious artist?...He had en-
chanted the public without an effort; he was the best-beloved of
modern writers almost from the outset of his career. But he had
in him at least as much of the French artist as of the middle-
class Englishman; and if all his life he never ceased from
education, but went unswervingly in pursuit of culture, it was
out of love for his art and because his conscience as an artist
would not let him do otherwise.

So it was with Shakespeare. In taking the theme of *Othello*
and altering it into *Cymbeline*, as in taking the theme of *Lear*
and altering it into *The Winter's Tale*, he failed, if we will;
but he failed by no intellectual decline; rather, in the
attempt to achieve something better, certainly more difficult,
possibly beyond reach.

(2) We may reasonably allow, moreover, that a great
artist, choosing to abandon something he has done consum-
mately for a shot at a longer range, is liable to miss his target;
and so widely, that in proportion as we applaud *Macbeth* or
Othello for masterpieces we are tempted to groan over
Pericles or *Cymbeline* as, in workmanship, puerile. Now
actually (as later I shall attempt to prove) the workmanship
of *Cymbeline*, whenever Shakespeare gets a chance to play
the old hand, is masterly, and the final scene almost the last
word in dramatic skill: as I hope also to demonstrate that

nine-tenths of the weakness of *Pericles* is most likely not chargeable upon Shakespeare at all, and certainly not chargeable upon the Shakespeare of that period, the playwright who had *Macbeth* and *Othello* standing to his record. Still it remains true that, when we get down to unmistakable work of 1610 or thereabouts, among strokes which attest the master, immixed with them and all the more flagrant by reason of the contrast, are many fumbling touches: and my contention is—inviting the reader to understand an artist's mind in operation—that such miss-hits are incident to the great artists when they turn from the dazzle of past achievement to attempt new range-finding shots into an unknown country.

(3) But lastly, on this point let us note how sincerely the man deals. He is occupied with forgiveness, reconciliation, the adjustment, under Heaven, of goodwill among men. But injured women do not forgive in a moment; stubborn enemies are not reconciled in a moment; old wrongs, hates, injuries, jealousies, suspicions are not allayed, redeemed, repented of, forgiven in a moment and made to acquiesce. The process is naturally a slow one: and its perfect success in actual life, if it is to be a durable appeasement and not a flash in the pan, usually depends upon its overmastering a real—often a prolonged and obstinate, but always a real, resistance. To forgive our enemies, to yield to conviction against our will—I put it to the reader as to a man of the world that, if their results are to be of any worth, these are *naturally* slow processes. To be sure, the final act of surrender, the stroke of return upon ourselves, may happen in a moment: but the *meaning* lies all in the continued sap and siege.

On the other hand, the working dramatist, having to tell his complete story in three hours, and by presented action, is at every turn invited to concentrate his effects, to bring all to a stroke which staggers or astounds. The way of the stage (if I may illustrate by a similitude) is the way of a flash of lightning; it is not the way of a long-drawn composing sunset.

In short, Shakespeare's aim in these last plays has brought him at last 'up against' the limitations of his art—which commonly happens in the end to men of genius who have mastered their craft within its technical limits. They arrive at a point where they have to posit this question: 'I have done all that this art of mine apparently allows. But it ought to allow more. Art ought to be coextensive and coterminous with life. Can I not break this or that technical barrier, to enlarge it?'

Now the drama was Shakespeare's medium. Without raising the question that life cannot be represented as a whole, but only in this or that aspect, by the separate arts of painting, sculpture, poetry, history, the drama, the epic; that no single art can ever hope to embrace it; I suggest that we ought to honour Shakespeare the more because, at the height of his skill, seeking to present a noble thing in life which the rules of his craft seemed to disallow, he turned his back on past success, defied the technical bars, and risked a made reputation—nay, cast it aside as one might cast an old cloak—to follow Nature.

Now let us descend again from these high problems of art to note certain small technical resemblances in our five plays.

(6)

It is fairly evident to me that, whilst Shakespeare was writing, the Burbages and others had been steadily increasing the scenic resources of the Elizabethan stage. I like to think that Shakespeare was all the while helping them with advice and suggestions; as he was certainly a party to the *coup* by which, on Christmas Eve 1598—to outwit a landlord who had exorbitantly raised their ground-rent—in the small hours of the morning the Burbages took down the whole structure of their theatre in Shoreditch, lock, stock and barrel, and carted it across the bridge to a plot of land they had secretly purchased in the Clink Liberty. We know that Shakespeare had a monetary interest in the Globe Theatre; a very ambitious speculation in its day and as a building one of the sights of London. And a reasonable knowledge of the world should assure us that when art such as the Elizabethan drama catches popularity, takes hold of the town, becomes the Court fashion, not only writers and actors, but carpenters, mechanicians, scene-painters—all concomitant in the business—vie with new inventions to improve it. That is business; that is how men behave. If the Shakespearean theatre had not improved, and even feverishly improved, its scenic capacities in the heyday of the Shakespearean drama, it must have contradicted every law of supply and demand.

But we have positive evidence, of which I will give you two or three items. We know, to begin with, that the Globe Theatre was set on fire and destroyed, on June 29th, 1613, through being too ambitious and letting off, in the wings, a salvo of chamber-cannon during an early performance (may-be the very first) of *King Henry VIII*, one of the plays we are considering. Act I, Scene IV, line 48, was the fatal point, and the signal a stage direction—'*Drum and trumpets; chambers discharged.*' Whereupon Wolsey, with proleptic significance, is made to exclaim 'What's that?' and his Chamberlain 'Look out there, some of ye!'

Again, whereas in *Twelfth Night* Shakespeare has to

start his play on the morrow of a shipwreck, in *The Tempest*
he opens with the actual scene of one.

Again let us take the great 'recognition' scene in *Pericles*
(Act V, Scene 1) and study the stage directions. They begin

On board Pericles' ship off Mitylene. A close pavilion on
deck, with a curtain before it; Pericles within it, reclined on a
couch

—all easy enough. The close pavilion is the alcove under
the old Elizabethan stage-gallery. It was usually curtained.
Curtained or uncurtained, it served for Imogen's or Prospero's cave; Juliet's vault, Polonius's hiding-place, Desdemona's bed, and so on. But now mark the addition:

A barge lying beside the Tyrian vessel. Enter two sailors,
one belonging to the Tyrian vessel, the other to the barge.

A little way on—

The Gentlemen and the two sailors descend, and go on board
the barge. Enter from thence Lysimachus and Lords....

Lysimachus whispers a Lord, who goes off in the barge.
Again, at line 64, the barge reappears and Marina disem-
barks.

The question whether or not in his later plays Shakespeare
has at his service some kind of painted scenery is a nice one,
and would take us here too long to discuss. But that he has
some newly-invented mechanism at his disposal the stage
directions hardly leave in doubt.[1]

For another point. All these plays include a dance in
masquerade or a supernatural vision; and most of them
include both. Now the Visions in *King Henry VIII* and
The Tempest are good enough: but I suppose that those in
Pericles and *Cymbeline* may fairly be reckoned as two of the

---

[1] I am aware that these stage directions are not Shakespeare's:
but they are implicit in the text.

worst futilities in the whole text of Shakespeare as we have it·
And here comes in an oddity: that the most inept and ill-
written and artistically childish thing in *Pericles*—the vision
of Diana—occurs in the very heart of the best writing in the
play; so that, while all else in the scene by force of poetry
vindicates it as late work, this interlude with its skimble-
skamble lines leads quite as effectively to the same conclusion.

We all know that towards the close of Shakespeare's life
the masque was coming more and more into fashion; and
how Ben Jonson took it up and developed it with the help
of scenic inventions by Inigo Jones.—Juno descending
from the clouds, Leda riding in on a swan, Venus with a
chariot of doves, the Graces sliding down a rainbow held by
Iris....It seems pretty clear that in his later days, as this
movement caught hold on the public taste, Shakespeare
began by employing its machinery to produce supernatural
effects genuinely dramatic and genuinely poetical—such as
the apparition of Banquo at the feast, the ghost on the
midnight platform of Elsinore as also that he half mockingly
used the device of the Interlude in the play-scene in *Hamlet*,
at first venting his irony on the players and anon converting
it to his own artistic purpose. But it is also evident to me that
as the taste for 'Visions'—preferably for visions of classical
goddesses—grew with the public, Shakespeare, loathing the
fashion, had to yield further and further to it: and it is
possible to hold that he paid his ironical homage to the
fashion either by writing these scenes as badly as he could
or by leaving the writing of them to any chance hack:

> No more, thou thunder-master, show
>   Thy spite on mortal flies:
> With Mars fall out, with Juno chide,
>   That thy adulteries
>   Rates and revenges.

> Hath my poor boy done aught but well,
>   Whose face I never saw?
> I died whilst in the womb he stay'd
>   Obeying Nature's law.

If Shakespeare wrote that, Shakespeare was deliberately playing the fool.

Indeed, turning to Act IV, Scene 1, of *The Tempest*, and considering it beside these other interludes, I feel inclined to suggest that some of the impatience (so unaccountable to Miranda)—

> Never till this day
> Saw I him touch'd with anger so distemper'd—

which Prospero exhibits as he closes the Masque of Iris, is not wholly unconnected with scorn of a performance which to the fine spirit Ariel he has already described as 'another trick.'

> Go bring the rabble,
> O'er whom I give thee power, here to this place.
> Incite them to quick motion: for I must
> Bestow upon the eyes of this young couple
> Some vanity of mine art. It is my promise
> And they expect it from me.

For a last minor point common to these later dramas, I would have the reader observe how prominent a part is played in them by the sea, with its adventurings, its ship-wrecks, castings-ashore, recognitions, appeasements afar of jealousies and cabals begun at home. All the true *Pericles* begins and ends on shipboard. Even Bohemia has its sea-coast, on which the waif Perdita is cast. At the critical point in *Cymbeline*—Heaven knows why—every character in the play has all sail set for Milford Haven; and *The Tempest* is *The Tempest*. In this again we may suspect an improvement in mere stage mechanism as well as catch a hint of a great wise mind voyaging out for a shore, somewhere within the ring of the 'still-vex'd Bermoothes,' where all this human evil is composed. I have read and marked disquisitions by learned men gravely doubting if Shakespeare, a Warwickshire man, ever saw the sea in his life. His knowledge of it is so different from theirs, who have so regularly spent their vacations at the sea-side and watched the bathing-machines come rolling in!

(7)

But by far the most important point of likeness in these later plays is that they all deal with human reconcilement: and of that reconcilement by far the most important point of likeness is that it always comes about through the young and for the young. Throughout his last years it would seem that Shakespeare's mind brooded over one hope, now playing with it and anon fiercely asserting it—'The sins of the fathers shall *not* be visited on the children!' Perdita shall be happy with Florizel, Miranda with Ferdinand. The turbulence of Henry VIII shall end with a christening. Imogen shall be clasped by her lord and her brothers inherit a kingdom. She shall have her happy hour with her father, as Marina with Pericles, as Cordelia with Lear—and not die of it, as poor Cordelia died.

Not one of these five plays can be labelled 'Comedy' or 'Tragedy.' All end happily; but all fetch happiness to shore out of shipwreck and suffering. Some, as we proceed to examine them, we shall perceive to be weak. But even in their weakness we shall perceive the effort of an artist whose later word, after he had sounded Comedy and Tragedy from *As You Like It* to *Othello*, was 'Behold, I will make all things new.'

CHAPTER XII

PERICLES AND KING HENRY VIII

Popularity of *Pericles*—A new sensation—Epic in terms of drama—The authorship of the first two Acts—The evidence of workmanship—Verse tests—Authenticity of the brothel scenes —The recognition scene—The different verdicts of the library and of the stage—Historical plays as pageants—The authorship of *King Henry VIII*—Moral unity the highest.

(1)

HEMINGE and Condell excluded *Pericles, Prince of Tyre*, from their First Folio edition of Shakespeare in 1623; nor did it appear among his collected plays until the Third Folio of 1664. Yet Heminge and Condell must have been familiar with it: for it happened to earn a very considerable popular success. For this we have not only the silent evidence of the book-trade—it was published in quarto, with Shakespeare's name, in 1609, and republished in the same year; a third quarto appeared in 1611; a fourth in 1619; a fifth in 1630; a sixth in 1635. We have assertative evidence as well. The first quarto, on the title-page, boldly advertises it as 'The late and much admired play called *Pericles, Prince of Tyre*.' One Robert Tailor, in the prologue to *The Hogge hath lost his Pearle*, writes:

> And if it prove so happy as to please,
> We'll say 'tis fortunate like *Pericles*.

And, in 1646, one S. Shepherd:

> With Sophocles we may
> Compare great Shakespeare: Aristophanes
> Never like him his Fancy could display—
> Witness the Prince of Tyre, his *Pericles*.

Lastly, testimony to the play's success with the public is accumulated, as on a backwash, by the number of critics who notice it to reprobate it; beginning with Ben Jonson and his characteristic sneer:

> Some mouldy[1] tale
> Like *Pericles*.

The play, then, certainly achieved success in its day, though it were but (as the French say) a success of scandal. I think there may have been another reason for its taking the town. It gave—like the 'revue' or the cinema of to-day—a new sensation. We may call these new sensations cheap, vulgar, tawdry; and so perhaps they are. We may, comparing even *Pericles* with *Hamlet*, demand of the public

> Have you eyes?
> Could you on this fair mountain leave to feed,
> And batten on this moor? Ha! have you eyes?

But Shakespeare, like every other great dramatist, wrote for his public; and we, laying aside our account with human frailty, must note that in art, as in life, men will have reaction, novelty—reaction even from the best; that transience qualifies even the attainment of a Pheidias, a Raphael, or a Shakespeare, because transience lies at the root and runs in the sap of all human pleasure. We cannot even conceive of human enjoyment apart from this qualifying transience. Good folk (as I observe them), being quite unable to

[1] The curious epithet 'mouldy' agrees with our theory—that *Pericles* was an old play exhumed.

imagine Eternity—that immense emptiness in which Time is not, and to-day and yesterday and to-morrow and a thousand years are as one; in the awful space of which everything stands still; in which the man who died in this war is alive and without apprehension of any war; in which the most exquisite flower of pleasure known to us has neither season in which to unfold, nor season through which to fade—good folk, unable to imagine this, or at any rate to keep a hold on such a conception, reduce it to Everlasting Life, Everlasting Bliss, which are simply life and bliss conceived in an endless prolonging of Time. Take it so, and I ask: How is our conception of everlasting bliss, of any bliss at once intense, ecstatic and perpetual, to be referred to any happiness of which any one of us has had experience? As Jowett puts it dryly, in his introduction to Plato's *Phædo*:

Where is the pain that does not become deadened after a thousand years? Or what is the nature of that pleasure or happiness which never wearies by monotony? Earthly pleasures and pains are short in proportion as they are keen; of any others which are both intense and lasting, we can form no idea....To beings constituted as we are, the monotony of singing Psalms would be as great an affliction as the pains of hell, and might even be pleasantly interrupted by them.

We are men, in short; 'sublunary things'; and our best in art, which in overweening moments we call 'immortal,' is by its very nature the slave of transience. 'There is nothing immortal but immortality,' says Sir Thomas Browne. The phenomenon itself vanishes, but

The Form remains, the *function* never dies.

The masterpiece is achieved and done for: there are to be no more *Macbeths*, no more *Othellos*, because men will

not have them—and Shakespeare himself resigns himself to
their demand for novelties. The function continues in chase
of new experiments.

The public, on the one hand, has a craving for novelties
in art; and the artist, on the other, a correspondent craving
to invent them—and not, be it noted, a base craving, merely
to open a new market, but a spiritual ambition, the last
infirmity of all noble workmen: to improve the best, break
the known barriers of rule, and master a new province for
Art. These two reasons converge to explain not only why
Shakespeare, having written *Othello*, went on to write
Pericles, but also (though it be a minor matter) why *Pericles*
took the town as it did.

(2)

For, obviously, it was a new thing, or an attempt at a new
thing; an attempt, by boldly casting over all unity of time,
to present in terms of drama what naturally belongs to epic
or romance. Let me insist on this, for it is of capital importance. In *Pericles* our workman Shakespeare boldly lays
hand on a theme proper to epic or the romantic novel—a
theme which had already done duty in both (in the *Confessio
Amantis*, and in a novel by one Laurence Twine, entitled
*The Patterne of Painefull Adventures: Containing the most
Excellent Pleasant and Variable Historie of the Strange
Accidents that Befell unto Prince Apollonius, the Lady
Lucina his Wife, and Tharsia his Daughter*)—and displays
in dramatic form a long, diffused story, supposed to cover
a lifetime. He is doing, in fact, precisely what Sir Philip
Sidney in a pretty mocking passage of the *Apologie for
Poetrie* laughed at bad playwrights for doing:

Now of time they are much more liberall. For ordinary it is
that two young Princes fall in love. After many traverces she

is got with child, delivered of a faire boy, he is lost, groweth a man, falls in love, and is ready to get another child, and all this in two hours space; which how absurd it is in sence, even sence may imagine, and Arte hath taught, and all ancient examples justified.

So, after all, Shakespeare's was nothing new as an attempt. What he achieved was to make a popular success of the absurdity, and a partial artistic success that encouraged him to improve on it in *Cymbeline* and *The Winter's Tale*; for these are long-drawn romances turned into dramas; by more cunning machinery, indeed, but unmistakably bearing the same stigmata as *Pericles*—the stigmata of the epical romantic tale, not of the drama.

The time supposed to be occupied by the action of *Pericles* is about sixteen years. *The Winter's Tale* has an interval of sixteen years between its third and fourth Acts, with various minor intervals of days and weeks. The chronology of *Cymbeline* is baffling and in places absurd (the speed, for example, of Iachimo's coming and going between Italy and Britain cannot be reconciled with any means of human locomotion known to Shakespeare. He could hardly have achieved it on a motor-cycle, with a steamer ready and waiting at Calais). But actually, as any intelligent reader must perceive, the author is feeling back towards unity of time. We do not see the King's sons stolen, and anon, through this and that device, watch them grow up—as we see the infants, Marina and Perdita, cast away, and are supposed to watch or imagine them growing up. We come upon Polydore and Cadwal ready-grown, and have it rehearsed to us how that they are the lost Princes, Guiderius and Arviragus. Yet the supposed action of *Cymbeline* must cover many months. Now, the supposed action of *The Tempest*—the whole of it—covers but three or four hours at the most, and the actual performance takes almost three.

And so, after advancing such excellent reasons why Shakespeare wrote *Pericles* at such and such a date, and why he made it such and such a play, let me proceed to show that he did nothing of the sort.

(3)

I will not go so far as to say that Shakespeare could not, at any time of his life, have written the first two Acts. He was great but careless. I believe, indeed, that he touched them up, the odious opening scene more particularly. Even in the rhyming lines I should be sorry to deny the Master in two or three passages. For example:

> See where she comes, apparell'd like the spring,
> Graces her subjects, and her thoughts the king
> Of every virtue gives renown to men!

Or:

> Yon sometimes famous princes, like thyself,
> Drawn by report, adventurous by desire,
> Tell thee, with speechless tongues and semblance pale,
> That without covering, save yon field of stars,
> Here they stand martyrs, slain in Cupid's wars.

Those last four words make me hesitate. But I will swear that if (as I profoundly disbelieve) he wrote these two Acts at any time of his life, he did not do so within a dozen years of his writing the rest of the play.

The scope of this inquiry confines me to such evidence as may be found in Shakespeare's workmanship. I pass over evidence of other kinds—evidence marshalled by Delius, Fleay, and others—which seems to me conclusive. I pass over all questions whether a man called Wilkins wrote the earlier part of the play. I care not who he was, so long as he was not Shakespeare. My only business is to suppeditate, by examining the workmanship, a conclusion already based on stronger evidence. Evidence on any point of dubiety concerning Shakespeare may be external or internal, may be derived from records, from allusions in the text, from verse-tests, from half-a-dozen studies other than the neglected one—of principles of workmanship—which I am here trying to pursue. Sometimes the witness of one sort will preponderate, sometimes that of another: and just here I am cheerfully playing second fiddle.

Now, that Shakespeare was trying, in *Pericles* and its successors, to convert epic into terms of drama is no warrant for inferring that he who had written *Othello* was, even in waywardness, so little of an artist as to be incapable of telling a story.

Yet in *Pericles*, as we have it, that is just what he could not do. Some two hundred years later, Mary Lamb, having to write out the story of *Pericles* for young people, started thus:

Pericles, Prince of Tyre, became a voluntary exile from his dominions, to avert the dreadful calamities which Antiochus, the wicked emperor of Greece, threatened to bring upon his subjects and city of Tyre, in revenge for a discovery which the prince had made of a shocking deed which the emperor had done in secret; as commonly it proves dangerous to pry into the hidden crimes of great ones.

Thus in one sentence—the last clause mere comment— Mary Lamb dismisses the whole of the first Act! The second Act she treats a little more tenderly, bestowing on it a full paragraph of four sentences. In her whole narrative, which—even though, as a tale for the young reader, it omits all the coarse business at Mitylene—covers some twenty-one pages, Acts III, IV, and V occupy more than twenty pages; Acts I and II less than one.

What does this mean? It means that a great deal more than a third of the play (in fact, it is nearer a half)—a solid block of writing, and that at the beginning, or just where in ninety-nine dramas out of a hundred you find the board laid, the game planned, and those opening moves developed which give the trend toward the climax—it means that all this has scarce anything to do with the story, and no *necessary* bearing on it whatever!

I have granted that *Pericles* is what Aristotle would call an 'epeisodic' play. 'I call,' says Aristotle, 'a plot "epeisodic," in which the episodes or acts succeed one another without probable or necessary sequence. Bad poets compose such pieces by their own fault; good poets to please the players.' I go farther and grant that Aristotle is right when he says in the *Poetics* (ix, 10), 'Of all plots and actions the epeisodic are the worst,' and again, in the *Metaphysics*, 'Nor does Nature seem to make episodes out of her happenings, like a vile tragedy.' Still, it remains inconceivable to me that Shakespeare, being the master he had made himself, should in these later years be guilty of such a blunder. It would mean, not that he was incompetent, but that, being competent, he was wantonly practising incompetency. As the American said, contemplating a certain leader of the English Bar, 'A stutter may be an affliction, and a hare-lip an act of God, but side-whiskers are a man's own fault.'

Nor is it any answer to say that all the nasty business of Antiochus and his daughter lay at hand ready-made in the pages of Gower and of Twine's novel. To be sure it did. But what of that? Shakespeare did not huddle into *Macbeth* or into *Cymbeline* everything he found in Holinshed, or into *Antony and Cleopatra* everything he found in North's

Plutarch. In selecting what is essential, in casting out what
is irrelevant or cumbersome, lies one half of a great artist's
secret. So what I adduce is *artistic* evidence that Shakespeare (or at any rate the later Shakespeare, with whom
alone we here concern ourselves) did not write Acts I and
II of *Pericles*, as we have it. Yet such evidence is almost
superfluous, since all the verse-tests put the question quite
out of doubt. Rhymed endings swarm throughout these
two Acts. There are 171 lines in the very first scene, and
46 of them rhyme. So, or almost so, it goes on until
Act III opens, with Pericles on shipboard; and just there,
where the true story opens, the rhymes suddenly cease. Save
as a tag to close an Act there are scarcely another six rhymes
(outside of the prologue and the silly 'vision') in the whole
of the play. The diction, the phrasing, moreover, turn
suddenly into right Shakespeare. Let us listen to Pericles as
he questions Marina:

> Prithee, speak:
> Falseness cannot come from thee; for thou look'st
> Modest as Justice, and thou seem'st a palace
> For the crown'd Truth to dwell in...
> Tell thy story:
> If thine, consider'd, prove the thousandth part
> Of my endurance, thou art a man, and I
> Have suffer'd like a girl. Yet thou dost look
> Like Patience gazing on kings' graves and smiling
> Extremity out of act.

Can any one doubt the authentic voice there?

(4)

So Delius and Fleay and Sir Sidney Lee and Dr Gol-
lancz are undoubtedly right in ruling out Acts I and II as
un-Shakespearean, or at least not Shakespearean of this

period. But I hold some of them to be as undoubtedly
mistaken in ruling out the brothel scenes (Act IV, Scenes II,
v and vi) as un-Shakespearean. I will swear that Shakespeare wrote them. For the reader's consent, I will ask him
to examine these scenes side by side with the corresponding
ones in *Measure for Measure*, and then dare to deny that
both are by the same hand. Next, I refer him to a paragraph
(equal truth and wisdom not to be bettered) from Professor
Sir Walter Raleigh:

Measure for Measure and the fourth Act of *Pericles* (which
no pen but his could have written) prove Shakespeare's acquaintance with the darker side of the town, as it might be
seen in Pickt-hatch or the Bankside. He does not fear to expose
the purest of his heroines to the breath of this infection: their
virtue is not ignorance; "'tis in grain: 'twill endure wind and
weather.' In nothing is he more himself than in the little care he
takes to provide shelter for the most delicate characters of
English fiction. They owe their education to the larger world,
not to the drawingroom. Even Miranda, who is more tenderly
guarded than Isabella or Marina, is not the pretty simpleton
that some later renderings have made of her: when Prospero
speaks of the usurping Duke as being no true brother to him,
she replies composedly:

> 'I should sin
> To think but nobly of my grandmother.
> Good wombs have borne bad sons.'

Shakespeare's heroines are open-eyed; therein resembling
himself, who turned away from nothing that bears the human
image.

No: the very greatest artists are not afraid of ugliness;
since only by understanding, by plumbing the mire of our
nature, can the beauty that springs from it be shown in
highest triumph. Spenser *wrote* exquisitely; nor is Una's
chastity a cloistered, though it be a fugitive, virtue. But how

thin is her purity, how but a figment of allegory her innocence, compared with the courageous virgin chastity of
Marina at bay in the house of hell, or with the fierce wifely
chastity of Imogen!

There was (as we know) in the Middle Ages an extreme
sentence of law, under which a woman might vindicate the
jewel of her reputation by walking over red-hot plough-
shares. Even such an ordeal by fire is braved—and trodden
without flinching—by Marina and Imogen.

But there is yet another and thoroughly *artistic* reason
why Marina should suffer these things. Her mother,
Thaisa, is to appear in the final Act as the lost wife restored
after many years—a favourite device of Shakespeare's, first
tried in the *Comedy of Errors*, repeated in *Much Ado About
Nothing*, again here in *Pericles*, once again in *The Winter's
Tale*. But let us distinguish. The *Comedy of Errors* is
comedy, or rather, broad farce. In *Much Ado* and *The
Winter's Tale* the hidden Hero and Hermione have both
been cruelly wronged; and their revelation at the shrine
abases the souls of the men who suspected them. Thaisa,
risen from the grave, has no such reproach wherewith to
confront Pericles, by whom she had been wronged by no
single deed, but loved in life and cherished in memory.
Therefore, it *must* be upon the daughter Marina—as it
needs not be with the daughter Perdita—that you charge
the audience's sense of affliction vanquished, of port at-
tained after tempest endured.

In fact, we must understand what Marina had endured
in Mitylene before we can express the full beauty of the
recognition scene in *Pericles*. It has not—no need to say—
the terrible beautiful grip of that scene in *Lear* where
Cordelia is reconciled with her father: because, to begin
with, Pericles has been no agent of Marina's suffering, as

Lear has been the prime agent of Cordelia's; and secondly, there is nothing in Pericles himself to beat his soul down as Lear's—nothing to justify the lovely broken anguish of—

Cordelia.   O! look upon me, sir,
And hold your hands in benediction o'er me.
No, sir, you must not kneel.

Lear.   Pray do not mock me:
I am a very foolish fond old man,
Fourscore and upward, not an hour more or less;
And, to deal plainly,
I fear I am not in my perfect mind
      ...Do not laugh at me;
For, as I am a man, I think this lady
To be my child Cordelia.

Cordelia. .   And so I am, I am.

Lear. Be your tears wet? Yes, faith. I pray, weep not:
If you have poison for me, I will drink it.
I know you do not love me; for your sisters
Have, as I do remember, done me wrong:
You have some cause; they have not.

Cordelia.   No cause, no cause!

Pathos to rival *that* no workman can write into *Pericles,* for the simple reason that it is not in the story, which holds no anguish comparable for a source of tears. Nevertheless the recognition scene in *Pericles* has a delicate beauty of its own: and the more we study that beauty the better we understand how it depends on Marina's having endured the worst of the world as an orphan; on the much it means to her to find a father; as we see how much more thereby, in the last Act, is summed up in her cry of discovery, as she runs and kneels to Thaisa:

      My heart
Leaps to be gone into my mother's bosom!

(5)

I shall conclude this chapter with a very few words upon another play, *King Henry VIII*, which I set beside *Pericles* not as coming next to it in date (for it certainly does not) but because, like *Pericles*—and by even more general consent —it is allowed to be in great part the work of other hands than Shakespeare's. And I shall here dismiss it briefly because it is a Historical Play, and, as such, belongs to a *genre* of its own, and has an artistic intention quite apart from that of the Comedies or of the Tragedies, or of the romantic Tragi-comedies with which we are here concerned; relying on different dramatic effects, and obeying therefore different rules of workmanship. I will only ask the reader here and on this point to bear always in mind that Shakespeare wrote to be *acted*: that very often a scene or a whole play of his over which we doubt in our library convinces us and vindicates itself when performed on the stage (as a captive fish, that lies dull and half dead in the hand, will, if restored to its element, revive, sport and flaunt again in its own lovely colours); and that, though on the stage to-day it disappoint us, the reason may yet be that the producers have mistakenly over-dramatised or over-sophisticated it, and so have missed the proper simplicity of the *genus*.

I think a historical play should usually be taken much as we take a procession in tapestry; should be treated on the flat, so to speak; that, without troubling our minds about dramatic concentration and high reliefs, we should allow the picture to unroll itself, and trust the audience not to be offended by abrupt intervals or inconsequences. I think, in fact, that some of us who a few years ago were helping in various historical 'pageants' did by our experiments— foolish as they often were—learn something of the right way with these historical plays, though it were only to trust an audience to take much for granted cheerfully. For a certainty we learned something, and had a sense that, by unlearning much more, we were harking back towards the secret.

But I have a better reason for speaking briefly of *King Henry VIII*. It is that, after time spent on comparing theories of Shakespeare's share in it, Fletcher's share, others' share, the problem of separating its authorship remains insoluble to me. I do not yet know, and shall not attempt to tell.

One or two points, however, may be established.

(1) The main business of Katharine is indisputable Shakespeare. We have only to compare her trial scene with Hermione's in *The Winter's Tale* to convince ourselves. And, as Dr Johnson noted, 'the genius of Shakespeare comes in and goes out with Katharine.'

(2) Katharine's 'vision' should not, being beautiful, have its beauty taken for evidence that Shakespeare invented it. Most of the visions in his later plays are so rankly bad that to a just mind any excellence in it ought to point the other way. (Yet my private opinion is that Shakespeare did invent it: because it belongs to the business of Katharine, which is his, and because the apparitions do not open their mouths.)

(6)

If we insist on judging *King Henry VIII* as a drama (setting aside for the moment all questions of mixed authorship), its workmanship has perhaps no one capital flaw to compare with the flaw of *Pericles*; but it misses its purpose no less fatally. *Pericles* consumes two Acts in getting at nothing at all, and starts afresh. *King Henry VIII*, after starting with a promise in the Prologue to make us weep over the spectacle of high things brought low,—

> And if you can be merry then, I'll say
> A man may weep upon his wedding-day.

starts upon Buckingham, works his fate to a climax, drops it, starts upon Katharine, works hers to a climax, drops it, starts upon Wolsey, works his to a climax, drops it, and winds up with a merry christening. The first four Acts might pass for a serious experiment in linking-up episodes to form a drama. But the fifth mars all, making all incongruous, dismissing us from the house of mourning with a poke in the ribs and a slap on the face. There is a unity which ranks above the famous unities of action, time, and place. It is a *moral* unity; which Aristotle forgot to mention for the simple reason that he could not conceive of a Greek writer offending against it. But the authors of *King Henry VIII* do so offend—that is, if we insist on taking it as a drama, not as a pageant. For my own belief, Shakespeare had nothing to do with the last Act, in which the artistic offence is found.

For the other flaw—that of the three climaxes—my own belief again is that Shakespeare was experimenting with the historical play much as he had experimented in *Pericles*, *The Winter's Tale*, *Cymbeline*: that he saw, or thought he saw, a way to *draw out* drama over a long period of time and took for his theme the transitoriness of human ambition —which, when we come to think of it, can scarcely be better illustrated than by a *procession* of men and women, each rising on another's misfortune, each in turn abased, and humiliated in the dust.

> Think ye see
> The very persons of our noble story
> As they were living: think you see them great,
> And follow'd with the general throng and sweat
> Of thousand friends; then, in a moment, see
> How soon this mightiness meets misery.

The date of *King Henry VIII* (or, to be accurate, of its production) is unfortunately pretty certain. As we know, one of its earliest performances set the Globe Theatre on fire. That is the kind of artistic event which gets itself precisely recorded in letters and diaries: and this one did. It happened on June 29th, 1613.

I say that the date is 'unfortunately pretty certain'—'unfortunately,' because it fixes the production of *King Henry VIII* a little after that of *The Tempest*; and the most of us would like to think of *The Tempest* as the final triumph upon which Prospero snapped his wand and buried his book. But, after all, *King Henry VIII* is anybody's child: while all of *The Tempest* is right Shakespeare. Let us 'make it so,' as good mariners say, after observing the heavens.

CHAPTER XIII

CYMBELINE

Johnson on the plot of *Cymbeline*—Imperfect sympathies—
Truth of imagination, of emotion, and of fact—A critical
disability—Shakespeare's magic—His work conditioned by the
Elizabethan stage—The theme of *Cymbeline*—The glory of
Imogen—Imaginary letter from Shakespeare to Johnson—
Echoes in *Cymbeline*—The whole greater than the parts—
Complexity of the plot.

(1)

AT the close of his commentary on *Cymbeline* Dr
Johnson thus dismisses the company:

This play has many just sentiments, some natural dialogues,
and some pleasing scenes, but they are obtained at the expense
of much incongruity. To remark the folly of the fiction, the
absurdity of the conduct, the confusion of the names and
manners of different times, and the impossibility of the events
in any system of life, were to waste criticism upon unresisting
imbecility, upon faults too evident for detection and too gross
for aggravation.

Now if this be the last word upon *Cymbeline*, or even if it
be rather more true than false, we may close our account
with the play. But (though I should tremble to utter it in
the presence of his ghost, and for more than one reason) I
confess that to me the Doctor's unfaltering pronouncement
tells little, and in a fashion not unlike that of the four

Caledonians who, being at a party when a son of Burns was expected, and hearing Charles Lamb say that he wished it were the father instead of the son, started up at once to inform him that 'that was impossible, because he was dead.' The essay in which Lamb tells this simple anecdote is headed 'Imperfect Sympathies.' I ask my readers to fix that term in their minds for a moment, while I attempt to establish and illustrate a principle of criticism, lacking which we shall be at a loss to understand, as *a fortiori* to enjoy, a vast deal of good literature, and this *Tragedie of Cymbeline* in especial.

There is a truth of imagination; there is a truth of emotion also; as well as a truth of fact. The first two are often found united, and all three not seldom. Yet all three are distinct; and he alone can be a critic of the first order who by fortunate gift of birth, or of training, has a sense responsive to all three indifferently, whether he catch them together or apart.

Let me give an illustration or two, and begin with one almost childish:

Once upon a time there lived a man immensely rich, who possessed town-houses and country-houses, retinues of servants, chariots, horses in stable—everything apparently, in short, that the heart could desire. But all this was marred by his beard, a bright blue in colour, at sight of which every woman felt a desire to scream.

Now this, of course, is untruthful to fact; historically unsound because lacking name, date, and evidence; scientifically (one would say) impossible; and, on top of this, offensive to credulity as soon as we reflect that a man so rich had money enough to dye his beard, if scruples of caste or religion forbade his buying a razor. But, the imaginative truth once granted (as childhood grants it with scarcely an effort), the rest of the story of *Bluebeard* at once becomes real. All of us, in our day, have felt the agony of Fatima as she calls up the stairway to the tower, 'Sister Anne! Sister Anne, do you see anyone coming?'

For another illustration, let me adduce one of the loveliest, most familiar stanzas in our poetry:

> Thou wast not born for death, immortal Bird!
> No hungry generations tread thee down;
> The voice I hear this passing night was heard
> In ancient days by emperor and clown;
> Perhaps the self-same song that found a path
> Through the sad heart of Ruth, when, sick for home,
> She stood in tears amid the alien corn;
> The same that oft-times hath
> Charm'd magic casements, opening on the foam
> Of perilous seas, in faëry lands forlorn.

Upon that, which all catholic taste admits to express the all but inexpressible heart of loveliness, Sir Sidney Colvin remarks:

In this joy he [Keats] remembers how often the thought of death had seemed welcome to him, and thinks it would be more welcome now than ever. The nightingale would not cease her song—and here, by a breach of logic which is also, I think, a flaw in the poetry, he contrasts the transitoriness of human life, meaning the life of the individual, with the permanence of the song-bird's life, meaning the life of the type.

In other words, nightingales (when you choose to think of it) have even shorter lives than men. True, *in fact*—in fact profoundly true! To what nonsense, viewed thus, it reduces Callimachus's famous lines, thus rendered by Cory:

> They told me, Heraclitus, they told me you were dead;
> They brought me bitter news to hear and bitter tears to shed.
> I wept as I remembered how often you and I
> Had tired the sun with talking and sent him down the sky.

And now that thou art lying, my dear old Carian guest,
A handful of grey ashes, long, long ago at rest,
Still are thy pleasant voices, thy nightingales, awake;
For Death, he taketh all away, but them he cannot take.

Death can and in fact does, of course, claim nightingales as
well as men. Yet was Victor Hugo talking like a fool when
he wrote 'The flowers, the flowers last always'? Hugo,
Callimachus, Keats are all uttering a truth outside mere
truth of fact: the same truth that Wordsworth utters more
didactically in his farewell to the River Duddon:

I thought of thee, my partner and my guide,
    As being pass'd away.—Vain sympathies!
    For backward, Duddon! as I cast my eyes,
I see what was, and is, and will abide.
Still glides the Stream, and shall for ever glide;
    The Form remains, the Function never dies;
    While we, the brave, the mighty, and the wise,
We Men, who in our morn of youth defied
The elements, must vanish....

'The function never dies.' The nightingale lifts the same
chant in this passing hour as

                        was heard
        In ancient days by emperor and clown,

and found a path through the sad heart of Ruth. The
nightingale, dying, transmits the invariable secret. We,
restless men, exhaust ourselves individually with 'the
weariness, the fever, and the fret,' and individually pass to
dust. The nightingale sings on.—That, I submit, is a 'truth
of emotion.'

But let us take any poetry. If we press the *Odyssey*,
Paradise Lost, even *The Ring and the Book*, as if we press
Bluebeard, Cinderella, Little Red Riding Hood—they are
almost always true to imagination, usually to emotion,

seldom to fact. Circe in fact no more turned the companions of Odysseus into swine than Cinderella's godmother turned the pumpkin into a gilt coach; Satan never addressed that speech of his to the fiends in council: at any rate there were no reporters present. And likely enough Mammon followed Belial with a plain 'Hear, hear'; content, like many another eminent financier, to let a clever youngster do his sophistry for him. Nay, if we take *The Faerie Queene* or *The Pilgrim's Progress*, or any great allegory, ancient or modern, what have we but a naked, deliberate, and successful attempt to inculcate truth by narrating that which never happened and never could happen? From the allegorist, deliberately didactic, let us pass to the lyrical poet in his ecstasy of love; take Ben Jonson's—

> See the Chariot at hand here of Love,
>   Wherein my Lady rideth!
> Each that draws is a swan or a dove,
>   And well the car Love guideth.
> As she goes, all hearts do duty
>   Unto her beauty,
> And enamour'd do wish, so they might
>   But enjoy such a sight,
> That they still were to run by her side
> Thoro' swords, thoro' seas, whither she would ride.

Or Donne's—

> As 'twixt two equal Armies, Fate
>   Suspends uncertain victory,
> Our souls—which to advance their state
>   Were gone out—hung 'twixt her and me:
>
> And while our souls negotiate there,
>   We like sepulchral statues lay:
> All day the same our postures were,
>   And we said nothing, all the day.

Or let us take Browning:

> This is the spray the bird clung to,
>   Making it blossom with pleasure....

Or Tennyson:

> The red rose cries, 'She is near, she is near';
>   And the white rose weeps, 'She is late...'

(pathetic fallacy)

> She is coming, my own, my sweet;
>   Were it ever so airy a tread,
> My heart would hear her and beat,
>   Were it earth in an earthy bed;
> My dust would hear her and beat,
>   Had I lain for a century dead;
> Would start and tremble under her feet,
>   And blossom in purple and red.

But it wouldn't, we know, any more than a spray blossoms with pleasure because a bird clings to it. The causation is quite unscientific. No, the truth in these passages is a truth of emotion coloured by imagination, or of imagination coloured by emotion.

I borrow that term 'Imperfect Sympathies' from Charles Lamb, because it exactly expresses a disability which, in whatever degree it afflicts any one of us, he should use all pains to overcome: and I lay stress on it because our enjoyment and understanding of this particular play *Cymbeline* depend so crucially upon adapting, even surrendering, our sympathy to it. In what follows I shall not repeat a number of things which are easily found in the text-books. If, taking it from the point of view chosen for these papers, I can persuade the reader to surrender his sympathies—or to surrender them a little more—with what Wordsworth calls

'a wise passiveness' to the exquisite story of Imogen, it will
be helping towards the best I can wish for him.

(2)

When we label the latest group of Shakespeare's plays by
the epithet 'romantic,' we attribute to them a common
something with which (as few will deny) Dr Johnson had an
imperfect sympathy. He was a great man, a masculine
critic: but the Woods of Westermain were not his province.
He was also a highly courageous man, and the dark menace
of those thickets would have no terror for him:

> But should you distrust a tone,
>   Then beware.
> Shudder all the haunted roods,
> All the eyeballs under hoods
>   Shroud you in their glare.
> Enter these enchanted woods,
>   You who dare!

Samuel Johnson would have dared, fast enough. He would
also have distrusted, and profoundly, not 'a tone,' but almost
every tone—the whole tone, in fact, of the performance.
As for the eyeballs under hoods and the rest:

> Thousand eyeballs under hoods
> Have you by the hair.

No! nor even by his wig!—He would just have said 'Shoo!'
gripped his walking-stick, and held on his way, contemp-
tuous.

'That,' it may be urged, 'is an argument *ad hominem*' or
(since we have mentioned the walking-stick) '*ad baculum*';
and, I may be told, it is all very well to say that Johnson

suffered from imperfect sympathy, or, as he would have phrased it, 'a stark insensibility,' but we have not yet answered his indictment. Well, to be sure it is a damning one, though all the counts are not equally formidable. If we admit it, very little is left to be said concerning the workmanship of *Cymbeline*.

And yet I am not so sure! I have a suspicion—a faint hope. If the indictment be true, and nevertheless I can ignore it and read *Cymbeline* with delight, then either I am a very great fool (a point I reserve) or Shakespeare is a magical workman so to charm me into forgetting faults so flagrant.

However he works his charm, it is not by hiding bad anatomy with an overlay of beautiful language. Though *Cymbeline* contains many exquisite lines, and more than one exquisite passage (notably, of course, the description of Imogen's bedchamber), its style on the whole is broken and difficult. It opens with a sentence that set every early editor emending until Johnson himself delivered the bewildered student thus:—'I am now to tell my opinion, which is, that the lines stand as they were originally written.' Professor Barrett Wendell quotes a hasty critic who said that *Cymbeline* sounds as if Browning had written it: and he instances, to illustrate the broken music of the play, the passage where Imogen receives Posthumus's letter bidding her meet him at Milford:

> O, for a horse with wings! Hear'st thou, Pisanio?
> He is at Milford Haven: read, and tell me
> How far 'tis thither. If one of mean affairs
> May plod it in a week, why may not I
> Glide thither in a day? Then, true Pisanio,
> Who long'st like me to see thy lord; who long'st—
> O! let me bate,—but not like me—yet long'st,

But in a fainter kind; O! not like me,
For mine's beyond beyond: say, and speak thick
(Love's counsellor should fill the bores of hearing
To the smothering of the sense), how far it is
To this same blessèd Milford.

'Here,' says the Professor, 'the actual sentence is only
"Pisanio…say…how far it is to…Milford."' True, and
the beauty of the passage owes little to felicities or flowers of
diction. But must we not see how beautiful it is *dramatically*
—that is, in workmanship? Note it to the last detail—the
irony of that 'true Pisanio,' addressed to the man even then
weighing how he can kill her; the irony of 'this same blessèd
Milford,' place appointed for her slaughter—she ('the
elected deer') crying for a horse with wings, to get the faster
thither!

But this is fine workmanship *on detail*, which Johnson
allows. 'This play has many just sentiments, some natural
dialogues, and some pleasing scenes.' His indictment is
concerned rather with the general structure of the story, the
'folly of the fiction.'

Well, let us take that. I said just now that his separate
counts are not equally impressive: and, for my part, I
attach very little importance to what he calls 'the confusion
of the names and manners of different times.' Shakespeare,
as I must keep repeating in these pages, wrote for an audience
in the Globe Theatre. He did not write for Dr Johnson.
He wrote for a stage which had little scenery or none; and
for actors who—as we may convince ourselves by glancing
over the wardrobe lists preserved to us—had a limited stock
of handsome, expensive dresses. Were some actor-manager
in these days to spend time and money in conscientiously
reproducing the scenery and costumes of Britain in the
actual Cymbeline's time, and then more time and money in

conscientiously reproducing the Renaissance scenery and costumes which befit Iachimo—were he to build up Imogen's bed-chamber in a 'constated' British palace of the age when our ancestors had but recently desisted from running about in woad (if indeed a few conservative country squires did not actually persist in it), what would he achieve? He would, by emphasising every absurdity to which Shakespeare was lordlily indifferent, make his production the more and more unlike that which, for the Globe stage, Shakespeare intended. The setting of *Cymbeline*, though nominally it belongs to Ancient Britain, and Milford Haven carries a homely, familiar sound, has no more actuality of date or place than Puss-in-Boots or Phæacia. If any age has a claim on it, we should choose the Renaissance; because amid so much that is generally true of all time, Iachimo's villainy has the peculiar smack of Renaissance Italy, and the plot comes out of Boccaccio—which, as seamen say, is 'nigh enough'—at any rate, is Italian. (I am aware that the plot is alleged to be found also in a work entitled *Westward for Smelts*, alleged to repose in the Ashmolean Library at Oxford.)

(3)

The gravamen of Johnson's charge lies in the words 'at the expense of much incongruity. To remark...the impossibility of the events in any system of life, were to waste criticism upon unresisting imbecility.' For a story, however far removed from truth of life, must be congruous in itself, congruous with truth of imagination. Even Puss-in-Boots is that. You cannot build artistically upon that which is merely freakish, inconsecutive. You put a certain *character* upon each person, and to that he must somehow or other be faithful. It is the very first rule laid down in the *Ars Poetica*:

> Risum teneatis, amici—
> Humano capiti cervicem pictor equinam
> Jungere si velit et varias inducere plumas
> Undique collatis membris....

Well, I cannot see that in aught essential *Cymbeline* violates this primary rule. The theme of the play is the vindication of Imogen after wrong endured. And here, as the secret of defence lies often in counter-attack, I turn on Dr Johnson and demand, 'Sir, in your preliminary compliments you are good enough to admit that "this play contains many just sentiments, some natural dialogues, and some pleasing scenes"; but why do you not include mention of the marvellous portrayal of Imogen? Over the martyrdom of Desdemona you could, in Heine's words, "froth like a pot of porter." How then comes this preoccupation with "some just sentiments," "some pleasing scenes," and this blindness to Imogen?'

For Imogen is the be-all and end-all of the play. She has all the wrongs of Desdemona, *plus* the serene courage to conquer them and forgive. She has all the fond trust of Desdemona, with all the steel and wit which Desdemona fatally lacks. Range out the great gallery of good women—Silvia, Portia, Beatrice, Rosalind, Viola, Helena, Isabella, Marina, Perdita, Miranda—Heavens, what a list!—and over all of them Imogen bears the bell.

I shall not descant upon Imogen. I might of my own preference substitute 'Miranda' for 'Perdita' in the following sentence of Swinburne's: but to every other word of it I subscribe with my heart. 'Though Perdita may be the sweetest of all imaginable maidens, Imogen is the most adorable woman ever created by God or man.' Hear her when Iachimo has spun his false tale of her husband's infidelity among chance Italian courtesans and counsels her 'Be revenged.' Hear the perfect dignity of love in innocence:

> Reveng'd?
> How should I be reveng'd? If this be true,—
> As I have such a heart that both mine ears
> *Must not in haste abuse*—if it be true,
> How should I be reveng'd?

Let the reader take these lines slowly with pause and pause between word and word, and it is odds if he can hold his tears for their very beauty. Hear her again, when Pisanio hesitates to kill her, and she, heart-broken, pleads to be killed.

> *Pisanio.*   No, on my life.
>   I'll give but notice you are dead and send him
>   Some bloody sign of it: for 'tis commanded
>   I should do so. You shall be miss'd at court
>   And that will well confirm it.
> *Imogen.*   *Why, good fellow,*
>   *What shall I do the while? Where bide? how live?*
>   *Or in my life what comfort, when I am*
>   *Dead to my husband?*

Hear her lastly when—but I shall reserve this lastly for the end of this chapter.

Many have sung the praises of Imogen: and not the least eloquent of them is Gervinus, who (with many tribal incapacities) brought to the study of Shakespeare a reverential mind, a noble modesty. Gervinus finds Imogen 'the most lovely and artless of the female characters portrayed by Shakespeare':

Her appearance sheds warmth, fragrance, and brightness over the whole drama. More true and simple than Portia and

Isabella she is even more ideal. In harmonious union she blends external grace with moral beauty, and these with straight-forwardness of feeling and the utmost clearness of understanding. She is the sum and aggregate of fair womanhood such as at last the poet conceived it. We may doubt if in all poetry there be a second creature so charmingly depicted with such perfect truth to nature.

I would add no word to Gervinus's eulogy, save perhaps this: for 'conceived' I should substitute 'achieved'—'The sum and aggregate of fair womanhood as at last Shakespeare *achieved* it.' For when I stand apart from their individual spells and study them, I can see all his previous heroines as parcels in a conception, of which—long shaped in his mind —he at last achieved this perfect portrait.

(4)

But here we come back strengthened to deal with Johnson's criticism.

If we agree with Gervinus; if we allow Imogen to be such a woman as that; then Shakespeare has done so marvellous a thing—a thing so far above other men's compass —that only the folly of inordinate expectation can deny it to be the very thing he was trying to do. What idleness, then, of presumption, when the man has done that almost impossible thing, and has done it supremely, to start lecturing him on this or that flaw in the machinery he used to accomplish it! If we, acknowledging the result, imagine that we can improve upon the means to it, then (if I may adapt Donne)—

> Then we have done a braver thing
> Than all the Worthies did:
> And yet a braver thence doth spring—
> Which is, *To keep that hid*.

Let us imagine Shakespeare from the Elysian Fields acknowledging the arrival of Dr Johnson's presentation copy, more or less in these terms:

'The author of *The Tragedie of Cymbeline* presents his compliments to the author of *Irene, a Tragedy,* and is in receipt of a commentary upon the earlier play. The author of *Cymbeline,* while grateful for the information that "this play has many just sentiments," etc.—the more grateful because it came as news to him—craves leave to observe that these compliments lie somewhat wide of the point: that, for his part, he had been inattentive to such things, or considered them but as subsidiary to a purpose which had long engaged his fancy: that of delineating a lady, wronged but forgiving, in whom his audience might recognise, or believe that they recognised, the completest of her sex. To effect this in the King's daughter, Imogen—who may be recalled as one of the prominent persons in the drama—he has to confess that he amassed many artifices as they came to hand, without considering their *separate* worth....The author of *Cymbeline* takes this opportunity of complimenting the author of *Irene, a Tragedy,* whose literary activities in other fields than the dramatic, and particularly in classifying the English tongue (licentiously abused by so many), he has followed with the liveliest interest. And he begs to remain,' etc., etc.

(5)

How did he do it? I grant that, when we start picking *Cymbeline* to pieces, we soon find ourselves puzzled, disheartened; as though at stand, in a cathedral of glorious windows, before an empty one demanding to be glorious as they, and—for material—at stand before a scrapheap of rejected glass. Cymbeline is Lear, but an inferior Lear; Iachimo is Iago, but an inferior Iago, a professional seducer without Iago's malignity as without his inward excuse. The wicked Queen is the Dionyza of *Pericles*. Posthumus is a weak Othello: Imogen has stepped down from her rank to him, as did Desdemona to wed the Moor. Here is a square of glass, with a label and a speech on it, signed Belarius, lauding the simple life in contrast with courts and royalties —good enough, yet not quite so good as that on the label in the exiled Duke's mouth in *As You Like It*:

> Now my co-mates and brothers in exile,
> Hath not old Custom made this life more sweet
> Than that of painted pomp?...

And here is a song, 'Hark, hark the lark,' in its setting for all the world like 'Who is Sylvia?' And here is Pisanio, the servant commanded to murder his mistress, but too merciful to do it—for all the world like Leonine in *Pericles* or the soft-hearted villain in *The Babes in the Wood*. As for this picture of a faithful lady putting on boy's clothes and turning page, have we not been tired of it by *The Two Gentlemen of Verona* and *All's Well That Ends Well*, not to dwell on similar masqueradings by Portia, Rosalind, Viola? When the *Tales from Shakespeare* were in progress, Charles Lamb wrote to Wordsworth, 'Mary's just stuck fast in *All's Well That Ends Well*. She complains of having to set forth so many female characters in boy's clothes. She begins to think that Shakespeare must have wanted—imagination!'

Yes, if you will, *Cymbeline* is constructed out of fragments, each like *something* Shakespeare had used before, and, if you will, every one inferior. Yet cannot we, if we aspire to be critics, get it out of our heads that the worth of any detail is separate, to be separately judged? Cannot we, even after so many great artists have told us, get it into our heads that the 'purple patch' is an offence, that the worth of every detail consists in just so much as it contributes—no matter how modestly—to the total effect? In great art the stone which the builder rejected may at any time become the head of the corner. Why on earth should it be a reproach against *Cymbeline* that in *Lear* Shakespeare did something better than *this*, in *Othello* something better than *that*, when out of the inferior *this* and *that* he has built the incomparable Imogen?

(6)

I hold, then, that Johnson made too much of the incongruities in *Cymbeline*. As *incongruities of fact*, where they do not assail the eye, they have only to be indicated to be admitted: but if we keep our gaze loyally on Imogen, they are overlooked or felt to blend into an *imaginative congruity* that leaves little for censure. My complaint rather, as I read the play (I have never seen it on the stage), lies against the complexity of the plot—a tangle of intrigues so multiplied that they, more than any incongruities, divert the mind from Imogen and worry me with the question, 'How on earth is the man going to unravel it all?' Thus I can well imagine the full effect on a spectator to be delayed until the curtain has fallen and he is walking away from the theatre: and the great masterpieces are always simpler, more direct, than this. Nor is the main thing—Imogen—the only thing that suffers from this delay. If we are interested in the plot itself, we must (as Professor Barrett Wendell has pointed out) give it 'a preposterous attention':

Until the very last scene, the remarkably involved story tangles itself in a way which is utterly bewildering. At any given point, overwhelmed with a mass of facts presented pell-mell, you are apt to find that you have forgotten something important. Coming after such confusion, the last scene in *Cymbeline* is among the most notable bits of dramatic construction anywhere. The more one studies it the more one is astonished at the ingenuity with which *dénoûment* follows *dénoûment*.[1]

In this amazing *tour de force*, which runs (in the Cambridge text) to 485 lines, Professor Wendell has counted for us no less than twenty-four cumulated *dénoûments*! An ordinary play has one, perhaps two, rarely so many as three. I shall, after referring the reader to his book, work out but a portion of the scene on a method which, less ample than his, confines itself to the wonderful development of 'recognition' (ἀναγνώρισις), out of 'recognition.'

The scene (Act V, v) opens with the stage-direction, *Cymbeline's tent. Enter Cymbeline, Belarius, Guiderius, Arviragus, Pisanio, Lords, Officers, and Attendants.*

Now of these:

(*a*) Cymbeline does not know who Belarius is; nor that Guiderius and Arviragus, whom he knights for their prowess in battle, are his own sons.

(*b*) Guiderius and Arviragus have no suspicion that they are the King's sons, but suppose Belarius to be their father.

(*c*) Pisanio knows nothing: and the Lords and Attendants are equally in the dark.

(*d*) Belarius, who knows all (so far), is still for concealing all.

The two youths are scarcely knighted before (line 23) *Enter Cornelius and Ladies*, who report that the wicked Queen has died in a frenzy of remorse, confessing that she had not only tried to murder the King's daughter, Imogen, by a swift poison, but attempted the King's own life by a lingering one. While Cymbeline, who had loved and

---

[1] *William Shakespeare: a Study in Elizabethan Literature*, 1894. English Edition, p. 358.

224 SHAKESPEARE'S WORKMANSHIP

trusted his wife fondly, staggers under this news, the
prisoners of war are led in (line 69). *Enter Lucius, Iachimo,
the Soothsayer, and other Roman Prisoners, guarded; Posthumus behind, and Imogen*—Imogen still in boy's disguise.
The situation now is:

(*a*) Lucius, the captive General, is a polite by-
stander. He knows nothing of the plot; but promptly
proceeds to beg ransom for Imogen, whom he believes
to be a boy in his service.

(*b*) Cymbeline thinks he must have seen the boy
(his daughter) before, somewhere; is strangely attracted, and offers generous ransom.

(*c*) Imogen is recognised by the faithful Pisanio
only: but—

(*d*) Belarius, Guiderius, and Arviragus recognise
her with stupefaction as the ghost of the boy Fidele—
the boy whose body Guiderius and Arviragus had,
a while ago, held in their arms, carrying it to burial.
They do not recognise Posthumus in his peasant's
disguise: but—

(*e*) Imogen (oh, trust her!) has recognised her
husband. She knows almost everybody on the stage:
and she shares with Guiderius and Arviragus the
knowledge that Cloten has been killed: but she does
not know these two to be her brothers, nor is she yet
acquainted with the full villainy of Iachimo.

(*f*) Posthumus knows the complementary half of
Iachimo's villainy, and very little beside.

(*g*) Iachimo knows neither Posthumus nor Imogen.
He is a villain caught in the dark.

(*h*) Cornelius holds the secret of the potion, and

(*i*) The Soothsayer knows just about as much as any
other soothsayer knows.

To resume—Lucius having begged his page's life, and the King having granted not only this but any boon the supposed boy may ask, all eyes are naturally bent upon Imogen. All present naturally expect the lad to ask, in his turn, for his master's life. The noble Lucius himself looks for this as a matter of course. Says he, while Imogen hesitates:

> I do not bid thee beg my life, good lad,
> And yet I know thou wilt.

She, however, with some seeming lack of heart, will take no account of him for the moment—and it cuts him to the quick. Even bare gratitude must come second to the vindication of her chastity, jewel of her soul. Here, with the villain Iachimo at her mercy—suspecting nothing, recognising neither of the victims of his foul practice—is a moment too precious to risk losing for the sake of anything in the world. She begs the King to step aside and give her some private hearing. Cymbeline grants this also.

> Ay, with all my heart,
> And lend my best attention. What's thy name?

'Fidele, sir,' answers Imogen: and upon that word leaves Belarius, Guiderius, Arviragus to an increased amazement. This *is* the boy then 'who died, and was Fidele'!

She and the King return from their conference. The King points a finger at Iachimo—'Sir, step you forth'—and Imogen, indicating the ring on Iachimo's finger, demands, as her boon, to know 'How came it yours?' Iachimo, caught in a trap, confesses his villainy: and his confession carries us to line 209, until Posthumus, on whom the truth has been dawning, breaks in upon the tale and reveals himself in an agony of rage and remorse. As the first gust spends itself in wild cries,

> O Imogen!
> My queen, my life, my wife! O Imogen,
> Imogen, Imogen!

Imogen herself, unable to bear the anguish of her husband's anguish, throws herself forward.

> Peace, my lord! hear—hear—

He, believing her to be a silly interrupting boy, turns fiercely and strikes her to earth.

At this point, then (line 229):

(*a*) Iachimo's confession has been made, to elucidate matters.

(*b*) Posthumus has declared himself.

(*c*) Imogen, her chastity cleared, is yet supposed to be dead. She lies on the ground, stunned by this last blow from her husband—his last blow and a physical one.

But this is too much for Pisanio, the only person on the stage who knows the supposed boy to be the real Imogen. He rushes on, lifts her head to his knee, crying:

> O gentlemen, help!
> Mine and your mistress! O, my lord Posthumus,
> You ne'er killed Imogen till now!

So *his* story, too, comes out: and his story reveals not only that she is the boy Fidele but (with Cornelius supplementing it) the whole vile complot of the dead Queen and how it chanced to be foiled. Therefore, Imogen being revealed for Imogen, she anticipates Posthumus' remorse by running to him and holding him in her arms, that only fail as his arms conquer them in a stronger clasp. Shakespeare wrote many

plays more perfect than *Cymbeline*: but he never wrote five
lines more exquisitely poignant than these:

Imogen. Why did you throw your wedded lady from you?
        Think that you are upon a rock, and now—
                (*embracing him*)
        Throw me again!
Posthumus.   Hang there like fruit, my soul,
        Till the tree die!

We have only yet arrived at line 265; and in the remain-
ing 221 lines of this marvellous scene there are yet some nine
or ten complications and *dénoûments* left for the audience to
follow. But on this passage I am satisfied to call a halt and
claim that *Cymbeline* has vindicated its author.

'O mighty poet!' was all that De Quincey could utter,
arising stunned from perusal of *Macbeth*. 'O mighty poet!'

May not we, closing *Cymbeline*, exclaim 'O mighty
craftsman!'?

CHAPTER XIV

THE WINTER'S TALE

The Winter's Tale—Echoes of *Pericles*—Fusion of tragedy and comedy—Futility of hard definitions—False criticism of its structure—The author's aim—An honest failure—The jealousy of Leontes—Some careless workmanship—The fate of Antigonus—The part of Autolycus—The recognition scene—Deliberate faëry—Weakness of the plot as a whole—The unapproachable love-scene.

(1)

IMAGINE a gallery hung with tapestries and having many side-doors to left and right, with passages that lead into mysterious parts of the house; or a long garden alley out of which by-paths branch and are lost in glooms of shade and echoes of lapsing water, faint, unseen, at times distant and anon close at hand. At close of day in such a place, you will be haunted first by the uncanny feeling 'I have been here—just here—before, either in this life or in some previous one,' and next by whispers, footfalls, shadows, that form themselves at the crossways ahead and fade down them as soon as surmised.

So, at the close of Shakespeare's day, are we haunted as we follow *The Winter's Tale*; and by many ghosts, but chiefly by the ghost of *Pericles, Prince of Tyre*. Indeed (to speak fancifully a little longer of a play that cannot be criticised without fancy), I cannot read these two plays in close succession but I am constantly put in mind of Coleridge's allegory, *Time, Real and Imaginary*, to give it a new application:

> On the wide level of a mountain's head
> (I knew not where, but 'twas some faëry place),
> Their pinions, ostrich-like, for sails outspread,
> Two lovely children run an endless race—
> A sister and a brother.
> This far outstripp'd the other:
> Yet ever runs she with reverted face
> And looks and listens for the boy behind:
> For he, alas, is blind!
> O'er rough and smooth with even step he pass'd
> And knows not whether he be first or last.

Like *Pericles*, *The Winter's Tale* slips a long interval of years between its third and fourth Acts, like *Pericles* employing a chorus to beg our forgiveness for the breach made in the sacred Unity of Time. They are yawning gaps, too: fourteen years in *Pericles*, sixteen in *The Winter's Tale*. But of course we recognise them to be necessary as soon as we see what Shakespeare is trying to do; which is, to reconcile the mistakes, wrongs, sufferings of one generation of men and women in their hopes for the next. 'The fathers have eaten sour grapes, but through their repentance and under God's mercy the children's teeth shall *not* be set on edge.' That is the recurrent task of our Shakespeare in these his last years, in the sunsetting:

> On the wide level of a mountain's head
> (I knew not where, but 'twas some faëry place).

And as yet Shakespeare, master of resources though he was, could hit on no device to avoid these gaps; having to present, in an action of some three hours, the children Marina and

Perdita first as babes exposed, helpless as innocent, to the surge of the sea or the beasts of the forest, anon as maidens grown up to reunite parental hearts long astray, redeem inveterate wrongs, cancel old woes, heal the past with holy hope.

(2)

Critics have accused *Pericles* and *The Winter's Tale* of this common fault: that each has a double plot which is also a separated plot—separated by the break between Acts III and IV. In a previous chapter we have examined the double plot of *Pericles*. In *The Winter's Tale*, it is urged, the first three Acts make a complete independent tragedy. By the end of them the boy Mamilius is dead; Antigonus is dead; and—far worse—for aught we know Hermione is dead, of a broken heart. The words of the Oracle are fulfilled; and Leontes, childless as well as wifeless, is very righteously left to a lifelong remorse. So far Shakespeare has worked strictly in terms of tragedy; and the action, tragically conceived, has been tragically rounded off. Then (say the critics) in the last two Acts, after a supposed interval, Shakespeare tacks on a complete independent comedy, which, picking up the thread of the story at its most tragic point, conducts us out into a garden of pleasant romantic devices where old wrongs meet to be reconciled as in this world they never do and never are.

I lay little store by this fault-finding. To start with, I think it unfair to drag *Pericles* into the comparison, since (as we have proved to our satisfaction) the first two Acts of *Pericles* are not Shakespeare's work; and therefore in opposing its last two Acts against its first three the critics oppose them against work for two-thirds of which he was not responsible; whereas in setting the last two against the

first three Acts of *The Winter's Tale* they are dealing with
work for which he is wholly responsible. Here, if faulty
workmanship be detected, Shakespeare and Shakespeare
alone is to blame.

Next, ruling out *Pericles* for this reason and taking *The
Winter's Tale* by itself, I find the fault-finders pedantic.
They seem to me to be enslaved by stock definitions. 'Here,'
they say, 'in Acts I, II, III, we have Tragedy; there, in
Acts IV and V, we have Comedy. *Therefore* Shakespeare is
guilty of the attempt to work into one drama two different
stories in two separate categories of Art. Q.E.D.'

Quite so. *That is precisely what Shakespeare was attempting to do.*

In a world where Nature mixes comedy with tragedy and
often shades one into the other indistinguishably, Art, if she
be Nature's mirror (as Shakespeare held), must always be
impatient of hard definitions. They have their disciplinary
uses: again and again while he is learning his trade they may
restrain the artist from 'mixing up things that differ'—
which Horace rightly put in the forefront of his *Ars Poetica*
as the prime offence against Art. But in the end they must be
for him a matter of tact rather than of strict law, which *de
minimis non curat*. They are, after all, conventions: they are,
at the best, inductions from the practice of great artists who
have gone before; as Æschylus, Sophocles, Euripides pre-
ceded Aristotle, and but for them he would have had not
only no theory but nothing to theorise about. As he goes on,
the great artist with a sense of growing power conceives a
desire to improve the best. At the same time he perceives
that in Art, as in Nature, truth is a matter too delicate to be
grasped by definition. *La Vérité consiste dans les nuances*;
and, in the division of labour between him and the critics, it
is his, not theirs, to lead the way in discovery.

Be this granted or not, no one can begin to understand Shakespeare's later plays who does not perceive that they have one common and constant aim—to repair the passionate errors of men and women in the happiness their children discover, and so to renew the hopes of the world; to reconcile the tragedy of one generation with the fresh hope of another in a third form of drama which we may call 'romantic' if we will.

Moreover—and for a minor point—it is not true of this particular play, *The Winter's Tale*, that Acts I–III make a rounded play in themselves. A number of threads are deliberately left hanging. For example, while the doom of the Oracle has been exacted, its promise of hope yet waits to be fulfilled—*The King shall live without an heir if that which is lost be not found.* The pith of an oracular response lies always in the riddle, and this is the sole riddle in the answer brought by Cleomenes and Dion from Delphi. 'That which is lost' is, of course, Perdita, as her name tells us: and the story of her putting away has already been introduced, and very carefully, into Act III. We do not know, to be sure, that Hermione lives: yet if, as members of the Globe audience, we know our Shakespeare of old, we ought to have guessed, in Paulina's protestations, a something held up his sleeve. I grant that it takes a guess, and that Leontes must by no means be allowed to surmise the truth.

But—to return to my main argument—if the critics be unintelligent who condemn the general structure of *The Winter's Tale*, they multiply stupidity when they proceed to convert and use it in condonation of certain flagrant faults: as, for example, when they argue that *because* Shakespeare, by compressing two plots into one play, overcrowded the time at his disposal, *therefore* we must overlook the monstrously sudden growth of Leontes' jealousy; that he left himself no room to develop it rationally: or, for another example, as when Gervinus, to excuse the unworkmanlike trick by which Shakespeare scamps the recognition scene between Perdita and her father, sagely pleads that 'The poet has wisely placed the event behind the scenes; otherwise the play would be too full of powerful scenes.'

I shall return to both these examples. Just here I wish to say that, the purpose of these pages being less to give information about Shakespeare than to suggest ways of reading him by which we can increase for ourselves our profit and delight, I have no quarrel with any critic on the mere ground of fault-finding: for I hold that as a rule he does us better service who draws our attention to apparent faults than he who glosses them over with ready explanations or quick assurances that they are beauties rather than blemishes.

If we can discover for ourselves that an alleged or an apparent fault is, or is not, a real fault, we bring off a critical success, however small: our first business in this world being to judge for ourselves. It is a historical fact that Shakespeare invited the applause of the Globe Theatre audience, and it should cost our modesty no great effort to rise to that average. Or we may forget the Globe audience and remember only that Shakespeare is addressing *us*.

But if we would be critics, our first task consists in discovering what the author is trying to do. This discovered, we understand where his true difficulties lie, and when we come upon an apparent fault in his work we can pretty easily determine whether to condone it—nay, perhaps even to admire it—as an honest attempt that has fallen short, or to condemn it for a piece of scamped and careless workmanship. Thus in *The Winter's Tale* the gap between Acts III and IV comes of honest failure to do an extremely difficult thing, yet a thing well worth doing, which Shakespeare essayed again and again until at length, in *The Tempest*, he mastered it. But the play abounds in flaws far less venial.

(3)

I begin with the jealousy of Leontes. This is actually baseless as Othello's: and it has far less excuse than Othello's, for it lacks both a villain to suggest and circumstances to feed the delusion. It is caprice of self-deception, a maggot suddenly bred in a brain not hitherto supposed to be mad. 'During less than twenty lines,' says Professor Wendell, 'Leontes is carried through an emotional experience which in the case of Othello had been prepared for by above two Acts and, when it came, occupied nearly two hundred and fifty lines. Lacking due preparative, it strikes us as monstrous.'

Granted that Leontes, as contrasted with Othello, has a naturally jealous disposition—then, *why are we not warned of it?* Camillo and Antigonus must surely, as observant courtiers, have sounded their master's nature and detected its master-weakness. But Camillo, who opens the play, hints no such knowledge: it comes upon him in Scene II like a thunder-clap. Antigonus and all the rest of the courtiers are simply bewildered: Leontes strikes them as a man snatched out of his wits. And what of Hermione herself? She has been Leontes' wife for several years, and an attentive wife. Yet she has no inkling at all of this master-weakness. The revelation of it in Act II, Scene I, outrages not only her honour but her understanding....Then, I say, if neither the courtiers nor Hermione have guessed, *a fortiori* we are not prepared. I ask any candid reader of the play if the surprise

of Leontes' insane jealousy does not hit him, as it hits everyone on the stage, like a blow on the face?

If, on the other hand, Leontes be not a man *naturally*
jealous, the awakening of jealousy, and the haste with
which it possesses him, shock probability no less. The
apologists on this side are even more at fault. They can only
suggest that Shakespeare lacked time and room to develop
the change in the man. But I take up the little volumes of
the Temple Shakespeare in which, for handiness, I have
been re-reading his later plays. I note that *The Tempest*, a
Court play, occupies 106 pages of print; *Pericles*, 116
pages; *The Winter's Tale*, 147 pages; *King Henry VIII*,
148 pages; *Cymbeline*, 169 pages. Now *The Winter's Tale*,
like *Cymbeline*, was written for the theatre: Doctor Simon
Forman's diary records that he witnessed a performance at
the Globe on May 15th, 1611. A short while before, he
had witnessed a performance of *Cymbeline* at the same house.
If, then, for *Cymbeline* Shakespeare could be allowed a
space of time correspondent with 169 pages of print, why
in *The Winter's Tale* had he to compress his action within
a space less by 22 pages—or between one-eighth and one-
seventh? We are dealing with workmanship, and this is an
eminently practical question, as any playwright will tell us.
Shakespeare *had* time, or could have found time, to make
Leontes' jealousy far more credible than it is. I maintain
that he bungled it.

(4)

But the play abounds in careless workmanship. Let me
follow up this really important flaw by instancing a few
lesser ones:

(*a*) The Oracle. 'It seems,' says Coleridge, 'a mere
indolence in the great bard not to have provided in the

oracular response (Act II, Scene II) some ground for Hermione's seeming death and sixteen years' voluntary concealment'; and Coleridge even suggests how it could have been conveyed in a single sentence of fifteen words. Shakespeare let the opportunity go. The resurrection of Hermione thus becomes more startling, but at a total loss of dramatic irony.

(*b*) Prince Florizel in Act IV, Scene IV, appears in shepherd's clothes. 'Your high self,' Perdita tells him,

> The gracious mark o' the land, you have obscur'd
> With a swain's wearing.

Yet before the end of the scene he is exchanging a fine court suit for Autolycus's rags.

(This, by the way, would seem to argue some imperfection in the text as it has reached us; since obviously such a blunder could not have survived the first dress rehearsal. Yet, strange to say, *The Winter's Tale* seems to be about the most carefully printed play in the whole of the First Folio.)

(*c*) Next let us take the fate of Antigonus: and let me begin by quoting Professor Sir Walter Raleigh on the fate of this poor man, disposed of in 'the most unprincipled and reckless fashion':

Up to the time of his sudden death Antigonus has served his maker well; he has played an important part in the action, and by his devotion and courage has won the affection of all the spectators. It is he who saves the daughter of Hermione from the mad rage of the King. 'I'll pawn the little blood which I have left,' he says, 'to save the innocent.' He is allowed to take the child away on condition that he shall expose her in some desert place and leave her to the mercy of chance. He fulfils his task, and now, by the end of the third Act, his part in the play is over. Sixteen years are to pass, and new matters are to engage our attention; surely the aged nobleman might have been allowed to retire in peace. Shakespeare thought otherwise; perhaps he felt it important that no news whatever concerning the child should reach Leontes, and therefore resolved to make away with the only likely messenger. Antigonus takes an affecting farewell of the infant princess; the weather grows stormy; and the rest must be told in Shakespeare's own words.

Antigonus.   Farewell;
The day frowns more and more: thou'rt like to have
A lullaby too rough: I never saw
The heavens so dim by day. A savage clamour!
Well may I get aboard! This is the chase!
I am gone for ever!

                       (*Exit, pursued by a bear.*)

This is the first we hear of the bear, and would be the last, were it not that Shakespeare, having in this wise disposed of poor Antigonus, makes a thrifty use of the remains at the feast of Comedy. The clown comes in to report, with much amusing detail, how the bear has only half dined on the old gentleman, and is at it now. It is this sort of conduct on the part of the dramatist that the word Romance has been used to cover. The thorough-paced Romantic critic is fully entitled to refute the objections urged by classic censors against Shakespeare's dramatic method; but if he professes to be unable to understand them, he disgraces his own wit.

This is soundly said; and yet Sir Walter has not plumbed the deep damnation of Antigonus's taking-off. Its true offence is against economy of workmanship. The bear is a naughty superfluity.

Students of this play may find a little profit and much amusement in an acting version prepared by John Kemble for Drury Lane, in 1802. Let me quote the precedent passage as printed by Kemble; or rather a part of it, chiefly for the sake of its stage-directions.

Antigonus says:

> Blossom, speed thee well!
> There lie: (*laying down the child*)
> And there thy character: (*lays down a paper*)
> There these: (*lays down a casket*)
> Which may, if fortune please, both breed thee pretty,
> And still rest thine—(*Rain and wind*)
> The storm begins![1]

There we behold the child Perdita laid with wealth in jewels and the evidence of her high parentage beside her. All we have now to do as a matter of stage-workmanship is to efface Antigonus. But why introduce that bear? The ship that brought Antigonus is riding off the coast of Bohemia and is presently engulfed with all her crew. The clown sees it all happen. Then why, in the name of economy, not engulf Antigonus with the rest—or, better still, as he tries to row aboard? I can discover no answer to that. If anyone ask my private opinion why the bear came on, it is that the Bear-Pit in Southwark, hard by the Globe Theatre, had a tame animal to let out, and the Globe management took the opportunity to make a popular hit.

(*d*) Next, for Autolycus: I challenge anyone to read the play through, seat himself at table, and write down what Autolycus does to further the plot. Let me not deny the knave his place in the picture. That is appropriate enough, and delightful. But as a factor in the plot, though from the

---

[1] Kemble is all wrong with his commas, as is the Cambridge text. The casket and papers cannot breed Perdita pretty. How should they? The right reading is, of course,

'Which may, if fortune please, both breed thee, pretty,
And still rest thine—The storm begins!'

moment of his appearance he seems to be constantly and elaborately intriguing, in effect he does nothing at all. As a part of the story he is indeed so negligible that Mary Lamb in the *Tales from Shakespeare* left him out altogether. Yet Autolycus is just the character that Charles and Mary Lamb delighted in. Again I give you my private opinion: which is that Shakespeare meant to make a great deal of Autolycus, very carefully elaborated him to take a prominent and amusing part in the recognition scene, tired of it all, and suddenly, resolving to scamp the recognition scene, smothered him up along with it.

(*e*) This brings us to the greatest fault of all: to the recognition scene; or rather to the scamping of it. To be sure, if we choose to tread foot with Gervinus and agree that 'the poet has *wisely* placed this event behind the scenes, otherwise the play would have been too full of powerful scenes'; if, having been promised a mighty thrill, in the great master's fashion, we really prefer two or three innominate gentlemen entering and saying, 'Have you heard?' 'You don't tell me!' 'No?' 'Then you have lost a sight'—I say, if we really prefer this sort of thing, which Gervinus calls, 'in itself a rare masterpiece of prose description,' then Heaven must be our aid. But if, using our own judgment, we read the play and put ourselves in the place of its first audience, I ask, Are we not baulked? In proportion as we have paid tribute to the art of the story by letting our interest be intrigued, our emotion excited, are we not cheated when Shakespeare lets us down with this reported tale? I would point out that it nowise resembles the Messengers' tales in Greek tragedy. These related bloody deeds, things not to be displayed on the stage.

It is a question of simple ἀναγνώρισις—Leontes recognising Perdita as his child; and the Greek tragedians never weaken the dramatic effect of ἀναγνώρισις by removing it out of sight of the audience. Ἀναγνώρισις (Recognition) and περιπέτεια (Reversal of Fortune) are in fact the two hinges upon which all Greek drama turns.

But apart from our own natural expectation, and apart from all rule of tragic workmanship, let us test Gervinus with his 'otherwise the play would have been too full of powerful scenes' by what we know of Shakespeare; who never flinched from cumulative effect, but on the contrary habitually revelled in it. Did he suffer us to lose that breathless moment when Sebastian and Viola stand and gaze and con each the other, incredulous?

One face, one voice, one habit, and two persons!

Did he cast Lear's recognition of Cordelia into *oratio obliqua*? Did he cut out anything from *Macbeth* or from *Hamlet* because 'otherwise the play would have been too full of powerful scenes'? Or let us consider *Cymbeline*. In *Cymbeline* we held our breath while Shakespeare accumulated no less than twenty-four *dénoûments* within the space of one final Act! And in Leontes' recognition of his daughter there is nothing at all to weaken—rather everything to strengthen and lead up to and heighten—the great recognition of Hermione.

Why, then, did Shakespeare shirk it? That I cannot answer, save by borrowing the words of Elijah:

Cry aloud: for he is a god; either he is talking, or he is pursuing, or he is in a journey, or peradventure he sleepeth and must be awaked.

—by which I mean no more than just this: The longer we consider these later plays that fall to be dated between the great tragedies and *The Tempest*, the more we are forced to feel that—to cast it in terms befitting the vagueness of the

surmise—'something had happened.' I am not referring to
that strange sunset atmosphere which so many have noted;
nor to that sublime confusion of dates and places which
some set down to carelessness, but which I believe to be
part of the method which deliberately sets the story in a
fairy haze, so that it belongs to no age but to all time. The
anachronisms in *The Winter's Tale* are as flagrant as those
in *Cymbeline*. 'Whitsun pastorals,' 'Christian burial,' Giulio
Romano, the Emperor of Russia, and Puritans singing
psalms to hornpipes, all contemporary with the Oracle of
Delphi—'the *island* of Delphi'! They jar us less than the
anachronisms of *Cymbeline*, but only because *Cymbeline*
professes to be history of a sort, whereas *The Winter's
Tale* but professes to be a tale: and Bohemia is as welcome
to a sea-coast as Prospero to happen on a West Indian islet
in the Mediterranean. 'Faëry—deliberate faëry' is the
answer—'the light that never was on sea or land'—but do
we not *wish* it was? Faëry—deliberate faëry: the nursery
tale of Snowdrop translated into *Cymbeline*; Danaë and the
floating cradle translated into *Pericles*: the Princess turned
Goose-girl, the disguised Prince, the clownish foster-father
and foster-brother, translated into this play.

No: I am not thinking of *these* touches, which may as
easily be beauty-spots as blemishes: but rather of those
laxities of construction, of workmanship, with which maybe
this paper has been disproportionately concerned: of the
tours de force also, mixed up in *Pericles* and *King Henry
VIII* with other men's botch-work, confused here, in *The
Winter's Tale*, with serious scampings of artistry.

(5)

Coming back to our strict enquiry into the workmanship
of *The Winter's Tale*, we must admit that the play never

lodges in our minds as a whole, is never compact as (for
instance) *As You Like It*, or *Much Ado*, or *Twelfth Night*,
or *Measure for Measure*, or as *Macbeth*, or *Othello*, or even
Antony and Cleopatra is compact, or as *The Tempest* is
compact. It leaves no single impression. We think maybe
of Hermione's most noble rebuke:

> Adieu, my lord:
> I never wish'd to see you sorry; now
> I trust I shall. My women, come; you have leave.

We think of her, grandly innocent, in the trial scene: or we
see her, in the last Act, the statue made life, in the hush of
the music, stepping down to forgive Leontes; brought to
him, like Alcestis from the grave; turning from him to
stretch hands over Perdita who kneels:

> You gods, look down,
> And from your sacred vials pour your graces
> Upon my daughter's head!

then, catching her, holding her a little away, searching her
eyes to make sure of bliss,

> Tell me, mine own,
> Where hast thou been preserv'd? Where liv'd?...

Or again we think of Paulina, that admirable woman in
Shakespeare's gallery; ancestress of Nurse Berry in *Richard
Feverel*, with a touch of Madame Sans Gêne; and of that
excellent scene in which she beards Leontes, and all the
king's horses and all the king's men cannot stay her tongue.
But first of all, when *The Winter's Tale* comes to our mind,
nine out of ten of us think of the sheep-shearing feast and
Perdita handing flowers—gem of all pastorals:

> I would I had some flowers of the Spring that might
> Become your time of day: and yours, and yours,
> That wear upon your virgin branches yet

Your maidenheads growing: O Proserpina,
For the flowers now that, frighted, thou let'st fall
From Dis's waggon! daffodils
That come before the swallow dares, and take
The winds of March with beauty; violets dim,
But sweeter than the lids of Juno's eyes
Or Cytherea's breath; pale primroses,
That die unmarried ere they can behold
Bright Phœbus in his strength—a malady
Most incident to maids: bold oxlips and
The crown imperial: lilies of all kinds,
The flower-de-luce being one....

—never the total play; but ever separate scene after scene,
and this the unapproachable one, in which Florizel and
Perdita, no active persons in the drama, find themselves the
centre of it, being young and innocent and in love. That is
all, but it is enough.

Love is enough: ho, ye who seek saving,
Go no further, come hither! there have been who found it,
And these know the House of Fulfilment of Craving....
These know the cup with the roses around it,
These know the World's wound, and the balm that
        hath bound it:
Cry out! the World heedeth not 'Love, lead us home!'

CHAPTER XV

THE TEMPEST

The three following chapters on The Tempest *were delivered as lectures before the University of Cambridge in the Michaelmas Term of* 1915, *and were prefaced by the following words:*

Here in Cambridge, in a second Michaelmas Term of War, it may seem an idleness to be talking about poetry. But I say to you that it is not. I say that an Englishman who, not having shirked any immediate services within his power, in these days improves and exalts himself by studying such a work of art as The Tempest, *lets ride his soul, as good ships should, upon a double anchor. There is the lesser anchor of pride, that, happen what may, here is something our enemy can as little take from us as he can imitate it: that the best part of revenge is to be different from our enemy and hopelessly beyond his copying, whatever he may destroy. But there is also the better anchor of confidence, that in a world where men just now seem chiefly to value science for its power to slay, we hold to something as strong as it is benign, and careless of death, because immortal.*

I

Date of *The Tempest*—Cunningham's discovery—His rehabili-
tation—Dr Garnett's theory—Elizabeth of Bohemia—Probability of the play's revision for a nuptial ceremony.

(1)

EVERYBODY knows that *The Tempest* is the first
play printed in the First Folio of 1623: which, for
aught anybody knows—indeed almost certainly—was its
first appearance in print. Why Heminge and Condell, the
editors, gave it that pride of place is a puzzling question if
we choose, but not at all beyond conjecture. I shall suggest
one or two reasons before I have done: but the best answer
lies in the fact that no editor of taste has ever disobeyed the
First Folio's lead; as neither, of course, did Charles and
Mary Lamb in their *Tales from Shakespeare*. And yet
almost everybody allows *The Tempest* to be a late play; one
of the latest, if not the very last, that Shakespeare wrote.

I hope in the following enquiry—still using the method
we applied to *Pericles, Cymbeline, The Winter's Tale*—to
lay before the reader some arguments for believing that *The
Tempest* was Shakespeare's very last play; by which, of
course, I mean the last of his sole authorship, putting aside
King Henry VIII and *The Two Noble Kinsmen*, of which
he was but part author. I think most of us would like to
believe *The Tempest* his last work and to cherish the fancy
(originated, I believe, by a poet, Campbell) that when
Prospero puts off his mantle, breaks his staff, and drowns his
great book

        deeper than did ever plummet sound,

it is Shakespeare himself who in the ritual bids a long
farewell to his realm of magic.

Nevertheless we must not neglect such prosaic stuff as contemporary records, diaries, play-bills, audits. 'There is such a thing as "circumstantial evidence,"' says Thoreau, 'as, for instance, when we find a trout in the milk-jug.' There is also such a thing as direct external evidence: and before hazarding our criticism upon Prospero's island, we must beat off a coast less romantic.

Of direct external evidence to date *The Tempest* nothing was discovered until 1842, when Mr Peter Cunningham, a promising antiquary, edited for 'the Shakespeare Society' (of which he was Treasurer) certain 'Extracts from the Accounts of the Revels at Court in the Reigns of Queen Elizabeth and King James I.' Among these was an entry taken from the account-book for the years 1611–1612. It ran:

By the Kings Players	Hallomas nyght was presented at Whthall before ye Kinges ma^{tie} A Play called The Tempest

Apart from his growing reputation as an antiquary, men knew young Mr Peter Cunningham (son of Allan Cunningham, the poet) as an enthusiastic young man of twenty-six; a clerk, on Sir Robert Peel's appointment, in the Audit Office, where he rose to be Chief Clerk. His *Life of Inigo Jones* and his *Life of Nell Gwynne* still hold their own on the second-hand book-stalls, and his edition of Horace Walpole's Letters, though superseded for serious reading, recently had its life prolonged in a cheap reprint. Young Mr Peter Cunningham, then, had been searching for old papers in Somerset House; 'rummaging'—to quote his own words—

'in dry repositories, damp cellars, and still damper vaults.... My last discovery was the most interesting; and alighting, as I did, upon two official books of The Revels—one of Tylney's and one of Buc's—which had escaped both Musgrave and Malone, I at last found something about Shakespeare, something that was new, and something that was definite.'

For settling the date of *The Tempest*, at all events, nothing could be more definite or conclusive. To be sure, an entry that it had been performed by the King's players before the King's Majesty on Hallowmas night, 1611, did not prove this to have been the first performance. But the whole play wears the look of having been designed for a Court entertainment. Its brevity—2068 lines, which yet permits two masques, or *entr'actes* to be included—its fairy atmosphere, borrowed and sublimated from *A Midsummer-Night's Dream*, a play undoubtedly written for the Court—a hint here, there a turn of speech—all point the same way. And then the alleged date, 1611, was recognised as coming most acceptably pat upon the famous wreck of the Virginia Fleet off the Bermudas, or, rather, the return of the survivors to England. One of them, Silvester Jourdan, had written an account of it, dating his dedication Oct. 13, 1610: to which narrative, as well as to a pamphlet issued by the Council of Virginia, the play owes several small debts.

Scholars, in short, took the matter as settled: 1611 was the date. This, I say, happened in 1842.

Twenty-six years later—on April 26, 1868—Sir Frederick Madden, Keeper of Manuscripts in the British Museum, received a letter offering for sale two highly interesting documents of the time of James I—the Account Books of the Revels Office for 1604–5 and 1611–12. The writer stated that some thirty years before, when a Clerk in the Audit Office, he had found these papers 'under the vaults of Somerset House—far under the Quadrangle, in a dry and lofty cellar known by the name of the *Charcoal Repository*.'

'Had I been a rich man,' he went on, 'I would have presented these highly interesting papers to the Nation:' but, as it was, he would be content with any sum that the Trustees of the British Museum might see fit to give him. That the writer was a Scotsman you will have guessed from the phrase 'Had I been a rich man, I would have presented': an Englishman would have written 'I should.' But he signed a name familiar to the Museum authorities. They answered, asking him to state a price for the trove. He replied, 'I have written to Collier about the Revels Account I sent you: and he will write to you.' Two days later he wrote again—Collier keeping silence—'I do not think I am asking too much of the Trustees of the *British Museum*, when I ask *Sixty Guineas* for them.'

A more fatal reference could not have been given. For this Collier was the notorious John Payne Collier, who within quite recent memory (1858) had fallen like Lucifer from a world-wide reputation as the one man of genius among Shakespearean scholars to an equally wide dishonour as the most diabolically clever of Shakespearean forgers; the wickeder because, on the repute of his combined learning and ingenuity, documents above price had been entrusted to his private hands. He had used them all, forging entries upon them remorselessly. The story of John Payne Collier yet waits to be written as a study in perversity of genius. But this is by the way. He had been thoroughly exposed and ruined, some time before. The man who quoted him for an opinion on the price of a manuscript stirred up a name that stank.

Sir Frederick Madden made some enquiries; impounded the documents, and after a very brief interval had them handed over (May 26, 1865) to the Record Office, where they still abide among the books labelled 'Audit Office

Declared Accounts—Various.' He acted rightly, of course; since on the would-be seller's own admission, however he had come by them, these documents had been stolen from the State.

No action was taken to prosecute anyone. After a while, however, it leaked out that the would-be seller, a man who had been in unlawful possession of them for thirty years, and at length tried to palm them off on the British Museum for his own, was no other than the Peter Cunningham who in 1842 had published his discovery, among others, of the date of *The Tempest* in the 'dry repositories, damp cellars, etc.' under Somerset House.

The explanation lies just here.—In 1868 Peter Cunningham was a man broken by drink; retired, at the age of forty-two, out of the Audit Office, and now so far broken that his poor brain could scarcely distinguish between *meum* and *tuum*. During his clerkship the archives of the Audit Office, hitherto inaccessible to the general public, had been carted over to the Record Office *en bloc*, unsorted, unindexed. He had 'borrowed' a couple of volumes, taken them home, worked upon them. His bemused brain belike no more remembered that he had worked upon them and given his extracts a publicity to expose him than it saved him from the direst error of all—that of calling upon Collier, once the god of his adoration, to be judge, at that time of day, of the worth of what he offered.

There lay his fatal mistake: though it is doubtful if he ever realised it, to care. For the Museum Authorities pitied him, knowing his past, and took no steps. But as luck would have it, the 1604–5 entries, occupying two pages of the MS. book, were in a different hand from the rest of the script. These entries happened to include one performance of *Othello*, concerning the date of which play Shakespearean

scholars had been for years at loggerheads. The shadiness of
the whole transaction, mixed up as it was with the name of
Collier, at once raised the cry of 'Forgery!' No one
seriously contested it—'Cunningham and Collier are tarred
with the same brush,' 'Cunningham is Collier's jackal,'
'We have tracked Collier down with endless pains. Shall
we now have to start afresh upon Cunningham?' For Dyce
and Halliwell-Phillipps—two of the most judicious Shake-
speareans of that day—the question was at once decided on
Duffus Hardy's private assurance that the whole business
was a forgery. 'It only required a glance of the experts.'
'And now who is the forger? The conclusion that Peter
Cunningham is the man seems unavoidable.'

Meanwhile Peter Cunningham heard or heard not;
made no sign; at any rate offered no defence; secure against
prosecution for theft, went on drinking himself to death;
and so died, unprotesting.

His guilt was henceforth taken for granted. Even so
cautious a scholar as the late Mr Aldis Wright, commenting
on the once-authoritative extract relating to *The Tempest*,
says boldly:

It is now ascertained that this entry and all the others of a
similar kind contained in the books of the Revels numbered XII
and XIII, are undoubted forgeries.

Thus it came to pass that from 1868 and the hour of poor
Cunningham's exposure, for forty-odd years, the date of
The Tempest rested where it had relapsed, in uncertainty;
conjecture, however, still playing around the incriminated
1611, with which all verse-tests and other internal evidence
seemed, on the whole, best to fit.

But in George Vertue's Collection of MSS. there is to be
found another entry, and a certainly genuine one, concerning

our play: recording that it was acted by John Heminge (co-editor of the First Folio) and the rest of the King's Company of Players before Prince Charles, the Lady Elizabeth and the Prince Palatine Elector in the beginning of the year 1613. Prince Charles of course was he who afterwards became Charles I; the Lady Elizabeth she whom we know as Elizabeth of Bohemia; and the Prince Palatine Elector that ill-starred Frederic who came here to wed her and carry her off to strange romantic fortunes. In place of earlier certainty there now grew a fascinating hypothesis, started long since by Tieck and elaborated with rare critical skill and sympathy by the late Dr Garnett, that this authentic record of *The Tempest*, a court-play acted to adorn the nuptials of Elizabeth of Bohemia, refers in fact to its first performance; that *The Tempest* was written expressly for her bridal.

(2)

I wish I could believe it true. I would give much to be able to believe it true. For a long while I firmly held it to be true, as Dr Garnett's arguments had wound themselves in, conquering a willing belief. For who, knowing the story of Elizabeth of Bohemia, would not be fain to think of her and *The Tempest* together? There are a certain few women in history who in life fascinated the souls out of men, for good or evil, and still fascinate the imagination of mankind, though themselves have been dust for centuries. Helen of Troy is one, of course, and Cleopatra another. These two were wanton and light of love; but virtue, or the lack of it, skills not. For Joan of Arc is a third, a maid and a saint above saints; and Catherine of Siena, another saint, is a fourth; and a fifth is Mary Queen of Scots, who was what you will—except a saint. But of her grand-daughter,

252 SHAKESPEARE'S WORKMANSHIP

Elizabeth of Bohemia—wayward, lovely, extravagant, un-
fortunate, adorable and peerless—what shall I say? Let us
rehearse Wotton's lines on her:

> You meaner beauties of the night,
>   That poorly satisfy our eyes
> More by your number than your light,
>   You common people of the skies;
> What are you, when the moon shall rise?...
>
> You violets that first appear
>   By your pure purple mantles known,
> Like the proud virgins of the year,
>   As if the Spring were all your own;
> What are you, when the rose is blown?
>
> So, when my mistress shall be seen
>   In form and beauty of her mind
> By virtue first, then choice, a Queen,
>   Tell me, if she were not design'd
> Th' eclipse and glory of her kind?

'Th' eclipse and glory of her kind'—if that strike the
reader as court eulogy—rather better done than usual, but
yet court eulogy—I will tell him a better and more curious
thing. If he will read the history of the early 17th century
and track the influence of Elizabeth of Bohemia, he will find
that scarce ever a man came in range of her but he knelt her
sworn knight: and, what is more, he either followed her
hapless fortune to the last extremity, proud only to serve; or,
called away, he went as though a great illusion had broken
within him; as though having once knelt before a revelation,
thereafter, laying down pride, ambition, self, his ambition
and his content accepted the pursuit of a dream in which the
world were well lost. We may see this strange conversion in
Wotton, who wrote the stanzas I have quoted. We may see

it, wildly deflected, in Donne. We may trace it in the life of Sir Dudley Carleton. We may see it, more naïvely expressed, in this well-authenticated story.

A company of young men of the Middle Temple met together for supper; and when the wine went round the first man rose, and holding a cup in one hand and a sword in the other, pledged the health of this distressed Princess, the Lady Elizabeth; and having drunk, he kissed the sword, and laying hand upon it, took a solemn oath to live and die in her service. His ardour kindled the whole company. They all rose, and from one to another the cup and sword went round till each had taken the pledge.

We may see it—to make an end with the devotedest—in Lord Craven, a Lord Mayor's son, who, having poured blood and money in her service, ever constant, laid his last wealth at her feet to provide her a stately refuge and a home. Through all the story she—mother of Rupert of the Rhine—rides conquering all hearts near her, reckless, spendthrift, somehow ineffably great; and lifting, in a desperate cause, all those hearts to ride with her, despising low ends, ignoble gains: to ride with her down and nobly over the last, lost edge of the world.

I say it were pleasant to imagine *The Tempest* written for the bridals of this wonderful woman; to read this immortal play and think of Shakespeare breaking his staff before one who—if the sceptred race and the charm divine guaranteed aught—guaranteed all for the next generation, in whose hope good men live.

(3)

But there is a beggar at the gate of this joy: a dead beggar too; yet claiming our justice as in life he had fallen too low to care for it—let alone to clamour.

Peter Cunningham went unpunished by law. No proceedings were ever taken against him, and the authorities (it would seem) were equally careless of establishing his guilt to their own private and reasonable satisfaction. The name of Collier, which he had invoked so pathetically—from a lifelong habit of loyalty that could not realise what had befallen his admired master—sufficed to damn him out of hand.

Thus the matter rested until, some seven or eight years ago, there came along a man—Mr Ernest Law, learned author of *The History of Hampton Court*—who asked questions. He started with a prejudice against Cunningham: indeed, took his guilt almost for granted. But he examined the Revels Books and began to doubt: he spoke of his doubt to one or two officials in the Record Office, and found to his surprise that they, too, had some misgivings: 'though,' as he says, 'responsibility naturally obliged in them a more reserved attitude than was incumbent in an outsider, in questioning a verdict which, more or less officially adopted, had remained so long unchallenged.' Mr Law called in experts to his aid; ink and paper were examined microscopically; and the result was a little tractate, published in 1911, on 'Some Supposed Shakespeare Forgeries.' I do not see how anyone who reads with a judicious mind can deny that Mr Law proves his case; that Peter Cunningham, unlawfully possessed of these books, did not tamper with them in any way: and (what alone concerns us here) that the 1611 entries, at any rate, including that of *The Tempest*, are quite above suspicion.

So there we are, after forty-odd years, back at the old date: and *The Tempest* was not originally composed for the nuptials of the Princess Elizabeth.

(4)

Yet let us go softly! *The Tempest* was played in 1613 to grace those nuptials: and my mind harbours a fancy, and something more than a fancy, that in the play as we now have it—as Heminge, who acted in it on that famous occasion, redacted it for the 1623 Folio—we have the 1611 play adapted, improved, and cast in its lovely final form.

For *The Tempest*, as it stands, is obviously a court play; and as obviously intended to grace a wedding.

> Honour, riches, marriage-blessing,
> Long continuance, and increasing,
> Hourly joys be still upon you!
> Juno sings her blessings on you.

As Dr Garnett points out, you cannot cut away the Masque of Iris but you make impertinent Prospero's lines that immediately follow; by admission among the grandest— yes, and the delicatest—that Shakespeare ever wrote. For Prospero does not say, as so many misquote him—

> And, like the baseless fabric of a vision....

but—

> And, like the baseless fabric of *this* vision,
> The cloud-capp'd tower, the gorgeous palaces,
> The solemn temples, the great globe itself,
> Yea all which it inherit, shall dissolve;
> And like *this* insubstantial pageant, faded,
> Leave not a rack behind.

Yet I cannot find record of any nuptials meet to be celebrated thus on or about Hallowmas Night 1611. Now, the wedding of the Prince Palatine with Princess Elizabeth was occasion enough—as all the records prove—to summon *any* great playwright up from a country retirement, however obstinate; to call on him, however weary, to nerve himself for a last triumph, to put forth all his powers.

For the occasion was tremendous. London went wild over it. The festivities lasted for weeks. For a sample:

The first of these fêtes was a mock naval fight upon the river Thames, for which thirty-six vessels, 500 watermen and 1000 musketeers were put in requisition, besides four floating castles with fireworks. The scene to be represented was the siege of Algiers. On the bank of the Thames opposite Whitehall a mock town was erected, the bombardment of which was to form the amusement of the 11th of February. The King, Prince Charles, the Princess Elizabeth and the Elector, with their suites and many of the nobility, stationed themselves at the Palace windows; and at a signal given by the discharge of cannon the performance commenced. Thirty-six balls of fire arose from the castles on the river and descended, some in fiery rain, some in thousands of smaller globes. Then, mounted on cords attached to one of the vessels, an armed figure appeared, representing St George with his lance, and also a young maiden and an immense dragon. St George and the dragon had a long combat, hurling fires at each other, which served as torches to display the beauty of the maiden; till, at the end of half an hour, the dragon exploded with a terrific report; and then St George and the maiden sported with fires till both were consumed. When the smoke cleared away a mountain appeared in the water, and from a cave in its side issued a comet which discharged an infinite number of fusees, whilst a fiery stag, pursued by hunters, made a tumultuous rush into the water, where, after a brief chase, all exploded together.[1]

For the cost of it all, let us perpend this, bearing in mind

[1] I quote from the late Mrs Everett Green's biography of the Princess Elizabeth, first printed as one of her *Lives of the Princesses of England*, afterwards enlarged and issued as a separate volume. A new edition has recently been published.

how the purchasing power of money has diminished in these centuries (we may multiply by 12 and still be cautious):

The magnificence of the marriage preparations completely bankrupted the Royal exchequer...£53,294 was expended, exclusive of the bride's portion of £40,000.

Add the two together, multiply by twelve, and we get a sum considerably over a million of our money—nearer a million and a quarter. There was in the middle of it what in less exalted households is known (I believe) as a row. James I of England was, the reader will remember, also James VI of Scotland.

In a sudden fit of economy the Court was broken up: and to the bitter mortification of the Lady Elizabeth, the household provided for her husband was abruptly dismissed. Frederic, responding to the hint thus thrown out, gave intimation to most of the attendants who came over with him (but remained at the King's expense) that their visit had already been sufficiently prolonged.

Which reminds one of Mr Bennett in *Pride and Prejudice*, and how he persuaded his daughter Mary to quit the piano. 'That will do excellently well, child. You have delighted us long enough.'
The narrative ends abruptly:

The King, to save appearance, left town for Newmarket.

CHAPTER XVI

THE TEMPEST

II

Workmanship as evidence of date of *The Tempest*—Comparison
with *The Winter's Tale*—Gonzalo's commonwealth—Youthful
love stronger than Prospero's magic—An exquisite surprise—
The most beautiful love-scene in Shakespeare—Supposed
sources of the play—Its central theme—Difficulty of handling
reconciliation in a three-hours' play—Shakespeare's attempts to
overcome it—The Unities not *laws* but *graces*—Shakespeare's
'royal ease.'

(1)

FORTUNATELY—and by that word I confess a
prejudice—even when we have accepted the evidence
of the Revels Book that there was a performance of
The Tempest on Hallowmas Night (November 1), 1611,
before His Majesty in his new banqueting-room at Whitehall, we are still able to believe it the very last play written
by Shakespeare. No scrap of external evidence forbids
that.

In *The Winter's Tale* we have its one serious challenger
for the place. But we can certainly date *The Winter's Tale*
back to the early summer of 1611; for on May 15 our old
friend Dr Simon Forman, physician and astrologer, saw it
performed at the Globe Theatre, as he has recorded
(appending a sketch of the plot) in his journal, *A Booke of*

Plaies and Notes thereof, preserved in the Ashmolean
Museum at Oxford, and undoubtedly genuine. This ante-
dates the earliest recorded performance of *The Tempest.* I
would not press the point unduly: as still less would I insist
upon it as significant that when Ben Jonson jibed at the two
plays in the Introduction to his *Bartholomew Fair* (1614),
he spoke of 'those who beget *Tales, Tempests* and such like
drolleries'—using that order. Nor again, passing from
external evidence to metrical tests, can I pretend that they
settle the question, though I think it remarkable that in *The
Tempest* the percentage of blank verse with what we call
'feminine endings' is 35·4; easily the highest in the whole
of Shakespeare, 2½ per cent. higher than *The Winter's Tale,*
which beats *Cymbeline* by more than 2 per cent., which
again beats *All's Well That Ends Well,* which in turn beats
Lear and *Coriolanus;* and these six head the list. 'But this,'
an objector may say, 'is the evidence of straws.' Then let
me bring better, still using the method followed in my
former papers: that of testing each play by its workmanship.

(2)

For a beginning.—No one can read *The Winter's Tale*
and *The Tempest* side by side and fail to observe that they
contain a number of stage devices almost identical, but
turned to different account. Further, many of these devices
are so frequent in Shakespeare's later plays that we may
almost say they had become his final stock-in-trade. Let us
take a few examples.

(1) Perdita and Miranda (and Marina for that matter;
but we will not here deal with *Pericles*) are both Princesses
—the one royal, the other ducal—who as infants have been
exposed to almost certain death and cast away on a strange
shore.

(2) Both grow up in complete ignorance of the high fortune to which they are rightfully heiresses.

Miranda, questioned by her father—

> Canst thou remember
> A time before we came unto this cell?
> I do not think thou canst, for then thou wast not
> Out three years old—

can only answer

> Certainly, sir, I can...
> 'Tis far off
> And rather like a dream than an assurance
> That my remembrance warrants. Had I not
> Four or five women once that tended me?

(3) Both Perdita and Miranda owe their deliverance to a good honest courtier, who, charged to see their deaths, finds his heart melt at the last moment. We have the same device in *Pericles* and again in *Cymbeline*, and indeed it is one of Shakespeare's favourites.

But here observe how far more artistically he works it in *The Tempest*. As the reader will remember, Perdita's appointed executioner is the old courtier Antigonus; and in dealing with *The Winter's Tale* I had something to say of the unprincipled and reckless manner in which Shakespeare disposes of him. It sins against all true economy of workmanship.

But why kill Antigonus at all? Let us turn to *The Tempest* and remark well what greater skill it uses with his counterpart Gonzalo. To begin with, Gonzalo survives: which is poetical justice. Further, we see him on the island still true, after many years, to his character of loyal-hearted servant, still active in his loyalty, which in turn advances the action of the play. Is it not a delicate stroke that, when

Miranda first hears the story of her casting away, of all the shipwrecked company near at hand, though she knows it not, this old counseller is the man she desires to see? (But she is heart-whole yet, be it remembered, and has never set eyes on a personable youth.) Let us consider the lines in which Prospero relates their dreadful passage—

> Some food we had, and some fresh water, that
> A noble Neapolitan, Gonzalo,
> Out of his charity, who, being then appointed
> Master of this design, did give us, with
> Rich garments, linens, stuffs and necessaries
> Which since have steaded much; so of his gentleness,
> Knowing I lov'd my books, he furnish'd me
> From mine own library with volumes that
> I prize above my dukedom.
>
> *Miranda.*   Would I might
> But ever see that man!

So in the end he is not only one of the company that provides Miranda with cause for her most exquisite cry of

>   O wonder!
> How many goodly creatures are there here!
> How beauteous mankind is! O brave new world,
> That has such people in it!

But it is he who utters the great cry of reconciliation:

>   Look down, you gods,
> And on this couple drop a blessèd crown!

echoing unmistakably Hermione's invocation in *The Winter's Tale*—

>   You gods, look down,
> And from your sacred vials pour your graces
> Upon my daughter's head!

To resume our list:

(4) Both Perdita's and Miranda's fortunes turn cardinally on a storm and a shipwreck. I shall have something to say of the opening scene of *The Tempest* by-and-by. For the moment I note what nobody will gainsay: that its storm and shipwreck are ten times as well managed as the shipwreck in *The Winter's Tale*.

(5) Both shipwrecks happen off a coast 'in faëry lands forlorn.' For the compass-bearings of Prospero's island we may search the map as profitably as for the seaboard of Bohemia. The commentators chase it to the Bermudas, back to Lampedusa, and away again to Pantelleria, to Corcyra: but they never make its landfall; and why? It isn't there.

(6) To Miranda as to Perdita—both discovered as adorable and ripe for love—there arrives the Fairy Prince; who also happens to be the one youth in the world to heal the old wrong between their parents. Had Florizel been any Prince of otherwhere than Bohemia, Ferdinand any Prince of otherwhere than Naples, why then of course there had been nothing reconciled and, of course, no play. Yet— wait!—I go too fast. Ferdinand *might* have been made son of Antonio, usurping Duke of Milan: and there were possibilities in that. But so, whereas Bohemia had married Sicilia, Milan would have married Milan; cousin, cousin; the wrongful Milan the rightful; and the wrongful lover, as husband, would have become ruler and lord. I suggest that Shakespeare greatly refines on this by making Ferdinand the son of Alonzo, King of Naples, temporal overlord of rightful and wrongful in Milan: that thus he avoids a difficulty which did not occur in *The Winter's Tale*, and yet leaves room for reconciliation. Alonzo of Naples, albeit 'an enemy'— as Prospero says—'to me inveterate,' is not guilty in the

same degree as Antonio. His sin is, to have abetted the usurper's suit—

> Which was that he (Alonzo), in lieu o' the premises
> Of homage and I know not how much tribute,
> Should presently extirpate me and mine
> Out of the dukedom, and confer fair Milan,
> With all the honours, on my brother; whereon,
> A treacherous army levied, one midnight
> Fated to the purpose, did Antonio open
> The gates of Milan.

There was the crime, and I am to suggest some points on which the playwright scores (as we should say) by giving the conspiracy just that shape.

To begin with, he avoids making his Fairy Prince the son of an arch-villain. In any play this would go near to shock us; in a romantic play it would certainly revolt us. No doubt bad fathers before now have begotten good heirs, even as (to quote Miranda) 'good wombs have borne bad sons.' But Antonio is altogether too much of a scoundrel for us to delight in a prosperous wooing by any son of his, or at any rate to delight in a wooing the prosperity of which leaves his villainy not only unpunished but successful. In *The Winter's Tale* Perdita's father had done cruel wrong, but under the hallucination of jealousy. He is not a villain. Now Antonio *is* one, and bad in grain.

Next, by this shift of invention Shakespeare wins a further freedom—to *develop* Antonio's villainy: to make him go from bad to worse under our eyes, and in the natural manner of traitors; to plot, for further self-advancement, to kill the very man by whose patronage he had mounted. And (to have done with Antonio) the same shift of invention leaves him open, in the end, to the full and condign, if merciful, punishment that childless he shall see all his ambition laid in ruin, while the two realms he has sold his soul for pass, enhanced by union, to the daughter of the first good man, the son of the second, whom he has plotted to destroy.

As for Alonzo, King of Naples, he has been weak, and by being weak, has helped the old wrong. But he is a good man at heart, and we find him sufficiently punished by the two or three hours of anguish he has endured, believing his only son drowned.

Lastly, on this point (if the reader be not wearied with Gonzalo, who is an old favourite of mine), by this device enabled to show Antonio's second conspiracy in operation, Shakespeare (borrowing freely from Montaigne) is enabled also to give us a sketch—thrown out, as it were, in passing—exquisite in few lines, as genial as it is wise, humorous and yet wistfully attuned to the moral of the whole play, 'We are such stuff as dreams are made on'— a sketch, a parable too (if we will) of Gonzalo the old counsellor, rusé in politics but still faithful to Milan, while still beyond Milan he cherishes an idea of the perfect commonwealth not realisable on earth, though mayhap (he deems) it might be on some such island as this on which they have fallen—

Had I plantation of this isle, my lord—

The younger courtiers interrupt, mocking: but he persists—

> I' the commonwealth I would by contraries
> Execute all things: for no kind of traffic
> Would I admit: no name of magistrate;
> Letters should not be known; riches, poverty,
> And use of service, none; contract, succession,
> Bourn, bound of land, tilth, vineyard, none;

* * * * * *

> No occupation; all men idle, all;
> And women too, but innocent and pure;

No sovereignty...
All things in common nature should produce
Without sweat or endeavour: treason, felony,
Sword, pike, knife, gun, or need of any engine
Would I not have: but nature should bring forth
Of it own kind all foison, all abundance
To feed my innocent people.

Dreams, dreams of an old man! Yet still generous dreams;
and such as thousands of young men since Gonzalo have
indulged in; Coleridge—the early Coleridge—and Wordsworth, Blake, Shelley; in our own day William Morris
notably and Gordon of Khartoum. Thousands of eager
high-spirited men have seen the vision; and, illusory though
it may be, it *has* a call for the nobler souls among us. But
the young men around Gonzalo laugh; and he is old, tired.
'Will you laugh me asleep, for I am very heavy?' So he
sleeps, and awakes; to be rewarded, not with any new
heaven on earth, but (perhaps more happily for him, after
all) with the best earthly thing that could betide in a world he
has served worldlily yet worthily and well.

(3)

But it is time we returned to our Princes and Princesses.
I find Ferdinand an improvement on Florizel in more than
one way. Even his introduction is better managed. He is
drawn into the scheme, whereas Florizel's meeting with
Perdita merely happens. Old Antigonus on shipboard just
bumps on the first coast he comes to and deposits Perdita,
who in due course grows up and is chanced upon by her
lover. But Ferdinand, travelling the wide seas, is deliberately
caught in a vortex and sucked by Prospero's art and pre-
science through perilous foam to the island; where he woos
his maid predestined yet (such is the art) so that the wooing,

while it thrills *us*, thrills with a kind of amaze even Prospero, its contriver. That has always seemed to me one of the loveliest inventions in *The Tempest* and perhaps the most glorious: the manner in which love takes charge of two young hearts and carries them ahead of its contriver, leaving him with his magic at a standstill.

Great indeed is the 'picture' (as I believe stage managers call it) in *The Winter's Tale*, when Paulina pulls the curtain apart and discovers Hermione standing as a statue. But how much greater and more surprising, yet how infinitely more natural, that moment of art when the curtains fall open at the mouth of Prospero's cave and reveal——two lovers playing at chess and exchanging——well, silly sooth, if you will, but true for ever and to the end of all things :——

> *Miranda.* Sweet lord, you play me false.
> *Ferdinand.*   No, my dear'st love,
> I would not for the world.
> *Miranda.* Yes, for a score of kingdoms you should wrangle,
> And I would call it fair play.

There is, for the joy of the audience, a pretty grace-note of irony in 'for a score of kingdoms you should wrangle.' That is Shakespeare's plenty, 'God's plenty.' Let us pass it and ask ourselves, 'Was there ever, of human invention, a surprise more unaffected, more exquisite?'

(4)

Again, I find Ferdinand superior to Florizel (though he has not half the time granted him) in the spirit of his wooing, the decisive young courage with which he accepts menial work for the sake of winning his love. Ferdinand enters carrying a log bravely; doing just the same labour as Caliban has been tied to—precisely the same labour groaning under which Caliban called,

> All the infections that the sun sucks up
> From bogs, fens, flats, on Prosper fall, and make him
> By inch-meal a disease!

Miranda comes forward in eager pity:

>   If you'll sit down,
> I'll bear your logs the while; pray, give me that;
> I'll carry it to the pile.

Ferd.   No, precious creature,
> I had rather crack my sinews, break my back,
> Than you should such dishonour undergo
> While I sit lazy by.

Mir.   It would become *me*
> As well as it does you; and I should do it
> With much more ease: for my good will is to it,
> And yours it is against.

So opens the most beautiful love-scene in Shakespeare: who, by the way (after *Romeo and Juliet*), was instinctively chary of love-scenes save when he could handle them with raillery. Now the commentators, pondering on this courtship, and specially on Ferdinand's carrying logs under Prospero's harsh injunction, are all in a pother, wanting to know from what source Shakespeare can have borrowed it. The trouble begins in Warton's *History of English Poetry*. Warton had been informed by 'the late Mr Collins of Chichester'—Collins the poet, that is—that Shakespeare's *Tempest* was based on a romance, *Aurelio and Isabella*, printed in 1586, in one volume, in Italian, French, and English, and again in Italian, Spanish, French, and English in 1588.

Mr Collins had searched this subject with no less fidelity than judgment and industry: but his memory failing him in his last calamitous indisposition [poor Collins went mad], he probably gave me the name of one novel for another. I remember that he added a circumstance, which may lead to a discovery, that the principal character of the romance, answering to Shakespeare's Prospero, was a chemical necromancer, who had bound a spirit like Ariel to obey his call and perform his services.

But alas! no one has ever been able to find a copy of this once-popular work. So the commentators turn to a German play, *Die Schöne Sidea*, written by one Jacob Ayrer, a notary of Nuremburg, who died in 1605. There is a magician in this drama, who is also a Prince—Prince Ludolph: he has a demon or familiar spirit: he has an only daughter too. The son of Ludolph's enemy becomes his prisoner, his sword being held in its sheath by the magician's art. Later, the young man is forced to bear logs for Ludolph's daughter. She falls in love with him, and all ends happily. 'It is possible,' say the most recent commentators—I summarise it in the words of Mr Morton Luce in a very notable preface to *The Tempest* in the 'Arden' Shakespeare —'it is possible that Shakespeare used Ayrer's play'; for the English comedians 'were at Nuremburg in 1604, where they may have seen, and possibly themselves have acted, *Die Schöne Sidea*. But it is more likely that both writers derived the main incidents of their plots from the same hidden source.'

Well, there we have it—if we think it matters. But, to begin with, did anybody ever hear tell of a necromancer who had *not* a familiar spirit? And to proceed—Did anybody ever see a *young* commentator? Has any one ever met a commentator who once upon a time had been an infant? Did Theobald ever ride a cock-horse? Was there ever a knee that dandled Halliwell-Phillipps? Have the commentators ever listened to a nursery tale? Or, having listened, could they not remember or bethink them that of nursery-tales, of all fairy-tales, of all folk-tales immemorially old, from Spain to Siberia, from China to Zululand, from the South Pacific to Lake Erie and back to Iceland, there is no *cliché* so common as this—the witch or wizard; the only daughter; the adventurous prince caught and bound to carry logs or sweep stables; pity and young love that do the rest and bring all right in the end? It is as old as Hellenic mythology. Anyone who lists may find it more than a score of times repeated in the *Cabinet des Fées*, or in the late Mr Andrew Lang's multi-coloured series of fairy-books. *That*—and nothing less common to all mankind—is the basal plot of *The Tempest*. But we may catch stray echoes of it anywhere, up and down in Literature. Here is one, in a variant of style—

> When she is by, I leave my work,
> I love her so sincerely,

(which is, after all, what Ferdinand does, though he *says* he is ready to crack his sinews)

> When she is by, I leave my work,
> I love her so sincerely,
> My master comes like any Turk
> And bangs me most severely—
> But let him bang his belly full,
> I'll bear it all for Sally:
> She is the darling of my heart,
> And she lives in our alley.

(5)

By this time the reader may pardonably have forgotten that we are making a list of stage devices common to *The Tempest* and *The Winter's Tale*. We had, in fact, arrived at No. 7: and I might go on with Nos. 8, 9, 10, 11, 12—

mentioning, for example, that each contains a masque or performance in dumb show, with dancing; or that in both wild animals are introduced, whether real or personated; or that in each there is a great recognition (ἀναγνώρισις) in which the long-lost are found; or that both are romance, and neither tragedy nor comedy; or I might descant on what so many have noted—the quiet aureate atmosphere that besets and surrounds, embraces, steeps, makes its own, these two with all the later plays: all, but these two eminently, and with irradiation so subtle, so ethereal, so lambent, that no man can tell at whiles whether it be an after-glow borrowed from without and afar, or be rayed forth through the frame of the work as from an inmost altar wherefrom all smoke, reek, vapour of passion has been cleared and the fire has settled to burn with a steady heat. The light moreover is recognisably autumnal and yet the atmosphere breathes of the very dawn,

> So cool, so calm, so bright;
> The bridal of the earth and sky.

Old memories of wrong; all quarrels, jealousies, suspicions, hymns of hate on which men have fed and feed themselves between a dream and a dream—all meet to be forgiven; all melt to be transformed, renewed, made better; all pass into a mist which, almost before we recognise it as a mist of pity, is shaken, rent, scattered by the morning breeze of hope. *That* it is to be a man and strong: to be wise, and overwise, and weary wise; and to catch your salvation in hope.

> We are such stuff
> As dreams are made on—

says Prospero. But Miranda loves Ferdinand, and Ferdinand loves Miranda, and (thank God!) neither of them believes a word of it!

(6)

I hope to have convinced the reader by this time that *The Tempest*, repeating (or, since 'repeating' begs the question, shall we say 'resembling'?) *The Winter's Tale* in at least a dozen particulars, at almost every point improves on it. Still it may be asked, 'What of that? Artists are often careless, often fall back on their best, shoot short after shooting furthest....You yourself (I may be reminded) have described Shakespeare in these papers as a royally indolent man. Granted that *The Tempest* is the better, more accomplished, work of art, it does not follow that it came later in time.'

And that would be rightly urged, though I hope that the evidence has already some *cumulative* effect.

So now I will make confession of what convinces *me*. But to do this, I must in very few words re-traverse some ground we covered in my first paper on these later plays.

Every great artist tires of repeating his successes, but never of renewing his experiments. So, of two plays apparently upon one theme, *Othello* is followed by *The Winter's Tale*, a comparative failure: so, of two upon another theme, *Lear* comes first in time, *Cymbeline* second. And why?—precisely because *Othello is* an absolute artistic success, and *Lear*, if not an absolute artistic success, *is* a gigantic masterpiece. The account is closed, the two themes in turn, *as* themes, have been mastered, once for all. But they may yet be taken and inwoven with a third theme, truer in the end than either. Thus Shakespeare goes on; and if anyone choose to say that in *Cymbeline* and *The Winter's Tale* he falls, why, then, let us grant that he falls. But he falls by no intellectual decline: rather in the attempt to achieve something further, certainly more difficult and, it may even be, impossible. It

is with Art as with Love—and these are the twin passions
that tear and rend every artist's life:

> Love wing'd my Hopes and taught me how to fly
> Far from base earth, but not to mount too high:
>> For the pleasure
>> Lives in measure,
>> Which if men forsake,
> Blind they into folly run and grief for pleasure take.
>
> But my vain Hopes, proud of their new-taught flight,
> Enamour'd sought to win the sun's fair light;
>> Whose rich brightness
>> Moved their lightness
>> To aspire too high,
> That all scorch'd, consum'd with fire, now drown'd in
>   woe they lie.
>
> And none but Love their woeful hap did rue:
> For Love did know that their desires were true.
>> Though fate frownèd,
>> And now drownèd
>> They in sorrow dwell,
> It was the purest light of Heaven for whose fair love
>   they fell.

(7)

What was this new theme which Shakespeare sought to
engraft upon his old ones? We know it already. We have
followed it through *Pericles*, through *Cymbeline*, through
The Winter's Tale, here to *The Tempest*. It is Reconciliation. Desdemona sacrificed, dead by her pillow: Cordelia
limp in Lear's arms—

> Thou'lt come no more,
> Never, never, never, never, never!

That cannot be the end of it all! 'Nay,' you hear Shakespeare say, 'if I were God now....' (For anthropomorphism,

whether we pity or mock it, is not wholly base.) 'But,' says he, 'I am Shakespeare and feel myself a god, being able to create some few things. Then this shall *not* be the end. There may or may not be another world in which wrongs are redressed. But there *is* a continuance of this world in newer generations that we surmise—how wistfully! You promise heavens free from strife, but this warm, kind world is all I know: and in it (he says), as I am Shakespeare, Desdemona's fate and Cordelia's shall *not* be the last word, and the sins of the fathers shall *not* be visited on the children.'

And so we have Marina, Perdita, Miranda created for us: creatures of loveliness made to love and conceive children, renewing the promise of the world.

(8)

Just here, however, comes in the dramatist's difficulty. Shakespeare is henceforth occupied, and to the end, with reconciliation. But (as I have pointed out) reconciliation, forgiveness, the adjustment and restoration of goodwill between injured and injurer must be, in the nature of things, a slow process. And this, of all themes, is the most heart-breaking for a dramatist, who has to tell, and by presented action, his complete story in two or three hours. Again and again this difficulty beat Shakespeare; and on our way through the later plays we have seen the devices by which he covered defeat. In *Pericles* we had ancient Gower acting Prologue, quite in the fashion of those old pensioners who in some great houses trot a sightseer around the picture-galleries. We listen to him begging us, in Act after Act, to suppose that so much time has elapsed:

> I do beseech you
> To learn of me, who stand in the gaps to teach you
> The stages of our story.

In *The Winter's Tale*, between Acts III and IV, we have Father Time himself dragged in by the forelock, or beard, to exhibit an hour-glass and plead—

> Impute it not a crime
> To me or my swift passage that I slide
> O'er sixteen years and leave the growth untried
> Of that wide gap.

And then of a sudden, in *The Tempest*, Shakespeare brings off the trick! The whole action of the play, with the whole tale of ancient wrong unfolded, the whole company of injuring and injured gathered into a knot, the whole machinery of revenge turned to forgiveness, takes place in about three hours of imagined time, or just the time of its actual representation on the stage!

'Marvellous stage-craft!'? Yes. I would not make too much of the famous Unities, but though discredited as *laws*, they abide as *graces* of drama; and pre-eminently a grace is this *Unity of Time*, whereby the author, in Dryden's words—

sets the audience, as it were, at the post where the race is to be concluded; and, saving them the tedious expectation of seeing the poet set out and ride the beginning of the course, suffers you not to behold him till he is in sight of goal and just upon you.

'Marvellous'? Yes....But will anyone tell me that Shakespeare, having solved the problem which had beaten him— great master of his craft—not once only but thrice, turned back afterwards to imitate, in *The Winter's Tale*, old failures?

Such a thing does not happen.

Here I take leave to speak positively. We must all bring our small private experiences to the task of interpreting our Shakespeare. He is so truly a child of Nature, and so wise in her, that we feel we owe him that service hardly less than we owe it to Nature herself: we read him, reading ourselves into him:

> O Lady! we receive but what we give,
> And in our life alone does Nature live:
> Ours is her wedding-garment, ours her shroud.

And just here any man who has seriously devoted his days, or the best of them, to inventive art—no matter how feeble the result—can stand up without false modesty and speak with more authority than any commentator who, learned as we please in other things, has never been baptised, never initiated, never made one of the cult. An artist may—I think the greatest do, and must—care little for what he has done: as Shakespeare, we know, took no further care for a play once written. *As You Like It, Hamlet, Othello*—he tossed them over his broad shoulder, and whoso list might pick them up. But he—the artist—passes on to some new strange search; and of its object we divine nothing nor know more than this—that, until found, it is the essential jewel of his soul.

A friend, the other day, called my attention to a note—a memorandum—by the late Dr Furnivall:

> When I asked Browning what struck him most in Shakespeare, he said, 'The royal ease with which he walks up the steps and takes his seat on the throne, while we poor fellows have to struggle hard to get up a step or two.'

If ever a man in invention displayed that royal ease, yes, certainly it was Shakespeare. All his contemporaries bear testimony to this that Browning noted. If in any one play he steps to his throne more eminently a king than in all the rest, that play is *The Tempest*. But in previous lectures I

18-2

have tried to anatomise the artist that goes up—yes, so royally—to his platform to draw the curtain for the last time; and I think of Arnold's lines—

> These things, Ulysses,
> The wise bards also
> Behold and sing.
> But O, what labour!
> O Prince, what pain!

and of these other lines of Arnold's—

> Such, Poets, is your bride, the Muse! Young, gay,
> Radiant adorn'd outside: a hidden ground
> Of thought and of austerity within.

CHAPTER XVII

THE TEMPEST

III

Argument for *The Tempest* being a marriage play—Its position in the Folio—An imagined first night—The uses of the inner stage—The realistic accuracy of the opening scene —Landlubber criticisms—Coleridge on Prospero's 'retrospective narration'—The dignity of Perdita and Miranda— Shakespeare's sympathy extending to Caliban—The contribution of Stephano—Comparison of *The Tempest* and *A Midsummer Night's Dream*—Prospero—Danger of supposing autobiography—A play for all time.

(1)

ALTHOUGH, as we have seen in a previous chapter, *The Tempest* was pretty certainly presented at Court, in some form or another, on Hallowmas Night, 1611, it was quite certainly represented there early in 1613 to grace the nuptials of the Prince Palatine and the Princess Elizabeth, and almost as certainly played as we now have it, whether there had been a previous form or not. For while it seems we must reject Dr Garnett's main thesis, that Shakespeare wrote it for that great occasion, I hold this much proved all but unanswerably. As it now stands, it was written for Court, and to celebrate a wedding. I am even inclined to add 'a royal wedding.' Its brevity (for a monarch and his guests must not be unduly tired, nor a bridal couple either) is one small indication. Its economy of scene-shifting, unique among Shakespeare's plays, is another and stronger one: and by a paradox, the *stationary splendour* of its setting, a third. For it is observable that while a royal banqueting house, such as that of Whitehall, allows a more sumptuous frame than an ordinary theatre; and while for a royal performance it encourages rich dress in the players, with refinement of bodily motion and the speaking voice; and while again it lends itself, as we know, to all the apparatus of a Masque; it cannot—it could not then, as Windsor cannot to-day—compete with a professional theatre in what we may call the tricks of the trade. When at Whitehall or at Windsor we come to these, we come, if not to 'two trestles and a board,' at furthest to something like a glorified Assembly-Room.

Now, as Dr Garnett has pointed out, 'after the first brief representation of the deck of the storm-tossed vessel with which the play opens, there is practically but one scene.' For though the action occasionally shifts from the space before Prospero's cell to some other part of the island, everything is avoided which might necessitate a change of decoration. Neither is there any change of costume except Prospero's assumption of his ducal robes in the last Act: and this takes place on the stage.

But of course Dr Garnett's argument rests mainly on the two masques, and specially on the nuptial masque of Iris, Ceres, and Juno: which, if the real purpose of the play—or, as I should prefer to put it, the occasional purpose—be overlooked, appears so merely an excrescence that some have hastily supposed it an interpolation. But this cannot be. If we remove the masque, Act IV (already, as it stands, much shorter than ordinary) simply crumbles to pieces; while further, as we saw in our first paper, the finest passage in the drama goes with it. On the other hand, if we save the masque (and Act IV along with it), we cannot deny it to be a nuptial one. It explicitly says that it *is*.

Thus far I have been following Dr Garnett: and will but add three small points which seem to me to strengthen his contention:—

(1) The resemblance, subtler for its differences but not less assured, between *The Tempest* and *A Midsummer-Night's Dream*—a play undoubtedly written for Court and a wedding. With this I will deal by and by, when we come to Ariel and fairyland.

(2) The 'notion' of the play: A prince arriving at an island to win a bride; the island ruled by the bride's father, a benevolent or 'white' Wizard. James I specially prided himself on his devout counter-dealing with witchcraft. As we have seen, the witchcraft in *Macbeth* is contrived to flatter him.

(3) The place of *The Tempest* in the First Folio. Heminge and Condell knew, of course, that it was not his first play, but almost his last, if not (as I maintain) his very last. Then why did they lead off with it? Putting aside the hypothesis that by divination they set it there as the play of all others calculated to allure every child for a hundred generations to come into his Shakespeare, to be entrapped by its magic, I suggest that, being cunning men, they started off upon the public with their revered dead master's most notorious triumph; that this triumph had owed no little of its notoriety on the one hand to having fulfilled a great occasion—the Lady Elizabeth's spousals—that set all England afire; on the other to Court approbation; which, even in our days, the 'profession' (and Heminge and

Condell were actors) has been known to appreciate, and
not rarely to exploit.

(2)

The date is an early night of 1613, when the days are felt
to be lengthening. At Whitehall the Great Banqueting
House is alight, and, for the mirrors to multiply, the tall
candles shine on a company of men and women whose
rivalry, to the soul's neglect, in every trapping that will give
the body splendour, as in every luxury that can minister to
its inward appetite, has already made the Court of James I
a byword in Europe for prodigality; for the moment to be
envied or foreboded on, as a sensual or as a spiritual man
will choose. They have their hour, at any rate; and we may,
if we will, amuse ourselves by essaying to reconstruct the
scene in detail after the fashion of Macaulay. *Here* the
King himself seated, *there* Cecil, now Earl of Salisbury,
grave, sedate; *there*, made heir-apparent but a few weeks
ago by the death of his brother Henry, the boy Charles who
in time must step out from a window of this same banqueting-
room and lay his head on the block to pay for it all,

> While, round, the armèd bands
> Did clap their bloody hands

(for the more we study causes, the clearer we see that the
Great Rebellion really sprang from the Stuarts' congenital
nescience of any obligation in dealing with public money).
And *there* young George Villiers, and *there* young Edward
Herbert (later of Cherbury), gay as flies; and *there* my Lady
Harrington and Lady Grace Dudley; *there* Francis Bacon,
knight and Solicitor General; knowing most things but little
guessing that in course of time he would be accused of
having come to witness his own play....We all remember

the trick of it, and can refresh our memories by turning to the famous passage in which Macaulay arrays Westminster Hall for the trial of Warren Hastings.

But, seriously, I suggest that in visualising a play which so tenderly yet imperatively dismisses this transitory life of ours as such stuff as dreams are made on—a tale rounded by a sleep—we may profitably see it at the double remove; conjuring up, between us and the stage, all that brilliant company in the auditorium—now, with all the players, dead and gone almost as if they had never been: and especially that one girl in whose honour all is devised, Elizabeth, bride and 'Queen of Hearts.' A passage of Hazlitt's haunts me as I think of it:

We walk through life as through a narrow path with a thin curtain drawn around it. Behind are ranged rich portraits, airy harps are strung—yet we will not stretch forth our hands and lift the veil, to catch the glimpses of the one or sweep the chords of the other. As in a theatre, when the old-fashioned green curtain drew up, groups of figures, fantastic dresses, laughing faces, rich banquets, stately columns, gleaming vistas, appeared behind; so we have only at any time to 'peep through the blanket of the past' to possess ourselves at once of all that has regaled our senses, that is stored up in memory, that has struck our fancy, that has pierced our hearts....

So, for me, two curtains rise on *The Tempest*. First, between me and the stage I see that company gathered: and, pre-eminent, in the front row, the figure of this girl, this paragon, for whose sake so many gallant gentlemen were to lose this world and count it gain.

> See the chariot at hand here of Love
> Wherein my Lady rideth!
> Each that draws is a swan or a dove
> And well the car Love guideth.

As she goes, all hearts do duty
　　Unto her beauty;
And enamour'd do wish so they might
　　But enjoy such a sight,
That they still were to run by her side
Thoro' swords, thoro' seas, whither she would ride.

To-night she is a bride; as the histories attest, in love with her husband; and if we can hereafter, between whiles, steal an instant from Miranda and Ferdinand, let it be for her face, with lips parted as she leans forward and her heart goes out to follow the lovers' story. But for the moment I see her, a little reclined, her young jewelled wrists, like Cassiopeia's, laid along the arms of her chair; and, before her, that other curtain.

(3)

In the public theatres of that time, the main stage was uncurtained, and its front ran boldly out into the auditorium. Now I think that in the Banqueting House at Whitehall that front was flattened back so as to be almost, if not quite, straight; and that this straight proscenium very likely had a frontal curtain. But this matters little; for, like every Elizabethan theatre, public or private, the Banqueting House had an inner stage, and *that* of course had curtains. We have seen to what uses this second, inner, stage lent itself. It served as Juliet's tomb, and Hero's; for Hermione on her pedestal; for the play-scene in Hamlet; for Richard's tent; for Desdemona's bed-chamber and Imogen's; for Imogen's cave, too, and Timon's, and, in this play, Prospero's. We know that, since its curtains could be opened or shut at will, properties could be shifted behind them; and therefore whenever in an Elizabethan play we come on a scene that demands a certain amount of stage upholstery, we may at once be sure that it was erected on the inner stage.

In *The Tempest* this inner stage serves three purposes. It serves—

(1) for Prospero's cave,

(2) for the masque of Ceres and Juno (a scene within a scene), and

(3) lastly for what comes first—the shipwreck itself; since to present the deck of a ship in a gale many 'properties' are required: the foot of a mast, at least, some leading ropes, and running gear, odd cordage, raffle, spars, deck-hamper broken adrift; with lightning and thunder produced from the wings and the 'flies.' You cannot call your deck-hands up on to a naked stage, and set them to run about hauling on ropes which are not there and howling to imitate a gale. For properties on the *outer* stage, reading the play, I can find no more necessary to be provided than two chairs and clothes-line, all in Act IV.

(4)

So, to a bang and a rolling roar of thunder, the inner curtains fall open, and we are shown—out at sea beyond the island—the deck of a long-laboured ship: men running, shouting, cursing; master and bo'sun bawling orders; canvas banging with loud reports, wind whistling, lightning and St Elmo's light, and all that a competent stage-manager can adventitiously supply from the wings.

This opening scene has been criticised: but my poor nautical knowledge applauds it for a first-class gale. Of course ships are built nowadays on improved designs and can lie several points closer up to the wind: but even nowadays, caught, as Alonzo's crew were, full on a lee-shore, a man must trim his judgment to the force of the wind and what is called the 'scend' of the sea. This in shoaling water heaves your vessel shoreward all the while. Then, if your judgment tell you that your upper masts will carry the weight, you *may* claw off by piling on canvas and driving her: and it will be the bolder, happier chance that naturally tempts you. But with the gale beyond a certain force—and Prospero was not conjuring by halves—you have to reckon if your spars are man enough for it; and if in your judgment they are not, then to down their canvas, 'try her with main course' as the Bo'sun does in seamanlike fashion, and ride to it—even lowering the upper spars themselves—as could be readily done in an Elizabethan ship—and so ease her drifting to leeward: for aloft, now, they are so much useless cumber and hold the wind. We have to remember, too, that with an Elizabethan ship this moment for deciding on the second-best would necessarily come sooner than on a modern one. She was good enough in any sea-room. 'Blow, till thou burst thy wind,' the Bo'sun challenges heaven, '*if there be room enough*.' But this is just the point. He has no fear of her seaworthiness, but much fear of her capacity to nose off a coast.

In short, the storm is a good storm, and the master handles his vessel well, giving the right orders sharp and prompt. The critics criticise more plausibly when they come to the actual wreck. For Scene I ends on the cry, 'We split, we split, we split!' as if she was actually on the rocks and striking. In Scene II Miranda at first confirms this. She has seen

> a brave vessel,
> Who had, no doubt, some noble creatures in her,
> Dash'd all to pieces.

She hears the cry of the crew:

> O, that cry did knock
> Against my very heart!

She sees them suffer. Yet later on she appears to have seen the ship *founder*—a very different thing; and yet again we have a description of Ferdinand's swimming for shore and beating the surges under him; and by this time we know from Ariel that there has been no real striking or foundering:

> Safely in harbour
> Is the king's ship; in the deep nook where once
> Thou call'dst me up at midnight to fetch dew
> From the still-vex'd Bermoothes, there she's hid:
> The mariners all under hatches stow'd;
> Who, with a charm join'd to their suffer'd labour,
> I have left asleep.

But, to be frank, I make very little of these supposed inconsistencies. It is surely not difficult, when we have listened to Ariel—

> I boarded the king's ship; now on the beak,
> Now in the waist, the deck, in every cabin,
> I flam'd amazement: sometimes I'ld divide
> And burn in many places; on the topmast
> The yards and bowsprit would I flame distinctly,
> Then meet and join. Jove's lightnings, the precursors
> O' the dreadful thunder-claps, more momentary
> And sight-outrunning were not: the fire and cracks
> Of sulphurous roaring the most mighty Neptune
> *Seem* to besiege, and make his bold waves tremble—
> Yea, his dread trident shake;

and again—

> All but mariners
> Plung'd in the foaming brine and quit the vessel
> Then all afire with me...

—it is surely not difficult, remembering this to be a fairy coast and the conjured storm mixed with illusions, to reconcile the discrepancies. As for Miranda's account of it —well, I have seen two or three wrecks and come near sharing in one, and I do not want to see another. But whereas in one I have seen a ship strike and visibly go to pieces in three successive waves (the masts falling together like sticks of barley-sugar—all crumbled and gone in some fifteen or twenty seconds), in another it happened very much as Miranda saw it: a ship, a squall that blotted out every-thing, then a clear horizon again, but no ship. That was a small craft, almost a boat. But we have all heard tell how the *Eurydice* went down, racing up past the Needles with her gun-ports open, close to home. To those watching her from the cliffs the squall blotted her out, passed in less than a minute, and, where she had been, nothing but the waves ran. Such an interval would leave Ariel time for all his beneficent conjuring.

(5)

The play has advertised itself as *The Tempest*, and in the very first scene we are already in a first-class one. But patently this sort of thing cannot go on through the five Acts to come.

Well, of course it cannot: but now let the reader consider the craft of the opening scene, in the light of a First Principle which I will set in italics. *If you are an artist and are setting out to tell the incredible, nothing will serve you so well as to open with absolute realism.* If you want, for instance, to tell the incredible story of Robinson Crusoe, you put your hands in your pockets and begin—

I was born in the year 1632, in the city of York, of a good family though not of that county; my father being a foreigner of Bremen, who settled in Hull.

So, if you want to tell how Alice met with the most impossible adventures, you give the child an ordinary kitten, set her on a hearth-rug in an ordinary room, take her to an ordinary looking-glass and *walk her through it.* So the trick is done: and so, past the realistic shoutings and cursings of our Bo'sun—past the realistic trepidation and runnings to-and-fro of our passengers—we come to shore on the island, and

The rarity of it is—which is indeed almost beyond credit—that our garments, being, as they were, drenched in the sea, hold, notwithstanding, their freshness and glosses, being rather new dyed than stained with salt water.

To the extreme technical skill of the second scene, the wonderful protasis between Prospero and his daughter, which unfolds—better, I dare to say, than any prologue of Greek Tragedy, because, more naturally and pat on the moment of occasion—every item preparative to what follows, every word instructing us while it intrigues and enhances our curiosity, several critics have paid tribute. I certainly cannot improve on Coleridge's—

In the second scene Prospero's speeches, till the entrance of Ariel, contain the finest example I remember of retrospective narration for the purpose of exciting immediate interest and putting the audience in possession of all the information necessary for the understanding of the plot. Observe, too, the perfect probability of the moment chosen by Prospero...to open out the truth to his daughter, his own romantic bearing, and how completely everything that might have been disagreeable to us in the magician is reconciled and shaded in the humanity and natural feelings of a father. In the very first speech of Miranda the simplicity and tenderness of her character are at once laid open....

That speech, as you remember, touches for a moment on reproach, to slide off into a pity which for us and for

Prospero is innocent-stabbing irony—all the more deadly for being gentle and simple and direct:

> O, I have suffer'd
> With those that I saw suffer! A brave vessel,
> Who had, no doubt, some noble creatures in her,
> Dash'd all to pieces. O, the cry did break
> Against my very heart! Poor souls, they perish'd.

(6)

Now for Miranda. Every critic wants to write about her; but when we are all in love, what is the use? Specially and rightly they have noticed the chosen distance at which she is poised between the brute Caliban and the rarefied Ariel with his fellow-spirits haunting that isle of voices: she so straight, forthright, speaking out all her knowledge, though it be bluntly, laying her heart bare to the first summons of love—so confidently, being clean.

I will but add this. Through these later plays we cannot but note that Shakespeare, choosing a maiden for the central figure of each successive work, successively sublimates his conception of maidenhood until towards the end no one is fit to act Marina, Perdita, Miranda, unless she be actually a princess or fit to be a princess. I dare say that I love Beatrice or Rosalind as whole-heartedly as anyone who may happen to read this page. But they are different. One can imagine a Beatrice or a Rosalind enacted with just a touch of vulgarity and yet without offence. But in Perdita or in Miranda that touch were inconceivable.

> *Et vera incessu patuit dea.*

And (wonder of all!) this man, suborned to the stage of his time, making himself 'a motley to the view,' had to write the parts of Perdita and Miranda to be acted by boys! There

—just there—his genius, which has lured me since child-hood on the quest, adventurous though vain, to track its secret down—just there that wonder, which is the voice and harp of Ariel, vanishes and leaves me hopelessly foundered: even as this sort of thing drives us to go hackneying the hackneyed encomium, the full meaning of which, when he wrote it, Ben Jonson never guessed,

He was not of an age, but for all time.

This should keep us wary, when we deal with Shake-speare, of testing the workman too narrowly by the condi-tions of his craft. I may be accused of being proner than most to fall into this very sin. So let me admit that, while it seems to me constantly useful, and sometimes illuminating, to have those conditions in mind, it is a folly to think of Shakespeare as *limited* by them. He invented Lady Mac-beth and Miranda, and both to be acted by boys!

(7)

I shall say little more of Miranda: because in two memorable pages Coleridge has condensed all, or almost all, that can be said. I believe that before reading him, and therefore without his help, I have felt the exquisite touches (there are two) when Miranda in the first dawn of love lets slip from memory first her father's behest and anon his precepts—'*Thou shalt leave father and mother and cleave,*' etc. But it was Coleridge taught me the beauty of—

At the first sight
They have chang'd eyes

—which does *not* mean 'they have exchanged glances' but with literal truth indicates the decisive moment that happens in true love between man and woman.

But specially I would refer to words in which, specially of

Miranda, Coleridge expresses just this that we all feel of her.

In Shakespeare all the elements of womanhood are holy, and there is the sweet yet dignified feeling of all that *continuates* society, a sense of ancestry and of sex, with a purity unassailable by sophistry, because it rests not in the analytical processes but in that same equipoise of the faculties during which the feelings are representative of all past experience—not of the individual only, but of all those by whom she had been educated, and their predecessors even up to the first mother that lived.

I will add but this concerning her—yet I think it her last secret and the last secret of the play:—She is good. It has been pointed out that, of all the courtiers wrecked on the island, Gonzalo is the only *good* man, and he alone of them keeps his cheerfulness, his happy old courage. So, and more eminently, Miranda is good: she means nothing but good to the world and in return will credit it only with good—

> O brave new world!
> That has such people in't!

And so we behold her—a being good absolutely, and by breeding set above commerce and fear—how fearlessly she gives herself in that incomparable love-scene with which Act III opens!

Says Ferdinand:

> Wherefore weep you?
> *Mir.* At mine unworthiness, that dare not offer
> What I desire to give; and much less take
> What I shall die to want. But this is trifling;
> And all the more it seeks to hide itself,
> The bigger bulk it shows. Hence, bashful cunning!
> And prompt me, plain and holy innocence!
> I am your wife, if you will marry me;
> If not, I'll die your maid; to be your fellow

You may deny me: but I'll be your servant
Whether you will or no.

Fer.   (*As he kneels*).   My mistress, dearest;
And I thus humble ever.

Mir.   My husband, then?

Fer.   Ay, with a heart as willing
As bondage e'er of freedom. Here's my hand.

Mir.   And mine, with my heart in't.

(8)

Many critics (I repeat) have pointed out as a point of
artistry how delicately Shakespeare has set Miranda, clean
of mind as of body of lively flesh and blood, on the balance
between her father's two ministrants: Caliban, of the earth
earthy, and Ariel, rarefied almost to a mere spirit of the sky,
often a mere voice on the breeze: and we have just noted
how much better she is than either.

Now of Caliban I shall say (for in my opinion the monster
has been rather monstrously over-philosophised) only this—
that somehow he is not a bad monster. It may seem unfair
to drag Falstaff into a comparison; but the worst I want to
make of it is that our full-blooded Shakespeare, having set
himself to create something gross, sensual, could never help
sympathising with it, liking it, in a sense loving it. Even as
none of us can help loving Falstaff, so if Caliban were to
come fawning into the room, our impulse would be to pat
him on the head—'Good old doggie! Good monster!'—
that would be the feeling. To be sure he is a 'waster' in any
decent scheme of society; *fruges consumere natus*. In his
second remark (the first is occupied with cursing) he reveals
himself as shamelessly as might a crowned head of Europe—

I must eat my dinner:

This island's *mine*.

while, for his uncouthness of speech, I cannot help feeling that he gets back something of his own when he answers Prospero—

> *You* taught me language, and my profit on't
> Is, I know how to curse.

But on this Dr Johnson has an exceedingly sensible remark:

Caliban had learned to speak of Prospero and his daughter; he had no names for the sun and moon before their arrival; and could not have invented a language of his own without more understanding than Shakespeare has thought fit to bestow on him. His diction is indeed clouded by the gloominess of his temper and the malignity of his purposes: but let any other being entertain the same thoughts, and he will find them easily issue in the same expressions.

Here, for convenience, let me take Caliban's companions and co-plotters. Trinculo the jester is adequate and makes a good foil: but he makes little more; nor, do I think, did Shakespeare *desire* to do any more; having done his last and worst with jesters. For we think of the plays chronologically now: and for me Shakespeare should never write of a Fool again after the Fool in *Lear*. To have let that brave heart—the bravest in the tragedy, wherein, outcast for loyalty yet strong and alone, it helps its master through agony, and will draw a gay, courageous laugh from its worst twinges—to have let that heart go, without even remembering to kill it, allowing it not even the dignity to break in honourable discharge—to let it pass without recognition, naked, nameless, out into the wind and the night—well, Shakespeare was often careless, but in this he was cruel, criminal. I do not want any more Fools of Shakespeare after the Fool in *Lear*.

But Trinculo's recognition-scene with Stephano (Caliban

being used in it with the funniest plausibility) makes capital farce; and Stephano himself is, I dare to say, a master stroke of invention. I may be thought to speak extravagantly here, for his share in the action is not of first-rate importance. But let us consider his value in contributing *solidarity* to our trust in a play which throughout the artist had to watch against its becoming too ethereal, too pure and good

> for human nature's daily food,

and floating off into sheer phantasy. But an unmistakable British seaman turned loose to stagger through our isle of magic, with a bottle!—The scheme wanted but that: a priceless British mariner, staggering through all but to stare, and against Ariel's fine-drawn melodies hiccoughing back—

> The master, the swabber, the bo'sun, and I....

Truly I see the beginning of what they call 'our world-wide empire' in Stephano. Let the reader mistake me not: I see them also in Andrew Marvell's mariners, rowing, 'where the remote Bermudas ride,' and chanting

> In the English boat
> A holy and a cheerful note.

But I detect them also in this unholier drunken figure, bewildered, yet positive that all is to be risked.—

> I escaped upon a butt of sack, which the sailors heaved o'erboard....Tell not me! When the butt is out we will drink water: not a drop before.

That, with his immortal advice in extremity, 'Every man shift for all the rest,' gives the man's measure.

(9)

In a previous chapter, on *A Midsummer-Night's Dream*, I said something of Shakespeare's Fairies. If we read that play alongside *The Tempest*, we cannot miss, while acknowledging that all has changed in Fairyland, to be surprised, and almost with a shock, by a crowd of similarities. Shakespeare, as I cannot too often insist, never tired of repeating himself, of trying old inventions, with a difference, to produce new effects. But whereas in *Twelfth Night*, for example (last of the gay comedies), we see *As You Like It*, *Much Ado*, the first part of *Henry IV* translated into a pale lunar haze, in *The Tempest* we see the fairyland of *A Midsummer-Night's Dream* converted to quite another effect: rarefied, and made thereby not less potent but more potent.

(1) Both plays include a bridal interlude: and both *as they stand* were (I am sure) designed to celebrate a Court wedding.

(2) Both catch away this world to entangle it in enchantment by faëry.

(3) Both are noticeably short (*A Midsummer-Night's Dream* 2250 lines, *The Tempest* but 2068 lines), and near together in length.

(4) Of all the plays these two most constantly invoke and rely on *music*. Nor can any other play compete with these two in the number of passages that composers have set to music.

Here, by the way, let us note the touch of poetry in Prospero's demand for music as he prepares to break his staff—

> And when I have requir'd
> Some heavenly music—which even now I do—

He *says* it is to charm the senses of Ferdinand and Miranda,

but a few lines later he says it is to cure the unsettled fancy
of Alonzo and his courtiers; and I rather like to think he
invokes it for his own passing. I like to read in it the demand
expressed in Sully Prudhomme's lines, thus translated by
George du Maurier—

Kindly watcher by my bed, lift no voice in prayer,
Waste not any words on me when the hour is nigh.
Let a stream of melody but flow from one sweet player,
And meekly will I lay my head, and fold my hands to die.

Sick I am of idle words, past all reconciling,
Words that weary and perplex and ponder and conceal.
Wake the sounds that cannot lie, for all their sweet beguiling;
The language one need fathom not, but only hear and feel.

Let them roll once more to me, and ripple in my hearing,
Like waves upon a lonely beach where no craft anchoreth;
That I may steep my soul therein and, craving naught nor
     fearing,
Drift on through slumber to a dream, and through a dream to
     death.

(5) Let us next note as a fact highly curious, but abun-
dantly proved by experience, that of all Shakespeare's plays
these two *require* to be acted by (shall I say?) amateurs.
The amateur may miss or hit. The professional mummer
has never made any hand with either play; nor (I think)
ever will.

(6) In neither play—and in this again the pair stand
alone (if we omit *Timon of Athens*)—is there any real plot
to concern anyone. The story 'dies in the telling.'

(7) In both, the lowlier characters—Caliban and Company as well as Bully Bottom and Company—get ludicrously
mixed in the enchantment.

—and so on. Many critics have saved me the trouble of indicating how much more ethereal, yet withal how much wiser, is this last fairyland of *The Tempest* than that of Robin Goodfellow, Pease-Blossom, Mustard-Seed, and the rest—those rustic Warwickshire elves. I think it more useful, perhaps, to point out how curiously and—despite all the intervening years and for all Shakespeare had learnt in them—how hauntingly alike is the language.

> And never, since the middle summer's spring,
> Met we on hill, in dale, forest or mead,
> By pavèd fountain or by rushy brook,
> Or in the beachèd margent of the sea
> To dance our ringlets to the whistling wind....
>
> (*M. N. D.*, II, I, 82.)

> Ye elves of hills, brooks, standing lakes and groves,
> And ye that on the sands with printless feet
> Do chase the ebbing Neptune and do fly him
> When he comes back....
>
> (*Tempest*, V, I, 33.)

> Come unto these yellow sands,
>   And then take hands:
> Curtsied when you have and kiss'd
>   The wild waves whist....
>
> (*Ibid.* I, II, 376.)

Those echoes!—'Hark! now I hear them—Ding-dong, bell'! But technically, as a matter of structural workmanship, the difference lies in this, that whereas in *A Midsummer-Night's Dream* the fairy element runs free, to play its own irresponsible mischief, in *The Tempest* it works entirely at the behest—and, even when mutinous, strictly under the control—of one human mind.

(10)

So I come lastly to Prospero. Who is Prospero? Is he perchance Destiny itself; the master-spirit that has brooded invisible and moved on the deep waters of all the Tragedies, and now comes to shore on a lost islet of the main to sun himself; laying by his robe of darkness to play, at his great ease, one last smiling trick before taking his rest? Yes, spirit,

> thou comest from thy voyage:
> Yes, the spray is on thy cloak and hair,

Or is he, as so many of us have pleased ourselves to fancy, Shakespeare himself, breaking his wand, drowning his book, and so bidding farewell? Or is he perchance, as the late Dr Garnett preferred to conjecture—James I of England? If so, in the words of the Preface to the Authorised Version, 'Great and manifold were the blessings, most dread Sovereign, which Almighty God, the Father of all mercies, bestowed upon us the people of England, when first he sent Your Majesty's Royal Person to rule and reign over us'! But—to take this conjecture first—it has been observed, not without sagacity, that to flatter the royal and learned author of *Demonologie* by presenting him to himself in the guise of a sorcerer were a proposal beyond even Shakespeare's courage—to say nothing of his tact. And even for the rest, let us ever beware how we say of any imaginative author that (as the phrase goes) he 'has put So-and-so into his book.'[1] Dickens, to be sure, did it once or twice— not nearly so often as some folk suppose, but still once or twice or thrice—with unhappy results. For in truth it is not the way of the imaginative artist: and if the reader will not

[1] See, however, p. 279. A hint at royal James does not exclude a glance at Shakespeare.

take that from me he may take it from Aristotle. Poetry
never works on photographs, but on hints; never on persons,
individuals, save in one way which Sir John Davies told,
three centuries ago, in verse for us—

> From their gross matter she abstracts their forms,
>   And draws a kind of quintessence from things;
> Which to her proper nature she transforms
>   To bear them, light, on her celestial wings.

And so, by this very virtue of Universality, *The Tempest* is
—what you or I make of it; Prospero—what you or I make
of him. 'O Lady! we receive but what we give.'

Of *The Tempest* I make so much as this: that here at the
close of my three chapters I feel it almost a desecration to
have put hand—as my method enjoined—into the anatomy
of such a marvel. May I earn forgiveness by a final confession?

The lights in the royal banqueting-house are out. To-
morrow the carpenters arrive to take down poles, rollers,
joists—all the material structure of this play—and, a day
after, comes the charwoman to sweep up sawdust with the
odds and ends of tinsel. The lights are out; the company
dispersed to go their bright ways and make, in the end, other
dust. Ariel has nestled to the bat's back and slid away,
following summer, following darkness like a dream. But
here are we, three hundred years later, treasuring this play
in our hearts, as—set in the forefront of the 1623 Folio and
by wisest tradition kept there—it has for ten generations
allured English children to their Shakespeare.

> That was the chirp of Ariel
> You heard, as overhead it flew;
> The farther going, more to dwell
> And wing our green to wed our blue.

But whether not of joy, or knell,
Not his own Father-singer knew;
Nor yet can any mortal tell—
Save only that it shivers thro'
The breast of us a sounded shell,
The blood of us a lighted dew.

And I conclude by asseverating that were a greater than
Ariel to wing down from Heaven and stand and offer me to
choose which, of all the books written in the world, should
be mine, I should choose—not the *Odyssey*, not the *Aeneid*,
not the *Divine Comedy*, not *Paradise Lost*; not *Othello* nor
Hamlet nor *Lear*; but this little matter of 2000 odd lines—
The Tempest. 'What?—rather than *Othello* or than *Lear?*'
'Yes: for I can just imagine a future age of men, in which
their characterisation has passed into a curiosity, a pale thing
of antiquity; as I can barely imagine, yet can just imagine,
a world in which the murder of Desdemona, the fate of
Cordelia, will be considered curiously, as brute happenings
proper to a time out-lived; and again, while I reverence the
artist who in *Othello* or in *Lear* purges our passion, forcing
us to weep for present human woe, *The Tempest*, as I see
it, forces diviner tears, tears for sheer beauty; with a royal
sense of this world and how it passes away, with a catch at
the heart of what is to come. And still the sense is royal: it
is the majesty of art: we *feel* that we are greater than we
know. So on the surge of our emotion, as on the surges
ringing Prospero's island, is blown a spray, a mist. Actually
it dwells in our eyes, bedimming them: and as involuntarily
we would brush it away, there rides in it a rainbow; and its
colours are wisdom and charity, with forgiveness, tender
ruth for all men and women growing older, and perennial
trust in young love

INDEX

83
85